Swans
of the world

Sylvia Bruce Wilmore

Swans
of the world

———————

with 8 plates and
numerous line drawings by the author

TAPLINGER PUBLISHING CO, INC.
NEW YORK

First published in the United States in 1974 by
TAPLINGER PUBLISHING CO., INC.
New York, New York

Library of Congress Catalog Card Number: 74-3669
ISBN 0-8008-7524-9

Contents

———◆———

5

List of Illustrations

List of Illustrations

List of Illustrations

The drawings of the display behaviour of swans are based upon *Waterfowl Behaviour* by P. A. Johnsgard

CHAPTER ONE

Introducing the Swans

———◆———

Swans, with their long necks and large, graceful forms, possess a mystical quality and present an enthralling spectacle wherever they are gathered. Harmonising with the icy tundra, large colonies of Bewick's Swans nest by the estuaries of Arctic rivers during May, and the white forms of Whooper Swans fly in V formation across the coniferous forests and snow-capped mountains of northern Eurasia on migration to western Europe and south-east Asia, to avoid the frost that grips the waning Arctic summer.

The bays and inlets of the Pacific coast of North America are enhanced by snowy flocks of several hundred Whistling Swans during winter, while the majesty of the Mute Swan reigns over lakes and rivers in the more temperate parts of Eurasia, bearing in its proud demeanour a royal tradition, and myths and legends stretching back to prehistoric times.

Being accustomed to these sights, people of the Northern Hemisphere naturally visualise swans in their dazzling purity, but in Australia and New Zealand the strange and beautiful Black Swan swims in lagoons and estuaries, its black head curved gracefully on its slender neck, and its feathers undulating as though ruffled by a gentle breeze. Also of unique beauty, the Black-necked Swan glides on the numerous lakes of the temperate southern part of South America.

Swans are the largest and most regal of all the *Anatidae* family. They share the *Anserini* tribe with the geese. The *Anserini* together with the

Whistling Ducks (*Dendrocygnini*), form the sub-family *Anserinae*. This sub-family and two others known as the *Anserantinae*, which consists only of the magpie goose, and the *Anatinae*, comprising all the remaining ducks, make up the family *Anatidae*. This family, together with the *Anhimidae* family (the screamers), form the order *Anseriformes*.

Jean Delacour, who has written the most authoritative books on wildfowl, reclassified the *Anatidae* family in 1945. He placed five species of swan under the genus *Cygnus*, which is Latin for 'swan'. Another bird, the white Coscoroba of South America, which is something of an enigma to ornithologists, he placed under the swans with a genus of its own, classing it *Coscoroba coscoroba*.

There are two northern species of white swans: *Cygnus cygnus*, which includes the large Trumpeter Swan, *Cygnus cygnus buccinator* of North America, together with the slightly smaller Whooper Swan, *Cygnus cygnus cygnus* of northern Eurasia; and the other species, *Cygnus columbianus*, comprising the Whistling Swan, *Cygnus columbianus columbianus* of the Arctic regions of North America, and the smaller Bewick's Swan, *Cygnus columbianus bewickii* of northern Eurasia. These northern swans possess the most common and goose-like features of the *Anserini* tribe.

The other three species, although very different from each other in appearance, are in the evolutionary sense more closely related to each other than to the Northern Swans. Several authors specialising in waterfowl believe that two genera should be recognised—*Olor*, which is Greek for 'swan', being the genus for the Northern Swans, and *Cygnus*, to include the Mute, Black, and Black-necked swans. This classification is mentioned to emphasise the difference taxonomically between the Northern Swans and the remaining three species.

The Mute Swan, *Cygnus olor*, is a large white swan recognisable by a graceful S-shaped curve to its neck, in contrast to the erect posture of the Northern Swans. It is less wild than its northern cousins and was domesticated in some parts of Europe until the end of World War II. The Black Swan, *Cygnus atratus* of Australia, is dark-grey and black with white primaries, and the Black-necked Swan, *Cygnus melano-coryphus* of South America, has a black neck and white body.

Swans have much in common with geese but one significant difference is in habitat: swans breed in the colder parts of the world both north and south of the Equator, with the exception of Africa, while true geese are restricted to the Northern Hemisphere. Also geese graze mostly on land whereas swans frequent fresh and brackish waters where they can find an abundance of water plants. All waterfowl are adapted to aquatic life; their webbed feet, with three front toes connected by a membrane, act as paddles, and their bodies are widened for stability on water, aided by their dense plumage which provides insulation and buoyancy. They also have a large oil gland near the base of their tail, with a small downy tuft around it which acts as a wick when the birds preen themselves. The gland is large and well developed, and it was previously thought that the oil kept the plumage waterproof; but in fact oil glands are also found in non-aquatic birds. The most recent opinion is that the gland secretion is a source of Vitamin D taken by the mouth with feather particles when the birds are preening.

The *Anserinae* can be distinguished from other waterfowl by their long necks and goose-like shape and posture. Swans are proportionately more beautiful and majestic than geese, although their anatomy has much in common; but swans have longer and more slender necks, smaller heads, with naked lores (the space between the eyes and bill), and longer bills. A swan has 60 vertebrae, of which 25 belong to its neck. This is more vertebrae than any other bird, or mammal—even a giraffe. Swans use their necks to forage for aquatic plants, and prefer water between 0·5 and 1·2m (19·7 and 47·2in) deep. They up-end, like ducks, with their tails high above the water, and nip off shoots from the vegetation, sometimes pulling up whole plants with their long, broad bills. They rarely have the urge or necessity to dive, except in danger. Their bills consist of layers of skin which are comparatively soft, and only the tip, termed the nail, is thick and horny. The edges of the upper and lower mandibles which form the bill are serrated and enable the swans to tear off stalks and leaves.

The swan's palate is among the most complete of all the birds. The high, wide skull and powerful jaw muscles provide a strong grasp for securing food; both jaws have movement but the upper jaw movement is limited and does not hamper the swan's firm grip. The bony nail and the spiny texture of the tongue, with its serrated edges, help the swan to grip food and break it up, and they are also useful when the swan dabbles for vegetation. In common with other waterfowl the

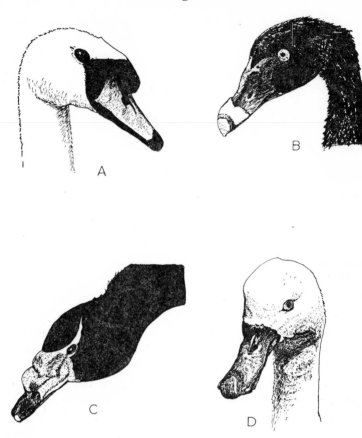

Swans' heads: A *the Mute Swan;* B *the Black Swan;* C *the Black-necked Swan;* D *the Coscoroba Swan*

swan's gullet is narrow and it lacks a true crop, but the glandular portion of the stomach, the proventriculus, performs the function of storing food which is later ground to a pulp by the oval-shaped gizzard.

Swans are vegetarians: their food consists of subaqueous vegetation and some graze on arable land. They also eat molluscs, grubs and insects that adhere to plants, and a certain amount of grit is always required to help digest the coarser foods. Feeding can take place by day and night as swans can select food by taste and touch.

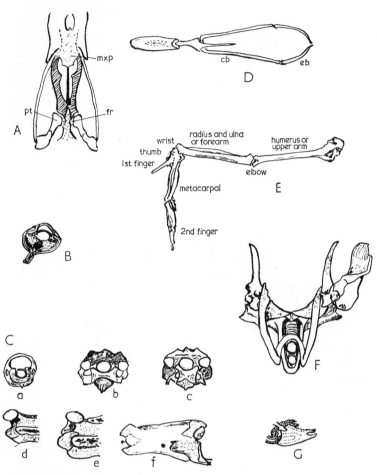

Parts of the Swan's anatomy: A the palate, desmognathous type—mxp palatal process of maxilla, fr articular facet on parasphenoid rostrum, pt pterygoid; B the eye, commonest 'flat' type, ventral half left eyeball, nasal side to the right; C cervical vertebrae, a atlas from front, b 4th vertebra from front, c 4th vertebra from behind, d median through 6th cervical side, e median section through 15th cervical, f 5th vertebra seen from left side—arrow in canal for vertebral artery; D tongue skeleton seen from below, cb ceratobranchial, eb epibranchial; E bones of swan's wing; F pectoral girdle of swan seen from front and showing trachea (cut short) entering sternum; G trachea outline (dotted) seen from left

The superb form of a swan is wonderfully adapted to aquatic life. Man has moulded yachts upon its structure which combines beauty with speed, the great breadth of its breast tapering narrowly to the rear like the stern of a ship. Their large, strongly webbed feet, set on short legs placed towards the rear of their bodies, act as perfect paddles which bear them through the water with exquisite ease. The legs are too far from the bird's centre of gravity for them to be efficient walkers and most swans have a clumsy waddle on land. Their feet, with the three strongly nailed toes, help them dig into the muddy surface under water to break up the bottom vegetation. They stand in the water and scrape their feet back, one after the other, then return to their floating position to pull up the dislodged food. The legs of swans and geese differ from ducks' legs, the network of scales on the front being square instead of shield-shaped.

Swans frequent both fresh and brackish water. Some species, such as the Bewick's, are well adapted to marine habitats. Two nasal glands which extract salt from the water are situated in a space in the skull above the eyes. They remove salt from the bloodstream and excrete it through the nostrils.

In flight, swans are magnificent. They fly with the neck fully extended and with their great wings—in some cases with a span exceeding the length of the body from tip to tail—beating in slow, regular movements. The Northern Swans, equipped for flying over great distances, have relatively longer wings than swans in temperate zones. A swan's wing is composed of the upper arm, known as the humerus, which is joined at the elbow to the forearm (comprising the radius—the outer bone; and ulna—the inner bone). As with the human arm there is a wrist, and this connects with a three-fingered hand. The thumb and first finger are joined to the junction where the metacarpal, or hand, meets the wrist, and the long second finger forms the wingtip. A bony knuckle at the bend of the wing is common in both swans and geese. This can act as a defensive weapon against predators or a bludgeon in combat. The wing of a swan has been known to break a man's leg.

In spite of their strength the wing bones are hollow, which saves much weight in flight. They are covered with a fine skin upon which the flight feathers grow. The eleven large stiff primary feathers which drive the bird through the air are attached to the wingtip, and these outermost feathers are emarginated, i.e. they are narrower on the front of the quill than they are on the rear vane-surface. Consequently when they are on the down-stroke the feathers part like fingers, and more air pressure is exerted on the wide vanes, causing each primary feather to twist like a propeller.

In common with all birds the base of the shaft of a swan's flight

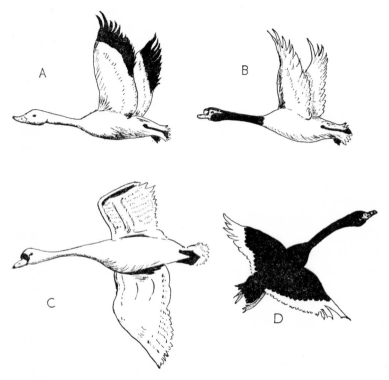

Swans in flight: A the Coscoroba Swan; B the Black-necked Swan; C the Mute Swan; D the Black Swan

feather is hollow for receiving nourishment while it is growing, but it is solid further up where it supports the two vanes. The inner vanes of all *Anseriformes* are stiffened. Each vane consists of hundreds of parallel barbs or filaments, and each of these is virtually a miniature feather carrying several hundred tiny barbules equipped with minute hooks, which mesh into the barbs, interweaving in a similar fashion to a very fine net. It has been estimated that there are approximately 1,600 filaments in the primary feathers of a Mute Swan, and a feather is 9–10in (23–25·5cm) long. The shorter, secondary feathers grow from the inner bone (ulna), and the 'thumb' bone forms an attachment point for the alula, a group of three or four small, vaned feathers used to stabilise flight. The tertiaries cover the upper arm; these feathers are an extension of the secondaries. The upper arm is moved by great flight muscles extending to the breastbone.

The feather structure of all the *Anatidae* is very similar: the feather tracts are extensive and are provided with a great number of relatively small contour feathers. These feathers give the body shape and provide insulation. The feather action is controlled by the involuntary dermal (skin) muscles which are attached to almost every feather follicle and can raise, lower, or move feathers sideways to assist flight manoeuvres. The contour feathers are similar to the flight feathers in structure having several filoplumes—weak, hair-like shafts with a tuft of short barbs at the tip, comparable to the 'hairs' on a plucked fowl. While the featherless regions are narrow and small in area, the feather tracts are broad and the feathers are placed close together. The contour feathers lie in parallel rows and are arranged obliquely to the long-axis of the body; in swans and geese the narrow, unfeathered space along the spine extends down the back to the base of the spinal column.

The flight of waterfowl is of a power-flapping type. As a group the body is heavy and the wings are proportionately small, giving them the smallest wing area per gramme of body weight of any group of birds. Whilst the wing load is still high, the larger species—including swans with their great expanse of wing—have the lowest wing load of the waterfowl, so that while the smaller ducks flap their wings over 300 times per minute, Mute Swans with their long, broad wings and strong chest muscles, give 160 flaps per minute. In a complete circle of a flapping stroke the wing-tips, which move faster and further than the rest of the wings, go through a figure-of-eight pattern with a wide loop at the top. They complete the up-stroke with a rapid snap which helps drive the bird forward. The driving force of the primaries on this stroke, though less powerful than the down-stroke, is especially important for large, heavy birds such as swans. Their feathers do not open

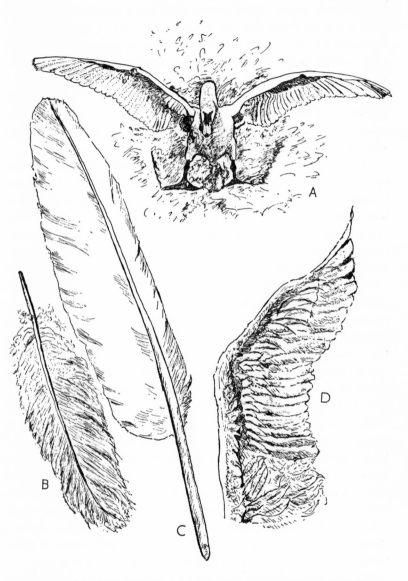

Wings and feathers: A the Mute Swan landing on water showing its six-foot wing spread; B the feather of a Mute Swan cygnet; C the feather of an adult Mute Swan; D the Mute Swan's wing

B

on this stroke to the same extent as those of smaller birds, since they require greater force, especially when taking-off or climbing. The flight speed in some swans is about 30mph, but this may vary from 18 to 55mph, migratory speeds being faster than speeds during local flights.

Swans fly at a height of anything from fifty to several hundred feet during local flights, but on long migratory flights they climb to altitudes of between 2,000 and 5,000ft, and higher, occasionally reaching 10,000ft, where it is much calmer than at lower altitudes.

The eddies of air caused by a bird in flight represent much wasted energy, but swans, geese and ducks are among the species which conserve some of this energy by flying in V formation on long journeys. Each bird gets extra lift from the slip-stream of the bird in front. Birds fly low when there are strong head-winds over the sea: they find the wind slowed down by friction and the waves. When the winds are behind them they move higher.

When landing, waterfowl throw their webbed feet forward to assist the braking action of their back-beating wings—they are not as efficient at landing as land-birds because the water cushions them against mistakes. The alulas are extended when the bird is landing and this prevents 'stalls' due to slow speeds.

The *Anserinae* differ from the other waterfowl in having only one yearly moult, which comes after the breeding period and renders the birds incapable of flying during the summer. The swan's flight and tail feathers are shed simultaneously. In breeding pairs this ensures that the parent birds stay with their young; the pen (female) moults first, then the cob (male). In this way there is always a parent to defend the nesting young. The non-breeding one-year-old and two-year-old birds gather in summer flocks (of some hundred birds) to moult. They moult earlier than breeding swans.

Another distinguishing feature of the *Anserinae* is that both sexes' plumage is similar, whereas the duck's plumage is different in the two sexes except in the eclipse moult when both sexes appear the same.

Both swans and geese have powerful and sonorous voices which are produced by a long windpipe set in the breastbone. The swan's windpipe is a long tube of cartilaginous and/or bony rings, one end leading to the mouth through the larynx and glottis, and the other dividing, just within the body cavity, into two bronchial tubes which lead to the lungs. In some swans these two tubes are enlarged for a part of their length. The male's voice is slightly more loud and metallic than his mate's deeper, lower-pitched call, although basically there is not a great deal of difference in their syrinx—the special organ birds have at the junction of the windpipe and bronchial tubes and which produces the bird-calls and songs. In swans, geese and ducks the syrinx has been found to consist of vibratory membranes which are supported by bronchial cartilages. The swan's windpipe is simple and does not possess a bony swelling called the *bulla*, which is common on the syrinx of ducks.

Swans, in common with geese, are very slow to mature. Ducks nest and mate in their first year but swans breed when they are three or four years old, or even older. It has been found that all species of *Cygnus* breed a year earlier in captivity, probably due to their having improved food supplies. They are aggressive during the mating and nesting season and defend their territory jealously. When the male has driven off an intruder he returns to his mate, posturing triumphantly, and if they are a pair of long-standing the female will answer with a similar display. This triumph ceremony of swans originated as an aggressive act—the result of the close approach of two birds—but has since evolved into the display of a strong emotional bond between the pair. It is essential for paired swans to have this strong bond as they must co-operate through the breeding season in protecting their territory and young. They mate for life in the majority of cases, and well established pairs remain together in close company.

Most swans control a large territory and are solitary nesters. They require light, warmth, territory, adequate food, a nest site and nesting materials to encourage them to breed. The female in particular is inhibited by cold, inclement weather, hunger, fear, lack of nesting materials or a nesting site. This disinclination to breed under adverse conditions is beneficial because it prevents reproduction at unsuitable times of the year.

The mating display among swans, while not as elaborate as the duck's ostentatious and noisy display, is a graceful and beautiful sight. The various species have slightly different forms of pre-copulatory display, but coition is basically the same. The female flattens herself with her neck half-extended out of the water, submitting to the male. Treading then takes place with the male gripping the feathers of the female's neck and thrusting his usually covert penis into his mate. The whole act only lasts 3–5 seconds. The sexual organs of both male and female swans are of the primitive type. Only waterfowl, ostriches and a few other birds possess an intromittent penis. Waterfowl also have the most primitive type of ovary: it is relatively long—three times as long as wide—and, as with other birds, it is on the left side; but there are rudiments of another ovary on the right side of female swans.

Both male and female swans take part in the building of their bulky, conspicuous nests from reeds and other available material. In common with geese they lack the instinctive action of transporting nesting material to the nest, and only build where there is an abundance of material. They pull up vegetation and pass it over their backs letting it fall first on one side and then the other. When the nest is built of reeds, in the water, the floating leaves help build up the area around the nest which of necessity must be firm and solid to hold two heavy swans. The swans choose a spot near shallow water, either on islets, banks or reed beds. The pen (female) adds down to the nest when her clutch is at least half finished. This down from her breast and belly is released by nibble-preening, an action probably stimulated by loose down and surface changes of the skin area. The exposed naked skin becomes warmer than normal as swollen vessels carry more blood to it, and this forms the brood patches. Birds' feathers are such efficient insulators that if they were not removed from the mother's underparts when she is incubating, they would keep much of her body heat from the eggs.

The pen lays a comparatively small number of large eggs—swans' eggs are among the largest in the bird world—they are never pure white, and are a rather extended oval in shape. The yolk forms about two-fifths of the weight of an egg, and the swan's egg being so large, the yolk is proportionately large. A swan chick itself is also large so that its relative body surface is smaller and it requires less energy to keep warm than a smaller bird. It can, therefore, retain the food from its yolk sac much longer, and after it has hatched it can live without food for a week. This being the case, a swan chick's mortality is highest in the second week—unlike a small bird whose life is in greatest danger during the first week after being hatched.

The pen lays her eggs every 2 days in the majority of cases; incubation starts with the last egg and the young hatch more or less together. Except with the Black Swan, only the female incubates the eggs, although the male may sit on the nest or guard it while she is away obtaining food. The average number of eggs in a clutch tends to be larger for species of swans which breed in middle, rather than in high or low latitudes. One reason for this difference in clutch size is the availability of food for the laying female, and another factor is that the larger the egg in proportion to the size of the laying bird, the smaller the clutch. To illustrate this, the weight of a Mute Swan's egg is 3·8 per cent in proportion to the weight of the swan's body, and the clutch size averages 6 eggs; whereas the Whistling Swan's egg is 4·0 per cent in comparison to its parent's weight, and the clutch on an average is only 5 eggs.

The incubation of swans' eggs is the longest in the *Anatidae* family, averaging from 30 to 36 days. The Northern Swans have the shortest period of incubation, and the Black Swans in the tropics have the longest period. Everything is speeded up in the higher latitudes to compensate for the short summer: the incubation period is shorter, and the young northern chicks mature quicker than those in temperate and tropical latitudes. In the Arctic, to counteract the shorter summer, the food supply is greater, which enables the cygnets to develop sufficient strength for migration with their parents in time to avoid the oncoming Arctic winter. The centre of the nest is filled with decaying vegetation which keeps it in the humid state necessary for incubation. Further moisture is supplied by the parent on returning from the water. The temperature of the nest must be 38° C (100° F) or over. The pen turns the eggs over with her bill and in some cases, when they have been disturbed and rolled out of the nest, she will instinctively roll them back in again, using a sideways movement of her bill to prevent them rolling to the side. The nest-building actions are continued by both swans during incubation.

When incubating, female swans lose weight, but they are more resistant to starvation than males because of a greater metabolism and an instinct to store a good supply of food before brooding. Different species of swans have different incubation habits but many of them start their moult at this time. During the last days of incubation the female spends a great deal of time preening and oiling her feathers. This she does by nibbling at her oil gland and rubbing her chin across it. She then spreads the oil over her breast and flanks with her chin, and nibbles amongst her feathers. The chicks become active inside the egg two days before hatching; they push their beaks through the shell membrane into the air sac and a faint cheeping, indicative of the chick taking in air, may be heard. A horny knob on the tip of the chick's upper beak (sometimes referred to as the egg-tooth) is used for breaking through the eggshell.

The swan chicks are nidifugous—that is the young hatch with their eyes open, are covered with down, and are able to run about and leave the nest almost at once. Most of them have a pale-grey and white down. They are wet when hatched from the protective fluid covering them inside the egg, but the warmth of the nest makes them dry and fluffy. They discover their oil gland at a day old, and when they manage to reach it they spend much of their waking time nibbling and oiling. In this way they receive Vitamin D from their mother's well oiled plumage and from their own oil gland.

In the swan tribe both parents help feed their young by pulling up plants from the bottom of the water and letting the chicks eat them as they float. The family instinct is very strong. The parents guard their young carefully through the fledgeling period, swimming with them, nesting with them, and in some cases carrying them on their backs under the protection of their wings.

The chicks communicate with their parents by a variety of sounds. The northern cygnets have a deep, slow cheeping, while the Mute, Black and Black-necked chicks have a lighter tone. A cygnet communicates with its parents by a series of cheeping sounds: when it is lost it holds itself erect and utters a loud cry; if it is cold and hungry its piercing cry is louder and more insistent. When it is tired its voice is low, soft and quivering; if hurt, its cry is shrill, almost like a scream. The mother answers with soft, low calls, and attends to their alarm calls immediately. Upon greeting the family, cygnets extend their necks and give loud cries; and their soft little cheeps when they are peacefully feeding and preening with the family help keep the brood in close contact with each other. This puerile cheeping sounds strangely incongruous from older cygnets, but apart from a hiss when alarmed this is their only way of expressing themselves and it is not until they start to fly that their voices change.

In the first year the cygnet's plumage is brownish-grey, gradually turning to white or black according to the species of swan. Their charcoal-grey bills change colour as they mature. Feathers first appear on the shoulders and underwing coverts. These are followed by the tail feathers and later, the underparts and sides of their body have their down replaced by feathers. Then the head, neck and back feathers appear, and lastly, after the secondary flight feathers, come the primaries.

Swan cygnets take longer to mature than any other member of the *Anatidae*; they do not adopt adult plumage completely until their third spring. When the parents' moult is over and they have their new plumage they teach their young to fly. In northern species the cygnets remain with their parents through the winter, accompanying them on their long and hazardous migration southwards. All breeds gather in flocks during the winter, and two-year-old birds begin their first attempts at courtship and mating, although many of these swans remain together as non-breeders.

All species of swans and geese are migratory to some extent, but those that breed in temperate climates only move around in search of food and water. Migration is stimulated by the decreasing amount of daylight in autumn, and the increasing amount in spring. These external factors cause internal hormone changes in birds, which encourage restlessness and the accumulation of reserves of fat which are up to half the body weight of the bird and act as fuel for a long journey.

All migratory birds have very keen eyesight—they are thought to navigate by assessing the rate at which the sun or stars move across the sky. A bird's retina is about twice as thick as that of man's and focuses rapidly and efficiently; it can also adjust quickly to changes in light intensity. A bird's eye is relatively larger than man's but only the cornea is apparent from outside. This is only a small part of the eye— the whole eye takes up nearly all of a bird's head, pushing the brains to the back. Birds have a functional third eyelid called the nictating membrane, which can cover the eye when the eyelids are open, and which has the function of a windscreen wiper, clearing rain and fog from the vision; it is also essential to waterfowl for protecting their eyes under water. The position of a bird's eyes in its head controls its visual field. Swans' eyes are of the commonest type, flat, and at the sides of their heads. They possess a wide field of vision, having both monocular and binocular vision, but their visual field is greater to the sides than to the front where the two monocular fields of vision overlap to form a single, narrow image; this makes them prone to fly into overhead wires because they cannot detect slender objects. They also have a very narrow rear overlap so that they possess nearly a full visual field and can detect approaching danger from all sides.

During the winter, swans spend much time feeding, bathing, preening, and making exploratory flights for food and water. They make an elaborate ceremony of bathing, ducking their heads and shoulders under water and rising rapidly with a scooping motion which sends the water over their backs. Then they rub their heads sideways along their flanks and folded wings. Finally, with loosely held wings they beat vigorously against the water, generously spraying their plumage. Sometimes they completely cleanse their plumage by somersaulting in the water.

After long flights wing-fanning relaxes their wing muscles: they raise their wings and flap them rapidly two or three times. They limber up their necks with head shakes and neck stretching, after which they straighten their necks and hold their wings closed before raising them above the body and stretching the neck forward and down. Another relaxing movement is spreading one wing backward and extending it parallel to the leg of the same side. Sleep is taken at midday and early afternoon as well as at night (except in cases of severe weather and shortage of food).

Swans depend largely on climatic conditions for their well-being and propagation. Major changes in the climate of the Northern Hemisphere brought about a warming trend in the 1940s which appears to have influenced a northern movement of Mute Swans during 1943-9, but in 1962 and 1963 the winters were very cold and a decrease of 25 per cent was noticed in the swan population. Snow and ice are the greatest hazards for the Northern Swans: if winter is still holding when they reach their tundra breeding grounds they will die of starvation. Rain dictates the migratory habits of the Black Swan as rainfall is very unevenly distributed in Australia. Flooding can destroy nests and prevent the birds from getting food. Food itself can become scarce. Around 1935 *Zostera marina*, a genus of eel grass, which is a favourite food of swans and other waterfowl, died all over the world. It disappeared from the eastern coast of North America; from Brittany and elsewhere in France; and from many brackish inlets along the British coast, resulting in a decline in the Mute Swan population where *Zostera* was their main food.

Swans are mainly peace-loving birds. They fight for territory and to protect their nest and brood, mostly attacking birds of a similar colour to themselves. An aggressive parent swan may kill anything from a dog to a small waterfowl should it interfere with its territorial rights or its brood, but, being a vegetarian, it will not eat its victim, however small.

It will be seen in later chapters how peacefully man and swans can live together. Swans are intelligent birds and even the wilder species can lose their fear of man when they live with him in mutual trust and respect. Apart from nature's way of natural selection, man has been the greatest enemy of swans: he has hunted them ruthlessly, claimed much of their habitat, and fouled their waters. Fortunately for these beautiful birds man has appreciated their ornamental value as far back as prehistoric times, and it is to be hoped that they will continue to enjoy the protection they have been granted during this century.

CHAPTER TWO

Swans through the Ages

———◆———

Swans have swum upon the Earth's waters for 30 million years, which gives them a far greater claim to antiquity than man with his existence only covering the past million years. But considering life on earth extends back in time for more than 2,000 million years, these hardy, beautiful birds are of quite recent creation.

Waterfowl, bearing some resemblance to those of today, evolved 115 million years ago, and according to the latest available figures for families and species in the class *Aves* (birds), set out in the *World of Birds* by James Fisher, they come twelfth in the 27 orders of birds compiled by the Swedish naturalist, Linnaeus, in the 1758 edition of his book *Systema Naturae*. Waterfowl are placed midway between the lower orders of birds such as the penguin and flamingoes, and the *Passeriformes* (perching birds) which are the most advanced. These birds—consisting of perching, countryside birds, such as sparrows—were not on earth until 60 million years ago, but they have increased greatly since the early Pliocene period because of their great adaptability and the spread of seed-bearing plants, such as grasses and sedges, which constitute their main food.

Waterfowl rely on water for their habitat, and although they lay large clutches and manage to survive hardships, large areas of marshland and water have been drained and built on all over the world without the water being reclaimed. It is useless to conserve a small area of wetland or marshland unless there is some guarantee that the water-table, which determines the environment, remains stable, because drainage or some other development in the surrounding country, even quite a distance away, can easily upset the water-level. Swans' habitats have therefore become restricted, and even the river banks are now crammed with factories belching smoke and pouring pollution into the water. These birds are creatures of habit and continue to build their nests where they are likely to be flooded or interfered with, and in many cases they have no alternative nesting sites.

Swans have inherited certain characteristics of reptiles—from which all birds descended. The long, sinuous structure of a swan's neck is reminiscent of a snake, and there has been found a probable relationship between a swan's bone structure in the wall above and around the eyes and that of a reptile. All birds' skulls have a certain similarity to reptiles, and their skeletons show many resemblances, especially with the sub-class *Archosauria* which includes pterosaurs, dinosaurs and crocodiles. There were 'bird-hipped' dinosaurs—as distinct from the 'lizard-hipped' dinosaurs of the Mesozoic era, 225–65 million years ago. The two orders of dinosaurs were distinguished by the structure of the pelvis. In the 'bird-hipped', as in a bird, the pelvic girdle was open in the front to accommodate egg-laying and was fused to the spine at the back. Very early in their history the *Archosaurs* adapted to running on their hind legs, and this form of locomotion became established in the ancestors of birds. Many of these dinosaurs had no front teeth— they developed beaks and were probably exclusively plant-eaters. But the nearer ancestors of birds are believed to be a group of reptiles called *pseudosuchians* which were flesh-eaters of the Triassic period, 225–195 million years ago, and whose scales gradually evolved into feathers. As the forelimbs of reptiles were relieved of walking they became available for conversion into wings. Birds developed two forms of locomotion as their limb girdles became more powerful and could support them on the ground and in the air. The trunk became shortened, the skull small and compact, the neck, as in swans, long and flexible, and the skeleton became lightened by a weight-saving adaptation known as pneumatisation which is a honeycombing of hollow bones by criss-cross struts to assist in flight. All these refinements took millions of years to perfect and the oldest known bird in fossil records, the Archaeopterex, had few of the advantages of the birds of today. Its name meant 'ancient wing' and it dates back to the late Jurassic period, about 150 million years ago. Its fossil was found at Langenaltheim, Bavaria, in 1861, and the distinct imprint of feathers in clay on an otherwise reptilian fossil confirmed Charles Darwin's pronouncement two years earlier, in his book *The Origin of Species*, that birds evolved from reptiles. The Archaeopterex was about the size of a magpie, it had the lizard-like head, toothed jaws, and boned tail of a reptile, and its wing bones terminated in three slender, unfused, clawed fingers; but its rounded wings, and long, rather wide tail were feathered. Its shape suggests it was a glider rather than a flier—it probably could not fly well but used its clawed fingers to climb trees.

The feather structure of the *Anseres* is regarded as the end of one line of evolution. The minute structure of the feathers is remarkably constant and the down plumules are evenly distributed. The most highly developed feather structure in this sub-order is found in the typical ducks. The geese come lower in scale and the swans even lower, forming a bridge between the *Anseres* and the *Ciconiiformes* (flamingos), which belong to the order of birds that evolved directly before them. Birds as we know them today are very different in appearance to their reptilian ancestors, but waterfowl still retain scales on their legs and lay eggs with shells.

All primitive animals and plants originally lived in the shallow tidal waters of ancient oceans. Since plants probably evolved in water and developed there long ages before they could adjust to conditions upon land, it is not surprising to find that water-birds were the first 'true birds'; they existed after the pterodactyls, creatures with bird-like features such as beaks and light bones and with slender bat-like wings of skin, and which lived during the Jurassic period when great changes were taking place in the plants of the Earth. The first trees bearing naked seeds took over from the spore-bearing giant horsetails and tree club mosses, and flowering plants made their first appearance and evolved rapidly in a climate of full warmth and sunshine. These 'true birds' were marine species called neornithes and they evolved during the following Cretaceous period, 135 million years ago. The *Hesperornis* resembled a huge, flightless diver, and the *Ichthyomis*, was a small tern-like seabird. Both their fossils were found in the Cretaceous shales of Kansas. A cormorant-like bird also existed, and the remains of a primitive flamingo have been found in Scandinavia, so that by this time the water-birds had already diverged widely in form and adaptation.

With the start of the new era, known as the Caenozoic, all warmth and lush tropical life was wiped out by a period of bitter cold ushered in by volcanic activity which, at its close, left the world looking more like the picture we know today. The giant reptiles such as the dinosaurs were wiped out and only a small number of reptilian species remained. The seed-bearing plants, and the birds and the mammals survived and came into their own. They had much change and upheaval to contend with while the great land masses were formed—these were the mountains we know today as the Alps, the Himalayas, the Rocky Mountains and the Andes. In the valleys between the mountains, lakes formed, and gradually the weather grew warmer again and birds very similar to those of today evolved. Swimming on an Oligocene lake, about 30 million years ago, was a swan-like waterfowl of the genus *Cygnopterus affinis*, which was something similar to the present Mute Swan but smaller and with a slightly shorter upper wing. This bird's fossil was found in Rupelmonde, Belgium, and another fossil of a similar species to the Mute but with a less well developed thigh bone, the *Cygnavis senckenbergi* of the Miocene period, 25 million years ago, was found in Germany.

Birds enjoyed their greatest variety during the Pliocene period, 13–2 million years ago. The climate was warm and nature thrived, and many species of birds emerged. Pierre Brodkorb of the University of Florida estimates that about 11,600 species were living around this time, a third more than exist today, which is not surprising bearing in mind that man, the hunter, had not yet made his appearance on Earth. Swans inhabited the Northern Hemisphere in company with the ancestral ostrich, primitive pelican, heron, duck, birds of prey, fowl-like birds, shore birds, owl, crane and many others. The phalanx (toe bone) of a species described as *Cygnus herrenthalsi*, believed to be of the *Cygnus* species, has been found from this age in the Herrenthals canal in Antwerp, and records of *Cygnus* without further description, have come from Italy, France, Russia and the United States of America.

The Earth's thriving flora and fauna were due for another setback during the following Pleistocene period, which began over 1 million years ago and was heralded in by the first of many glaciations of the Great Ice Age, an age memorable for prehistoric man coming into his own. The period was one of pressure and extermination. Great ice-sheets eliminated many plants, and the birds scattered. But even at the height of glaciation the ice never spread further south than what we now know as northern Germany, northern France, the larger part of the British Isles, small areas in the north of Asia, and about half of North America. Glaciation was followed at intervals by benign inter-glacial periods and the Earth's flora and fauna advanced and retreated with the warm and cold cycles. Swans were common in Europe during the Ice Age and there is plenty of proof of their existence in fossil form because their large bones had more chance of being fossilised under that age's extreme conditions than did the smaller birds' hollow bones which were very fragile. Swan fossils have been found in old river beds, lake beds, bogs and marshlands, and also caves where they were taken by predators such as hyenas and polecats. Later, in the Middle Pleistocene, primitive man hunted them with the axe and left evidence of his kill in caves.

The hardy *Anatidae* family managed to survive these climatic up-heavals but by nature's law of the survival of the fittest those species that could not adjust became extinct. Such was the fate of the *Cygnus equitum* whose Pleistocene fossil was found in the Har Dalaam Cave, Malta. This swan had a shorter and stouter forearm than any recent swan, which greatly impeded its flight and it could not have withstood flying long distances to beat glaciation during its migration to a breed-ing area. Adequate wing-span was needed to beat the glaciation, and the swans no doubt developed their strong wing muscles during this period; this is an inheritance that has given them such flying force that they can migrate hundreds of miles at a speed of 50mph. Their red flight muscles have evolved a plentiful supply of blood vessels which prevents them from tiring easily. In flight these muscles generate heat, and speed up the body's metabolism. This heat could overpower them if it were not regulated by their respiratory system, which in migrant birds is the most efficient of any of the vertebrates. The *Anatidae* family possess a pair of small, bright-red lungs and they also have at least nine thin-walled air sacs with interconnecting chambers through-out the body, which not only bring supplies of oxygen to the tissues for burning, but help to keep the temperature at a tolerable limit, probably through the evaporation of water.

Two other species of swan became extinct after the Pleistocene period. The *Cygnus falconeri*, a swan about one-third larger than the Mute, whose fossil was found in Zebbug Cave, Malta, had long fore-legs and short feet similar to those of a goose, and they were not practicable for swimming long distances. The *Cygnus olor bergmanni* was found in Azerbaidzhan in Transcaucasia, southern Russia, and this extinct swan's hip bone was found to be coarser and less refined than the Mute of today. It is interesting to find that the short-legged swans with large, webbed feet survived the strain of swimming at speed in rough Arctic waters or down fast-flowing glacial rivers. Fossils of the Whooper and the Bewick's Swans, both of the Pleistocene period, have been found in England, Ireland, Germany, France, Switzerland, Finland and Malta; and Mute Swan fossils of the same age, show that this swan also inhabited Europe, in Germany, England, Ireland, Portugal, Italy and Azerbaidzhan.

Although to this day swans mostly inhabit the colder regions of the world, they existed during the earlier, warm Caenozoic era and their webbed feet and unfeathered legs became a potential source of heat loss during the Ice Age. Evolution has eliminated serious heat loss by reducing the blood flow to the legs of waterfowl at low external temperatures, and by some kind of vascular heat exchange so that the blood flowing into unfeathered parts of the leg does so at a very low temperature; this is the reason the feet of waterfowl are always cold to the touch. Swans also remedy their heat loss by sitting on their legs. The swans' dense plumage has served them in good stead under icy conditions, their insulating feathers not only keeping them warm but melting the ice around them and so keeping water-holes open in which they can forage for food. The body temperature of birds is 106° F (41° C), and drops 2–3° when they are sleeping; but their heat production rises when the temperature falls, although, in spite of this, in very cold weather the body temperature may fall and if it falls beyond a certain point the bird will die of cold. For this reason it is vital that swans should have enough to eat in very cold weather and so keep their body temperature at a safe level. The Arctic swans swim all night, keeping a large passage of clear water free from ice so that they can feed and keep up the metabolism necessary to maintain the body temperature.

Swan fossils of both the Pliocene and Pleistocene periods have been found in the widespread deposits left from the great volcanic activity of the later Caenozoic era in North America. In the early Pliocene times before the Rocky Mountains were formed there was a broad plateau on the western side of North America. It was about 3,000ft above sea-level, and western-flowing streams opened out into broad valleys and lakes well supplied with water from the abundant rainfall which was greater than at the present time. The temperature was mild and nature flourished. Proof of swans enjoying these pleasant conditions has been found in the swan fossil described as *Cygnus hibbardi*, found in the Hagerman Lake Beds, Twin Falls County, Idaho. This was a species of swan similar to the Whistling Swan. For most part of this era, with the Mississippi already in existence, the Atlantic coast and the Gulf Coast were covered by sea, but during the Ice Age, America was glaciated as far south as Cincinnati, Ohio. From the discovery of swan fossils of the Pleistocene period it is believed the Mute Swan was indigenous to North America. A swan fossil described as *Cygnus paloregonus* was found in Fossil Lake, Malhem County, Oregon. This fossil belongs to the group of swans without the looped windpipe and with short legs and long toes, which points to it being more like the Mute Swan. Further proof of the Mute being a native of North America has been found in other large *Anserini* bones answering their description. The great Trumpeter Swan is also represented in fossil records of this period. They have been found in Florida, Illinois and Oregon.

Australia escaped glaciation in the Great Ice Age except in the southernmost point of New South Wales, and during this period the climate was wet and cold, providing the essentials for a flourishing vegetation. Such a climate was far more suitable to swans than the climate of Australia today, with its uneven distribution of rainfall. But waterfowl had to contend with hot and arid interglacial periods when their only refuge was the coastal regions. Under these conditions, and although the Australian continent was cut off from the mainland 60 million years ago and its fauna and flora are different from the rest of the world, it is interesting to find that although the Black Swan is unique in appearance it is biologically related to the *Cygnus* species.

Page 33 (*above*) A pair of Mute Swans and their cygnets; (*below*) male Mute Swan in aggressive posture guarding nest

Page 34 (*above*) Female Mute Swan on nest; (*below*) a pair of Trumpeter Swans

During the Pleistocene period it has been found there were two swans in Australia, both similar to the Black Swan. The *Cygnus lacustric* and the *Cygnus nanus* fossils were both found near Lake Eyre in South Australia. Both swans are now extinct. It is believed the existing Black Swan occurred prehistorically in New Zealand, but whether this be so or not, the fossil of another swan, the *Cygnus sumnerensis*, known to the natives as the 'Poua', was discovered in Morick's Cave, Sumney, New Zealand. It was of quite recent origin, and although considerably larger than the Black Swan, it was otherwise similar. It is thought to have existed on Chatham Island, New Zealand, from 1590 to 1690.

At the beginning of the Caenozoic era, 70 million years ago, the south of Britain was almost entirely covered by sea, with a long island south of the present River Thames. The climate resembled that of the East Indies, with a tropical flora, palm trees and tropical birds. Great volcanic activity shaped mountains during the following 40 million years, but few sedimentary deposits are preserved in Britain, and no bird fossils have been found previous to the English albatross of the Pliocene period, which was discovered in Suffolk rocks. From 1 million to 11,000 years BC glaciation prevailed most of the time, and, except in the south, Britain was covered in ice. Vast stretches of ice connected England with France, and animals could cross over ice to Ireland at times. During the interglacial periods the melting ice would raise the sea-level and divide these countries. All the time our islands were changing considerably in outline as well as climate, and it was not until the prehistoric era—about 5,000 years BC—that England was, in shape and climate, somewhat similar to what it is today. In the early part of the Pleistocene period, birds as we know them today—ducks, geese, cormorant and crow—enjoyed the interglacial climate with cave lions and hippopotami, but as the glaciation persisted fossils of only water-birds, among them the greylag goose and the Whooper Swan, have come to light from the river gravels of warm Holsteinian times. In company with these waterfowl, and in spite of such climatic extremes, native monkeys, cave lions and forest elephants still survived in England.

By this time man had arrived in Britain. A human skull was found at Swanscombe, Kent, dating back to 250,000 years BC. This man was one of the early Acheulian men who hunted with stone axes in

Europe and Britain, living in caves and feeding on boars, giant deer and birds. Swans, unused to man, must have been easy prey during their moulting period, and Whoopers, who breed under arctic conditions today, no doubt bred in the south of Britain when the rest of the country was glaciated. Towards the end of the Great Ice Age, man's interest in swans from an artistic and gastronomic viewpoint is found in the caves of the Cro-Magnon men who painted magnificent pictures of the birds and beasts of their period in caves in various parts of Europe.

When the last glaciation was over, the men of western Europe entered the Middle Stone Age and invented more sophisticated hunting weapons. These men were Eskimo-like in culture and lived in Yorkshire; they ate swan, duck, cormorant, goldeneye and jay. Sea-bird fowlers lived around the north of Britain during the following prehistoric period (from 8,000 to 3,000 BC). They left traces of sea-birds, geese and swans in their kitchen middens and caves. Their tradition as sea-fowlers still survives at Ness at the north end of Lewis, an island in the Outer Hebrides, and sea-fowling only ended at St Kilda, another of the islands, in 1930—there was only a handful of inhabitants left, which made life on the island impossible and they had to leave the island for the Scottish mainland.

As man progressed, farming was added to his hunting skill and he no doubt domesticated some of the birds which have been found in fossil form in the surface peats of southern Britain, particularly in the fenland. Thanks to the birds' large bones and love of water, Bronze Age fossils of Mute, Whooper and Bewick's Swans have been well preserved in bogs. By the Iron Age, 500 years BC, swans were revered: they were believed to be supernatural, myths and legends circulated about them, and symbols of swans were wrought in iron. In Scotland during the late Iron Age the countrymen built sophisticated fortresses, called 'brochs', against southern Iron Age and Roman raiders. These Scottish people hunted sea-birds, and Keiss and Orkney's Broch of Ayre gives us fossils of Whooper Swans along with those of the great northern diver, gannet, cormorant, gull and guillemot.

Apart from these sea-birds of the Iron Age the marsh causeway of the great lake-village of Glastonbury has yielded the bones of many birds. Fossils of the Mute and Whooper Swans, greylag goose, ducks of

Swan folklore: A *coffin of Tungus Shaman with wooden figures of swans on posts at each side (after Harva, 1938);* B *a swan engraving on stone from the Stone Age;* C *Adonis and Aphrodite riding in a chariot drawn by two swans, design from a vase (after Reinach, 1899);* D *swans and human figures carved on the Inishkeel slab, Ireland (eighth century);* E *figure of a swan in felt, decorating a carriage in a Pazyryk barrow, used in the Pazyryk Burials which date from*
400 BC

various kinds, and the dalmation pelican have been impeccably excavated by Arthur Bulleid and H. St George Gray. These marshes in Somerset's Vale of Avalon were probably the last British breeding ground of the pelicans. Glastonbury's townsfolk were engaged in flourishing industries of metalwork, textile-weaving and pottery from about 250 BC to the time of the Romans, and with so much wildfowl and game on their doorstep they were naturally bird-hunters and pelican-eaters.

The Greeks rose to power before the Romans and they were at their height of success in the fourth century BC. They held the Mute Swan in great esteem; it was wild in Greece during the time of Socrates, and he and Plato both believed that swans sang before they died. In his *Phaedo* Plato tells of Socrates' last words in the year 399 BC before he was put to death on a charge of impiety and corruption of the morals of the young. He said: '. . . you do not think that I can see as far ahead as a swan. You know that when swans feel the approach of death, they sing—and they sing sweeter and louder on the last days of their lives because they are going back to that god whom they serve . . .' Other Greeks and Romans, such as Aristotle and Marcus Cicero, believed in the swan song; but Pliny, the Roman naturalist, doubted the truth of it. He wrote: 'Some say that swans sing lamentably just before their death; but untruly, I suppose, for my experience with several has shown the contrary.' He was nearer the truth, at least in respect of the Mute Swan, for the only musical sound they make is with their great wings, which in flight hum like the notes of a cello.

The Romans were skilled in domesticating birds and had a taste for taming them; they kept various species of ducks and the greylag goose, the ancestor of the British domestic goose and they may even have been the originators of domesticating the Mute Swan during their sojourn in England, for it was used for food and kept in a semi-domesticated state in Britain before the Norman Conquest. Fossils of Mute, Whooper, and, it is thought, Bewick's Swans, have been found at Colchester dating back to somewhere between AD 43 and AD 400 when the Romans occupied Britain. But in the Dark Ages which followed the Roman retreat from Britain at the beginning of the fourth century AD, the only proof of swans in the British Isles is from Lake Lagore in County Meath, Ireland, where the Irish saints dwelt after St Patrick had converted Ireland in the fifth century. These good men depended upon wild food for a great deal of their protein, and also kept chicken. Among the chicken bones have also been found at least 14 species of wildfowl they included in their diet, among which were Whooper and Bewick's Swans. It was the fate of the Whooper Swans still to be slaughtered for food when the Dark Age Vikings terrorised the northern waters of Europe. These Scandinavian pirates colonised the Shetland Isles, and many seabirds and wildfowl fossils from this period have been discovered in Jarlshof in Shetland. The Whooper Swans of Iceland and Greenland must also have been hunted by the Vikings during their sojourn in those countries, and the tradition of hunting these wild, aloof birds has only been broken in Iceland during the last hundred years.

The sacredness of the swan spread throughout Europe and became woven into the tales of King Arthur and the Knights of the Holy Grail in the mythical figure of the Swan Knight. There is no authentic answer to the origin of the Swan Knight; according to Wolfram Van Eschenbach in his thirteenth-century poem, 'Parsifal', the Swan Knight was Lohengrin, son of Parsifal, in the King Arthur cycle of the Holy Grail. Other names for the Swan Knight have come to light. John Rous, the Chantry Priest of Guy's Cliffe between 1477 and 1485, described him as Eneas, an ancestor of the first Saxon Earl of Warwick. In his version Eneas was one of the five children of a multiple birth. Matabrune, the wicked grandmother, changed all the children, except Eneas, into swans with collars and chains of gold around their necks. This gold was later said to be made into a cup which the Duke of Warwick bequeathed to his son, Richard, in his will of 1 April 1400. Rous, who drew Eneas holding this rich, jewelled vessel, claimed he had drunk from it at Warwick Castle.

The legends have it that Lohengrin, the Swan Knight, came from King Arthur's court to Nimwegan, Holland, sailing in a boat drawn by a swan which was in reality his brother upon whom his wicked grandmother had cast a spell. Lohengrin refused to go on his travels without his brother. When he landed at Nimwegan, Lohengrin was just in time to hear the Duchess of Bouillon plead with the Emperor Otto to protect her daughter, Beatrice, from Renier, the Duke of Saxony, who was trying to usurp her heritage. Lohengrin killed

Renier and married Beatrice after exacting a promise from her that she would never question him about his birth, for if she did he would be forced to leave her.

When their daughter, Ida, was seven years old, Beatrice could restrain her curiosity no longer and upon questioning Lohengrin about his origin he sadly had to tell her he must obey his destiny and leave her. He then sailed away in his swan-drawn boat.

A slightly different version is given in a book in Faversham Abbey which seems to contain the earliest English reference to the Swan Knight story. In this the Swan Knight rescued the widow, the Duchess

The Swan Knight, taken from a fifteenth-century painting of the swan knight Lohengrin, arriving at the court of King Henry to defend Elsa

of Bouillon, from Renier, and then married her. In this version and the French *History of the noble Helyas, Knight of the Swanne*, Ida, their daughter, is said to have married Eustace II, Count of Boulogne, and Ida's children claimed to be descendants of the Swan Knight. One of them was Godfrey of Bouillon, the leader of the First Crusade, who became known as Protector of the Holy Sepulchre. This in part was true, but Ida was in actual fact, the sister of Godfrey, the last duke of Lower Lotharingia, who was invested with the dukedom by Emperor Henry IV in 1089. When he died in 1100, Lower Lotharingia was separated into principalities, and the various rulers inter-married, all claiming descent from the Swan Knight. The Swan Knight cult spread to most of the western European countries, including Britain. Swans were moulded from gold and silver and the nobility who claimed descent from the Swan Knight wore swan badges. Among these so-called descendants of the fabulous knight were many English kings and peers; they wore swans as crests upon their helmets and as supporters of their shields and banners. King John of France bore two swans as supporters, and in 1476, King Christian of Denmark had a silver swan with a golden chain upon his seal.

During feasts, swans were feted and the Swan Knight was honoured. Philip the Good, Duke of Burgundy, gave a banquet in 1453, and before the feast there was a model of a ship in full sail upon the principal table. It had an armed knight standing inside wearing a coat bearing the full arms of Cleves, it was drawn by a silver swan harnessed with a golden collar and a long chain, and at the end of the ship was a castle with a falcon floating in the river beneath. This scene represented the story of a valiant knight who sailed on the Rhine to the Castle of Cleves and married the princess, by whom he had children who were descendants of the Duke of Cleves. It was proclaimed at the feast that there would be a joust in which the Knight of the Swan would encounter all contestants, and the knight who gave the best performance would win a rich golden swan on a golden chain from which hung a ruby.

Although there were many assertions that the dukes of Cleves founded an Order of the Swan, the real Order was founded in Brandenburg in 1443 by the margrave, Frederick II. The collar of this Order had a silver swan suspended from it below the figure of the

Virgin and Child. This Order died out after 1525 when the House of Brandenburg adopted the reformed religion; but when Mary Eleanor, sister and heir of the Duke of Cleves, married Albert of Brandenburg, a new and more important descent from the Swan Knight was formed. Anne of Cleves, the fourth wife of Henry VIII of England, brought her swan badge to England, and the Order is still commemorated in England in the 'White Swan' public houses.

The majestic beauty of swans seems to have captivated the English aristocracy from the twelfth to the sixteenth centuries. Poets wrote of the Swan Knight, and books were painted and chronicled showing the descent of various families from the legendary figure. King Edward I may have founded an Order of Swans, for it was customary during his reign for knights to make their vows of arms 'before the Swan'. This custom was practised when Edward held the 'Feast of the Swan' on Whit Sunday, 1306. It was the most splendid feast since Arthur was crowned at Caerleon and it copied the style of the Arthurian banquets. Two great swans, covered with a network of gold and little bells, their necks encircled with golden chains, were brought in by the heralds to the sound of trumpets. The knights were then ordered to make their vows of arms before the swans.

Another proof of the high esteem Britain held for swans was the mention of their being brought from Cyprus by Richard I during the Crusades. He probably only brought a few pairs, for the journey from Cyprus was long and hazardous and it is doubtful whether swans crowded in the hold would have survived. Swans were plentiful in western Europe and already semi-domesticated in Britain, so it seems unlikely that Richard, already impoverished by the Crusades, would have incurred the cost of importing swans from such a distance.

The Mute Swan was kept in semi-domestication in England as far back as the reign of King Edgar in 966; during that year the Abbots of Croyland were granted the right by Charter to take possession of stray swans. The swan is the only bird to be classed as a stray or 'estray', as it was formerly called. In Jacob's *Law Dictionary* (1732) an 'estray' is defined as: 'Any beast that is not wild found within a Lordship and not owned by any man . . . and Swans may be estray as well as beasts, and are to be proclaimed . . .'

In the Middle Ages great stretches of country in England were waterlogged and covered with dense reed beds and meandering waterways which formed an ideal habitat for swans and other waterfowl. Large stretches of East Anglia were under water, and the Mute Swan was hunted and netted for food there until it disappeared as a wild bird, but it was saved from extinction by the fenmen realising its potential and semi-domesticating it. As it nested along the rivers and waterways, the men caught the wild cygnets when quite small; they hand-reared them, pinioning them before they were fully fledged and placing them on their own waters. These swans' progeny were treated in a similar manner and gradually the wild species became extinct. The same process was taking place on the River Scarpe and other rivers in Belgium and northern France.

Swan-keeping became a profitable concern in England by the thirteenth century. Swans were protected from indiscriminate ownership by royal grant, and besides being kept for food, they were valued as a status symbol by the nobility who owned them to grace their lakes and ornamental waters.

The history of the Mute Swan in England is colourful and eventful. In deference to this regal bird, and indeed to all the swans, it is preferable to let them have their individual histories in later chapters.

CHAPTER THREE

The Mute Swan

(*Cygnus olor*)

———◆———

The beautiful form of the Mute Swan, swimming majestically on the waters of the temperate zone of Eurasia, has an aura of mystery and tradition around its shining white plumage. Of all the swans, the Mute Swan has been the one most associated with legends and history; it has been revered by kings and lauded by poets, and even to this day it is protected by royal grant in England.

Mute Swans have been domesticated in northern Europe for centuries. Up to the eighteenth century all Mute Swans in England were semi-domesticated, and they were farmed in the Netherlands for their down and food, and as ornamental birds, until after World War II. Now they are virtually wild everywhere, but in some countries, especially Britain, they retain much of their semi-domesticated nature, frequenting public waters, seeking food from man, and living mainly a residential life. Because of their domestic history more is known about the Mute than any other swan.

The proportions and posturings of the Mute Swan are more harmonious than those of the other swans. It is distinguishable from the Northern Swans by its naked black forehead and lores (the space between the eyes and head), and the black knob at the base of its deep-orange bill. Its nostrils are nearer the base of the bill than in the Northern Swans and it has a black, horny, oblong nail at the tip. Unlike the Northern Swans its culmen (the ridge on the top of a bird's bill) has no concave depression. In posture the Mute favours the Black

The Mute Swan, mating, display and nesting: A *mutual head turning;* B *rubbing flank feathers with bill;* C *upper part of the neck thickened, lower part thinned, folded wings lowered, swans facing each other;* D *precopulatory head-dipping and raising—when lifted from the water it is shaken with a circular movement;* E *postcopulatory display;* F *nesting swans*

Swan: it raises its wings in aggression, often when swimming peacefully, and at times it swims with one leg extended backwards and sideways over its back, with the web uppermost to dry it. When dry it brings the leg adroitly forward and inserts it under the cover of the flank feathers. Also, in common with the Black Swan, it tucks one leg under its plumage and stands on the other when on land. The female, as in all swans, is smaller than the male, with a smaller knob on the bill.

On water the Mute carries its long, pointed tail in a slightly uptilted position contrary to the downward curve of the Northern Swans' tails. It wags its tail, apparently in pleasure. The graceful carriage of its long, thick neck and slightly lowered head, form an S-shaped curve. It does not give the impression of being 50–60in (127–153cm) from bill to tail, nor of weighing 18–35lb (8–16kg), as it sails with superb ease on the water. Mute Swans are the heaviest of all flying birds, with the Trumpeter Swan a close second. Sometimes they attain 44lb (20kg) in weight in Britain, and there has been an instance of one weighing 50·7lb (23kg). The great muscles across its breast give it width, and its body tapers narrowly towards the rear, offering a minimum of resistance to the rippling water.

The graceful appearance of the Mute on water is strangely lacking on land. Its heavy body looks awkward as it waddles on its short, black legs and large, webbed feet measuring 6½in (16·5cm) from leg to middle toe. These paddle-like feet are set to the rear of the body, a position which, although handicapping the bird on land, allows the legs to function most efficiently in water in the combined duties of propeller and rudder.

The pre-flight movements of the Northern Swans are lacking in the Mute and before taking off, its strong wings, spanning 4–5ft, have to flog the water for some 20–30ft before acquiring sufficient air through them to soar clear. Once in flight it flies well, and can fly up to 50mph, but with its heavy body, it avoids flying over ground higher than 500ft. At the famous Abbotsbury Swannery in England a swan named 'Guardsman' was recorded as having a wing span of 12ft.

The swan's voice is by no means mute, although it is not as loud, and in some cases as frequent, as in any of the other species because its windpipe of some 27in (69cm) in length is almost straight. It emits a

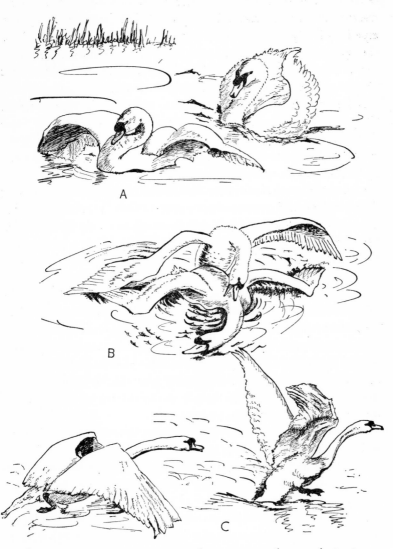

The Mute Swan, postures: **A** *territorial aggression—male swan chasing intruder;* **B** *male swan attacking intruder;* **C** *male swan in pursuit of escaping intruder*

series of noises. If annoyed or excited, it gives a loud snort which can rise to a shrill trumpeting if it is really angered. It also hisses like a goose, especially if frightened, when it gives a loud, rasping hiss and adopts the aggressive posture; but it has a gentler hiss used as a form of greeting. It also produces a friendly 'chirring' sound, and the mother bird gives a cry similar to a puppy yapping when calling to her brood.

Mute Swans make up for their weaker voice by their aggressiveness. They have the strongest territorial instincts of all the swans and once they have established a territory they are very possessive. Some of the most spectacular battles among birds take place between male Mute Swans. The aggressive swan pounds through the water after an intruder, using simultaneous foot strokes and raising the elbows so that the secondaries and tertiaries form a graceful arch over the back, and at the same time pressing his neck well down and throwing his head back. Upon meeting the intruder he turns his flank towards him, bows his head and erects his neck feathers, at the same time hissing and moving his head from side to side. The two swans fight breast to breast, often with their necks entwined and beating each other with their powerful wings. These battles can continue until they are exhausted or one of the birds is injured. The ultimate intention of the aggressor is to push the other's head under water and attempt to drown it. The aggressive posture is assumed also for intruders of other species—but only within the swan's territory. Once the aggressor is outside his territory he will draw his feathers close to his body in the submissive posture which he uses in time of fear or when mating.

When the male has driven off the intruder he will return to his mate, and in triumph they meet breast to breast, then stretch their necks, and at times the male will gently rub his neck against his mate's before returning to normal. Their victory is expressed vocally by a prolonged snorting.

Once a pair of swans have established a nest site the male will continue to defend his territory, but when there are non-breeding or immature swans on his waters, although he makes a show of battle, the combat appears to be for the most part more of a ceremonial pageant. The birds seldom harm each other. The mated swan will adopt the 'busking posture'—wings arched—and chase the younger swans over the lake. Eventually they face each other sideways, rear up in the water with necks outstretched and flap their wings violently. The actions are graceful with a suggestion of 'waltzing', and the swans appear to be enjoying themselves; it seems this contest has become established as a form of entertainment. Sometimes the female, if not brooding, joins in.

Generally, Mute Swans are solitary nesters: they prefer to nest about one and a half to two miles apart even on large lakes and expanses of water with a rich food supply. If the aquatic vegetation is adequate a pair of Mute Swans will inhabit fairly small ponds, but they must have enough escape distance to enable them to take flight. Exceptions to their solitary nesting, occur at Abbotsbury, and Radipole Lake, near Weymouth, southern England, where there is abundant food, and 30–50 pairs breed in both regions. The greatest breeding grounds of the Mute are now the waters and marshes of Denmark. They have been recorded from Lim Fjord in Jutland, southwards to Fyn Island and Køge Bay in south-east Zealand. They were depleted to three or four breeding pairs in Denmark in the 1920s as a result of the hunters' greed, but the Danes remedied this by granting them full protection in 1926, and by 1966 there were 2,500 pairs on their waters. Where nesting is unfavourable, rafts are sometimes laid out to encourage the swans to build their nests. Space is confined on Denmark's islands and here again the swans have rejected their territorial habits and breed in colonies, mainly on the Baltic coast.

In Sweden this swan was originally wild, and breeding occurred sparsely until the 1920s when numbers of Mutes, probably fugitives from Denmark's predation, established breeding grounds in most of southern Sweden up to Dalecarlia and Gastrikland in the north. Before the 1950s the swans bred mostly in the sheltered, reed-edged bays of inner archipelagos, but since then they have branched out along the coasts. They sometimes breed on the lakes of Nassjon, Blakne-Hoby and Bjorketorposton Fridlevstad. There is a breeding population in the Netherlands of about 2,500 pairs, half of which congregate in Zuid Holland. Poland has seen a great increase in breeding Mute Swans: in 1958, some 3,600 pairs were counted. Breeding is also widespread in northern Germany.

A census taken in Britain revealed that the density of swans' nests was highest in south-east England and continued to be high along the Thames Valley and into the Midlands as far as Cheshire. Nesting swans

also favoured Norfolk, Somerset and Wiltshire. The breeding population was estimated at 3,500–4,000 pairs, for the years 1955–6. In Ireland
they breed in most counties and on some of the islands off the west
coast. There is scattered breeding in Scotland, and nests have been
found as far north as Inverness on the shores of the River Beauly.

Pairs of Mute Swans are found nesting in Iran, Afghanistan, and
south-west Russia in the shallow bays of the Caspian Sea. In 1969 there
were 200 swans breeding on Lake Agros in Greece. Small numbers of
breeding swans frequent the old river beds of central Mongolia, and in
the many small, mostly brackish lakes and marshes scattered over the
Gobi Desert.

Breeding pairs of Mute Swans have greater aggressiveness than non-
breeders and immature pairs, and for this reason have a powerful
ascendancy over them, securing the most attractive nesting sites. Also,
in common with the proverbial early worm, they take up their territories earlier in the year. Once a pair has secured a territory they
usually return to it year after year, and in many cases, make it a permanent base all the year round. The cob selects the nesting site but the
pen may reject it for another. Most swans breed in the proximity of
river systems, building their nests near small ponds, flooded gravel
pits, reed beds, small lakes, marshes, and even ditches, reservoirs and
sewage farms, preferring small stretches of water rather than large
expanses such as the Norfolk Broads.

Nesting is not begun in earnest until the swans are three or four
years old; they move around from flock to flock in their second year
before finally taking a mate. During the winter they usually pair and
have at least one non-breeding year together before nesting. Some
make a pretence of nesting, even building a nest before separating.
There is a slight tendency for the female to mature earlier than the
male, and she may often be a year younger than her cob. There appears
to be a real attraction between particular individuals of the opposite sex
and not just a pair-bond associated with the sexual life: they stay together outside the mating season and apparently enjoy each other's
company.

During mating, both birds adopt an affectionate or friendly posture.
The cob has a very pronounced knob at the base of its bill at this time,
and both birds' heads and necks are peculiarly thickened. Their necks

Page 51 A pair of Whooper Swans with chicks

Page 52 Whooper Swans on the frozen lake Hyo in Niigata Prefecture, Japan

are submerged lower in the water than at other times and they lay their plumage close to the body in a smooth line in the submissive posture. Their courting display is a graceful and beautiful sight consisting of mutual head-dipping, alternating with comfort movements such as preening the back and flank, head-rubbing in those areas, and even up-ending. They perform their movements together, and when raising their necks hold their heads side by side. The wings are held so low at this time that they are often dragging in the water. As the female sinks lower into the water the cob holds her neck with his bill and mounts her. After coition the birds rear up breast to breast, with necks extended and bills pointing upwards as they call with prolonged snorting. Then lowering their heads they turn them from side to side and subside into the water, treading vigorously. Finally, after a long and pleasurable bathe they partake of an equally prolonged preen.

Contrary to popular belief, not all Mute Swans are monogamous; their marital status is very similar to man's. Some pairs breed together for years and are only parted by the death of one partner, and it has been found that there is some truth in the legend that a swan, having lost its mate, will not take another: one swan whose mate was shot, built a nest in the same place as usual and brooded on it for six weeks. But little flirtations, and even divorces, have been observed, the male indulging in a little light love-making on the side when his pen is nesting, and a pen and her brood have been known to swim off with a male who has driven her mate away. In an intensive study of mating Mute Swans, C. D. T. Minton found that 85 per cent of the breeding birds remained together.

The characteristic nest-building actions of the species are observed in the Mute Swan. The female builds where the male drops the material, arranging the reed stems, roots of water reeds, rushes and sticks, in a rough criss-cross fashion to form the outside of the nest, and adding decaying vegetation and some down to the interior. She sways her feet and body to mould out the depression in the centre until it is some 8in (20cm) deep. Nests vary in size according to the availability of the material; they can be from 3–5ft in diameter and 1–2ft high. If the nest is in danger of being flooded, the pen will build up the nest as high as she can to protect the eggs. When it is complete she sits upon it for all to see, like a snow-queen on a very untidy throne. She lays the eggs at two-day intervals, on average they number six but they can vary from two to a dozen. The Mute Swan's egg is the largest of the species, measuring 112 by 73·5mm (4·4 by 2·9in), and weighing 340g (12oz). Their elongated oval shape is of a greyish, bluish-green tinge.

It is awe-inspiring to see how long a pen will remain brooding: she rarely leaves her nest, except for short intervals to snatch a little food and this she usually does at night when the cob is on guard. Unsuccessful breeders often remain on the nest long after the incubation period of around 35 days; a pen in Scotland incubated for 56 days. When leaving, the pen does not cover her nest as the Northern Swans do, probably because of the cob's vigilance, and because of the greenish eggs acting as a camouflage against the rotting vegetation inside. Mature wild swans are usually very aggressive to all intruders at this time, but in some cases, tamer swans, especially if they are young, nest in populated areas and neither defend their nest nor their cygnets against man. If the first brood is destroyed by human predation, vandalism, or flooding, the pen may lay a repeat, but smaller, clutch after three or four weeks. Sometimes one of the parents is killed at this time and the other one has been known to carry on incubating alone. Although this is usually the female, a male Mute Swan has been known to incubate the eggs on the death of his mate.

When the chicks hatch they are fluffy balls of pale, greyish down with white underparts, weighing on average 220g (7·7oz). The down is rounded above the dark-grey bill and extends a very short way down; the legs and feet are also a dark, charcoal grey. In common with other waterfowl, swan chicks accept the first large moving object they see, which is usually their mother, but it could be a domestic hen which has reared them, or, in the case of a human being nurturing a rejected chick, the human will be imprinted upon the chick's consciousness and it will accept human fostering, becoming devoted to its substitute parent. A cygnet has been known to become attached to a large Alsation in the same way.

Although the chicks are capable of running about almost as soon as they are hatched, the pen keeps them in the nest for a day or two, and then the cob takes the first-hatched on the water. The second week is the time of high mortality for cygnets and it is estimated that, on average, a pair of Mute Swans only raise two young a year, the low

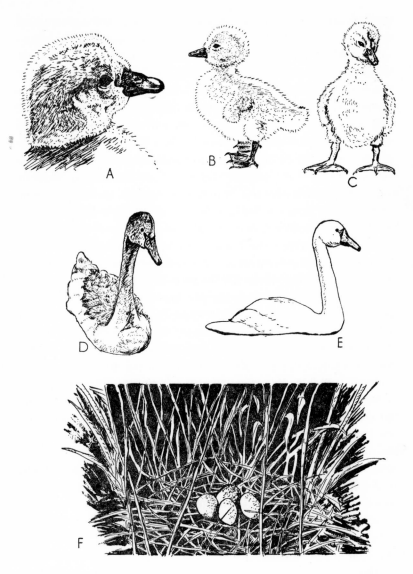

The Mute Swan, chicks, cygnets and nests: A *chick's head;* B *chick;* C *Polish chick (all white);* D *cygnet;* E *Polish cygnet;* F *nest*

figure being mostly due to predation by pike, foxes, crows and humans; but cold, wet weather can bring about death by disease.

Parent Mute Swan are a fine example of solicitude and vigilance. The family swim together, the pen leading and the cob keeping an eye on the brood from the rear. At first the chicks eat the plants their parents pull up from the water, but they gradually feed themselves, and after seven days they can dip their heads under water, and at around ten days old they attempt to up-end. The cob snorts fiercely at any sign of danger, and the pen gathers her brood together with her sharp little cry which is answered by the chicks' shrill cheeping. Signs of aggression accompanied by hissing are evident in two-week-old chicks. When they are tired the chicks board their parent's back, climbing up the slightly lowered part of the tail and gripping the swan's feathers to help haul themselves into the downy hollow of her back. When they are settled, the pen—and in some cases the cob— curves her wings inwards to form a protective cradle.

Gradually the chicks lose their fluffy appearance and grow into un-gainly, awkward cygnets. Their long necks are accentuated by their undeveloped wings and downy rumps. Feathers replace the down, their heads become brown and the face and neck a drab colour. As the cygnets mature, the brown feathers on their backs become drab and the white on their chin, neck, and underparts, becomes suffused with drab. When the flight feathers first appear they are pale drab with whitish tips in keeping with the wing coverts and alula. Their bills, legs, and webs remain grey until they are nearly a year old, and the naked lores and knob have not yet developed. Their shrill cheeping remains until they are four or five months old and is replaced by snorting, when, with fully fledged wings, they learn to fly. They flap a great deal as they discover the strength of their muscles and co-ordinate them with the air currents, until eventually they take to the air and fly across their territory without collapsing on the water. By this time they are about five months old and their parents have completed their rather slow moult.

The family often make flights together and sometimes as early as November the parents will one day return to their territory alone; or, with younger and less territorial parents, both they and their young will join the flocks on large areas of water. Sometimes the family remain until well into the New Year and by that time well mated parents, who are established in their territory, will demonstrate in no uncertain fashion their wish to be rid of their offspring. Some cygnets will return again and again to their nesting area, but they become confused by the quite vicious attacks of their parents and eventually remain in the immature flocks. This rejection by the parents is instinctively brought about by an inherent urge for self-preservation—they are aware their ever-hungry offspring will eat them out of their territory, and, with the expectation of next year's brood to feed, they have to preserve their food supply.

Swans that lose their mates during the breeding season carry on caring for the cygnets alone, be they male or female. Sometimes these swans possess strong territorial instincts and drive off prospective breeders the following year, often even chasing away a possible mate. Other swans, upon losing their mate, lose their aggressiveness, especially if they are unsuccessful breeders, and return to the flock in autumn, remaining there sometimes for several years without re-mating.

Throughout the first winter and spring, the cygnet's drab plumage gradually turns white, although some dark feathers may remain and it is not until the third spring, when they reach their maturity, that the birds are pure white. In the second year the bill changes to a pinkish tinge, and at maturity it turns orange, with the naked lores and black knob at the base. Cygnets do not move about a great deal until they are two years old and then they fly around more than any age group, searching for food and water and probable nesting sites. During the third year they are less mobile: they spend their autumn and winter, courting and pairing in the flocks. Once they have paired they are even less active, instinctively becoming territorial and ready to settle down to family life. In a healthy pair of swans the breeding cycle is continued year after year. The non-breeders move around more than breeders, returning to the flock during the moulting and winter seasons.

The Mute Swan is the main species of swan that has a moult migration. The immature one- and two-year-olds migrate in oblique lines to the protection of shallow waters along low and sheltered sea coasts; they need access to firm land or very shallow water because they cannot preen while swimming. Both male and female non-breeding birds shed their wing feathers at the end of July and their flightless period lasts 7 weeks. During this time they are rather timid, and very vulnerable. They often find mates in the moulting flocks, and the pairs move around together before joining the winter flock and eventually occupying a nesting territory the next spring. Unsuccessful breeders and non-breeders often take sanctuary in the same waters during this period. These flocks are found to be fairly constant in the English lowlands, and immature swans fly from the Thames Valley and the West Midlands to moult at Barrow-in-Furness in July, while 1,000 swans flock to the River Stour in East Anglia. More northern flocks, of around 322 birds, from Northumberland and Durham, congregate at Loch Leven in Kinross-shire for their summer moult.

In Denmark huge flocks numbering 100,000 birds gather near their breeding territory in shallow areas off the coast around Lolland and southern Zealand, and also in similar areas off the island of Amager and in Køge Bay. Smaller congregations are found in south Roskilde Fjord (30km west of Copenhagen) and on the west coast of Jutland at Ringkøbing Fjord. From 1557 to 1750 Køge Bay was well known as the hunting ground of the Danish kings who shot the flightless swans, and after that period the prefect of Scania was privileged to shoot swans on the Swedish side of the Sound. In some places in Sweden the swans were placed under protection as far back as 1910. Since 1926 when they were placed under full protection, they gather in hundreds along the east coast of the southern Sound.

Unlike the Northern Swans, Mutes seldom migrate great distances during the winter months: they live in temperate zones and rarely venture further north than 60–62° but move around in their regions seeking the warmer coastal areas during icy conditions.

Although there is no extensive migration of Mute Swans to England from Ireland or the continent or vice versa, there have been records of individual swans flying more than 100 miles during hard winters, both to and from north-west Europe. The flocks reach their highest numbers in July, but their population is swelled in January by paired breeders and their young, especially during severe weather, when they leave their territories to seek warmer waters in populated areas, such as

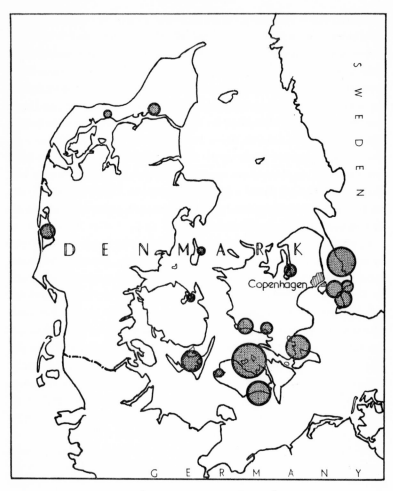

Moulting Mute Swans in Denmark

the Thames Estuary where they scavenge for human refuse, and around mills and distilleries where they find waste grain.

Although Mutes are vegetarians, they are more adaptable feeders than most swans. Their main foods are found in estuaries, coastal inlets, and small stretches of water; they prefer the depth to be 20–45cm (7·9–17·7in), where they can obtain their food by laying their chins flat across the bottom and breaking off the waterplants, sometimes pulling up whole plants and allowing them to be strewn on the water to be eventually disposed of by other waterfowl. It is possible for them to remain under water for 10 seconds, but when the water is deeper they up-end and can reach down to around a metre for about 13 seconds without having to come up for air. Swans require extra food before the annual moult as they lose on average 5 per cent of their weight at this time. Brooding females also eat enormously before egg-laying, to sustain enough fat for their long incubation.

The main foods of Mute Swans are *Potamogeton* (pondweed); *Chara* (stoneworts); *Myriophyllum* (milfoil); *Ruppia* (wigeon grass); and *Zostera marina* and *Zostera nanna* (eel grasses). They frequent salt-marsh meadows such as those along the south coast of Devon and Cornwall in England, where from April to June they will graze on succulents of non-aquatic vegetation such as *Triglochin maritima* (sea arrowgrass), *Plantago maritima* (sea plaintain), and *Puccinellia maritima* (salt-marsh grass). When the vegetation dries up later in the summer, they move to the river estuaries to forage among the *Zostera* meadows and take *Enteromorpha* (green algae). In Sweden the swans take small quantities of large green, brown and red algae and other submerged aquatic plants. They also graze on pasture grass and its roots, and the seeds of some aquatic plants such as *Scirpus* (club rush). Insects, molluscs, tadpoles and sometimes larger amphibians are taken in conjunction with plants to which they adhere, and swans have been seen straining to masticate and gulp down large fish which they have taken voluntarily. Wheat and bread are favourite foods of swans, and many swans living near towns depend a great deal on people feeding them. Complaints have been made by farmers in Britain of Mute Swans grazing on spring grass; fishermen also find them a nuisance because, they claim, they destroy the weed providing cover for fish and also eat the ground bait used to attract fish. The Home Office asked the Nature Conservancy to investigate the status of the Mute Swan in Britain, and under their patronage the Wildfowl Trust co-operated with the British Trust for Ornithology to carry out a census in the spring of 1961. In 1955 the BTO had already carried out a census from which it was estimated there were between 17,850 and 19,250 Mute Swans in Britain.

From the 1961 survey it was found that no drastic action was justified to limit or reduce the number of Mute Swans. No extensive damage to crops had been found by their eating the spring grass in certain localities. There was a certain cause for concern at the weed cover for trout being eaten in southern England, but up until then the loss of weed had been negligible and it was unnecessary to take any steps to reduce the swans' numbers unless they increased considerably. There was no evidence of them eating fish eggs, except in conjunction with waterplants. Wildfowler's complaints of swans interfering with other wildfowl during territorial aggressiveness were rejected as there was only a minute percentage of aggression reported, and ducks had been seen nesting peacefully within a few feet of a swan's nest. If provoked, certain male breeders can be aggressive and even drown large dogs by holding them under the water with their great wings— it therefore pays to be wary of breeding swans.

It was finally decided that although swans had increased greatly on the continent since they were protected, they had not reached pest status in Britain and should continue to be protected by law. Also it would still be a crime to kill a Mute Swan or interfere with its nest or eggs.

Sweden and Denmark also carried out intensive investigations to find whether the feeding habits of the large concentrations of Mute Swans in the Baltic and around the coast of Zealand were injurious to fishing, and here again the swans were exonerated and proved to be almost exclusively vegetarian.

After the 1955–6 census the Mute Swan population reached its peak in Britain in 1959, but fell to the 1955 level after the hard winters of 1961–2 and 1962–3. Severe cold, freezes the waters where swans obtain their food and they die of starvation. The royal swans on the Thames are protected from such hazards by swan-markers of the royal swans, and the Worshipful Companies of Vintners and Dyers, making regular journeys to the Thames bridges and inaccessible parts of the towpath to feed them with bread. They also open holes in the ice; and Michael Turk, the Vintner's swan-marker, on finding a swan with its beak frozen, held his hands around the beak until it thawed.

To assist the intensive investigation on Mute Swans the Wildfowl Trust, in 1960, supplied strong rings, and by the end of 1965 there were 14,000 swans ringed. From this it was found that the average annual mortality for swans ringed when under one year old was 40·5 per cent, and for birds ringed when over one year 38·5 per cent. There is possibly a greater survival in the third and fourth years of a Mute Swan's life than in the first two. Under perfect conditions a Mute Swan could live as long as fifty years, but their average age, after they have reached one year, and survived the dangers of growing up, is probably no more than from five to seven years.

The cause of death was diagnosed for 1,051 out of the 2,156 Mute Swans recovered in Britain between 1960 and 1965, and the greatest danger to their mortality was reported to be collision with overhead cables. The swan's huge wing-span can touch simultaneously two live conductors carrying as much as 33,000V. The violent flash-over caused by the shorting-out of this very high voltage kills a swan instantly, and also causes a fault in the line, blacking out quite a large area. A new and expensive type of PVC has reduced the damage caused by swans in some areas. In 1961–2 swans were the cause of 196 faults in the Eastern Electricity Board overhead network, but the number had dropped to 137 in 1964, owing to the fitting of these new conductors together with the fitting of high-speed reclosure switches.

The mileage of overhead cables and wires increases every year, and the growing tendency to run major power-lines along valley bottoms rather than on the hills, although advantageous in some ways, brings them more into contact with swans. In Kent, during two months in 1963, a quarter-mile stretch of power-line killed 21 swans—30 per cent of the local flocks. The greatest mortality from this hazard is among two-year-old birds when they are migrating to their first breeding grounds in March. Younger birds, whose deaths are 12·3 per cent less than the two-year-olds, are victims in October and November when they begin to fly. Unfortunately, because they are usually killed outright, swans have no chance of gaining experience in avoiding these wires. With their rather weak frontal vision swans have difficulty in changing their course when suddenly confronted with objects, so that besides hitting the narrow wires they also come into collision with cliffs, pylons, bridges and buildings.

Oil pollution has already been mentioned. This is a great hazard, especially to the one-year-old swans when they leave their parents to join the flocks along the coast. In 1956 a Thames oil barge sank at

Battersea and the oil spillage caused the deaths of 243 Mute Swans. At Burton-on-Trent a flock of 90 moulting swans was diminished to 15 by a major oil spillage in the River Trent. In Swedish waters oil is the chief cause of death in Mute Swans. Oiled birds have been treated with a very fine wood flour which absorbs the oil, but when rubbed off with a cloth does not eliminate the natural oils. This is a long process and the swans can experience serious internal damage if they ingest it while preening. After much research two Scandinavian chemists, Odham and Stenhagen, have found that the waxes produced by the preen gland of swans contain one or two major acids and alcohols with a complex mixture of minor components. These chemists treated oil-polluted birds at Gaulein, Scandinavia, with a synthetic wax incorporated into a mild, detergent solution, so that after cleaning the birds' plumage there was an adequate coating of wax left on the feathers which safeguarded the birds from becoming waterlogged and then sinking. After treatment 75 swans were successfully released.

Outbreaks of parasitical diseases occur in gregarious species of birds such as swans. They generally recover from these diseases but if the balance between them and the parasites is upset—such as with starvation—sickness and death follow. This was the case at Abberton Reservoir, Essex, in 1958, when 50 moulting swans (25 per cent of the flock), died from such diseases when the high water-level prevented them reaching their submarine vegetation. Some of the swans died of *Echinuria uncinata*, a genus of *Nematodes* (roundworms). This is ingested with food and has as its intermediate host, the freshwater crustacean, *Daphnia*, which carries the larvae in its body. Upon invading the swan's proventricular gland it causes ulceration, followed by enteritis and death. Other parasites which affected the swans were *Hymenolepis*, the commonest form of *Cestodes* (tapeworm), and *Trematodes* (flukes), which occur in the gut, duodenum, small intestine and rectum, or invade the respiratory system and blood vessels.

A summer of low water-levels brings the leech *Protoclepsis granata* in its train, and this can account for many swans' deaths.

Some cygnets suffer a bill deformity, the upper mandible being shorter than the lower one which causes them to put their heads on one side when feeding. Sometimes the skull is also affected. This deformity occurs in successive broods and is thought to be hereditary.

A number of swans taken to the Wildfowl Trust for post mortem were found to have died from avian tuberculosis. In this, as with pseudo-tuberculosis, the bird becomes weak, drowsy, and eventually unable to fly. The plumage loses its bloom, or, as in pseudo-tuberculosis, is ruffled. Other diseases were found to be nephritis (inflammation of the kidneys), enteritis, and pericarditis. Two birds were believed to have died from metal-poisoning after fragments of copper and zinc were found in their alimentary tracts. Another disease of Mute Swans is *Salmonellosis* (paratyphoid), which usually affects the gut and is diagnosed by great thirst, diarrhoea and convulsions. In chicks there are two peak periods in this disease, firstly when they are 3–5 days old, and then three weeks later. *Aspergillosis*, a fungal infection, is caused by a mould in certain soils and decaying vegetable matter. It produces lesions in the lungs and air sacs, and the birds show respiratory distress and have drab plumage. It is usually fatal.

Man accounts for a great deal of the Mute Swan's mortality. In the case of freshwater fishing the swans are more often the sinned against than the sinners. They become entangled in the lines, and if the fishermen do not retrieve them, the grazing birds are liable to swallow them hook, line and sinker, which causes great suffering and, if not attended to, eventually death. The Royal Swan Keeper and the RSPCA get as many as five calls a week in their various areas, asking them to release swans from fishing tackle. Human interference with swans and their nests, and egg-stealing, are all on the increase and have led to a decrease in procreation of recent years.

From the census of Mute Swans in Britain it was found that in the London area 1,229 swans frequented the river valleys, the most important being the Thames with its extensive tidal flats of clear water. Mute Swans were seen sailing on the river through the heart of London and along the coastal water as far east as Dartford, attracted by the refuse deposited by ships. Mr F. J. Turk, Her Majesty's Swan Keeper, believes swans increased on the Thames after World War I when they were less sought after for food, especially by gipsies.

Kent was found to possess as many as 1,048 birds. Norfolk had 900, of which a large proportion were a herd of non-breeders on Hickling Broad. Flocks of up to 500–700 birds remain on the River Stour in East Anglia throughout the year. In the counties of Worcestershire and

Staffordshire, where there are herds at Stratford-upon-Avon and Burton-on-Trent, the overall population is around 300 birds.

On the Fleet in Dorset there is a population of some 1,000 swans. A large number of these birds are to be found at the famous Swannery at Abbotsbury which has been in existence for at least 550 years, and originally belonged to the Abbey of St Peter, the great monastery of the Benedictine monks, who domesticated swans as a source of income. The monastery was dissolved by Henry VIII in 1541, and the same year it was purchased by Sir Giles Strangeways whose descendants have owned it ever since. The 700–800 birds there, are foot-marked, full-winged and virtually wild, although the many visitors have accustomed them to man. Before 1935 there were 500 swans on the Fleet, but with the disappearance of their favourite food, *Zostera marina*, their numbers decreased, and although both *Zostera marina* and *Zostera nanna* have returned, there has never been such a great concentration of swans. Fred Lexster, the present swanherd at Abbotsbury, belongs to the family who have been in charge of the swans for three generations and he can tell many tales, such as the swan that lived for 100 years, and another that was mated to the same pen for 40 years.

Swans were found to be less numerous in the highland areas of Wales and northern England, and mostly frequented the south-east of Scotland where 850 swans were counted. There was a flock of over 300 at Loch Leven in Kinross and over 70 at Leith in Midlothian. In Ireland there are some 5,000–6,000 Mute Swans. One flock in County Wexford reached 1,500 in 1946, and flocks of 500 are found regularly. Since the census, swan numbers in Britain have dropped by 25 per cent.

In Europe the Mute Swan is now protected, but during the nineteenth and early twentieth centuries, its population was very low. It has increased greatly since World War II and is now widespread in many parts of Europe with the exception of Norway, Finland, the northern parts of the Soviet Union; and the Iberian Peninsula and Italy in the south.

In Sweden the Mute has occurred in the wild state at least as long ago as the Iron Age. Since it was placed under protection in Sweden its numbers have increased and there are now 4,200 swans in the country. At Lake Tahern there are flocks of 1,500–2,000 birds in the summer, and during winter they are joined by family groups. In Holland the

estimated winter population is 15,000–20,000, mostly in Zuid Holland
and on the IJsselmeer. In January 1969, counts were made in north-
west Europe and it was estimated there were 14,800 Mutes in East
Germany; 4,450 in West Germany; 1,235 in Poland, and 116 in Finland. The Mute Swan, immortalised by Hans Andersen's fairy tales,
appears to be greatly respected in Denmark and claims a population of
66,000. In the Baltic Republics of Estonia, Latvia and Lithuania the
swan has become re-established after near extermination; there are

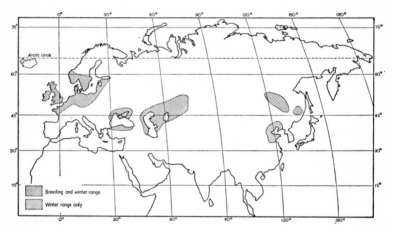

Habitat of the Mute Swan

now some 500 breeding in these countries. France possesses few swans:
there are 50–100 pairs in the north, and another 50–100 pairs on the
Mediterranean coast. There are few swans in Belgium, but Mutes have
flourished on Bruges canal for five centuries as the extraordinary result
of the murder of a tyrannous magistrate named Langhals, which means
'long neck' in Flemish. The people of Bruges beheaded him, and the
city was sentenced to keep 'long necks', or swans, at public expense
ever since. The swans are still fed by the city's employees every
morning.

Switzerland has a wintering population of some 3,500 Mute Swans,
mostly congregated around Lake Constance; and Greece retains the
legendary beauty of the swan on the Evros Delta. Austria has re-

peatedly introduced the Mute to the reed belts of Lake Neusiedl but although they have bred there, cold weather and predation by hunters have reduced their numbers. Now only about a thousand remain in Austria during the winter. Many of these feed among the shallow waters near the banks of the Danube in Vienna, and semi-tame swans are kept in the town's many picturesque parks during summer, to be taken to the ice-free waters of the Old Danube for the winter.

Further west, the delta of the Danube on the Balkan peninsula is one of the most important wetlands in Europe. In 1969 nearly 3,000 Mute Swans wintered there, protected from ice by frequenting the many brackish and salty lakes which have outlets to the sea. During the cold spells they feed on *Zostera marina* and about 150 species of algae, which grow in a shelf along the shallow coastline. In the delta area of Dobrudja, swans congregate on a flood-plain which embraces the Balta region of Russia, and has a wide belt of wetland with a sub-tropical climate and vegetation. When Rumanian winters are severe, swans migrate to the Bulgarian coast and to Turkey, where 217 swans were counted in January 1970. Beyond here swans occasionally winter on the Aral Sea, and further east on rivers in the low-lying area north of Tashkent, and on Lake Issk-koul in Kirgizstan where 400 swans were recorded in 1967–8.

On the western side of Mongolia there is a far-eastern population of Mute Swans along the Pacific coast in Korea and southern China, and some occasionally migrate to Japan. A pair of Mute Swans have been introduced to the Imperial Palace moat in Tokyo.

The Duck Research Group set up by the International Wildfowl Research Bureau calculated there were 73,300 Mute Swans in Europe and south-west Asia in 1968.

In Australia the Mute Swan was introduced as an ornamental bird for ponds and lakes, mainly in gardens and parks in the capital cities. It has been released on natural waters in northern Tasmania and south-west Western Australia, where it has become established but has shown no inclination to breed or greatly increase its range. On natural waters it breeds in late winter and spring, but it may breed at any time in sheltered parks where it is fed by the public. It was deliberately introduced into New Zealand in 1866, two years after the Black Swan, but whereas the latter has become completely acclimatised in its wild state, the Mute Swan remains restricted to ornamental ponds and a few small colonies in the Canterbury, Otago, Hawkes' Bay and Wairrapa districts. It has been seen in an apparently wild state in New South Wales and there is still the possibility it will eventually establish itself in Australia.

Long Island, North America, introduced the Mute to grace the lakes in its parks and the private waters of its country estates, long ago. Now the winter population exceeds 500 birds. In the north-eastern states its population has spread rapidly: the birds have broken away from the domesticated flocks and live in a wild state along the coast from New Jersey to Massachusetts. In the thickly populated lower Hudson River Valley the Mute has become firmly established, and its numbers in Grande Traverse Bay, Lake Michigan, have increased from a single pair in 1949, to a wintering population of 41 in 1956.

The flock of Mute Swans on Rhode Island are called Polish swans. They have a white colour phase which is distinct from the usual grey phase of the hatched chicks. These Polish swan chicks are pure white and remain so when cygnets. In their adult state they retain the fleshy-grey legs and feet of their infancy instead of the black limbs of the more common species. This white phase is caused by a pigment deficiency brought about by a gene carried in the sex chromosomes. The sex of an animal is determined by the combination of the X and Y sex chromosomes. In swans, as in all birds, the female genotype is XY which means there are two different chromosomes in its genotype which govern its sex. The male genotype is XX which means the chromosomes are similar. When a female Mute Swan inherits only one melanin-deficient chromosome she will be a white phase cygnet, whereas the male of the same parents will be normal; but if the next generation is produced by two of their offspring the brood will contain numbers of both grey and white cygnets of either sex.

Polish swans were given their name by a London poulterer who imported them from the Polish coast on the Baltic Sea. The ornithologist, Yarrell, saw them on the British coast in 1838, and thinking they were a new species, named them *Cygnus immutablis* (changeless swan). These swans occur more frequently in eastern Europe than the western region. It is thought they are the result of inbreeding, as they were bred by preference in the Netherlands to be sold as ornamental birds and for their feathers and flesh. In other parts of Europe they were left to breed and reproduce in preference to the grey cygnets who were sold for their succulent flesh. England has few of these leucistic swans, which is surprising considering the intense domestication of Mute Swans in the country. The normal Mute Swans take exception to these white cygnets, mistaking them for intruders, and sometimes attacking them, even if they are their own brood.

There are about 120 wild Mute Swans on the estuaries of the southern Cape Province of South Africa, where they were introduced from Europe fifty years ago.

With a gift of six swans from Her Majesty the Queen to the President of Brazil during the British royal tour in South America in 1969, the Mute Swan has now been introduced to all the continents.

The Queen sends her swans all over the world. Requests come into the Lord Chamberlain's office from every continent. He passes these to the Queen's Swan Keeper who decides whether or not to allow the applicant the privilege of possessing the swans. When he agrees, he selects the best pair he can find—he always sends them out in pairs, partly for breeding purposes and partly for company—and once they are captured, they are kept in a pen to have their health checked. No charge is made for the swans but the countries receiving them are expected to pay for the crating.

This privileged association of Mute Swans with man has been manifest since the ancient Greeks. By the tenth century there is proof of swans being domesticated in Britain, the Abbots of Croyland being granted the right by King Edgar to take possession of stray swans. By the Norman Conquest swans held an important part in the lives of the peasants in East Anglia, the Fens and other wetlands. In those days peasants could neither read nor write but they used signs to distinguish their swans, as the Romans did centuries before with their domestic stock. The earliest known swan-mark was that of the Prior of Coxford, Norfolk, in 1230. Unfortunately for the peasants, it was soon realised by those in power that swans were valuable game and by the fifteenth century swans were protected from indiscriminate ownership by royal grant; and an 'Act for Swans', in 1482, laid down that nobody could own a swan-mark and keep swans unless he had freehold lands and tenements to the yearly value of 5 marks above all yearly charges, which, with a mark worth approximately 160 pence, was a fair sum in those days.

Swan-keeping became very profitable, and consequently the Mute Swan was nurtured and protected as no other bird can claim to have been. In 1274 the price of a swan for food was fixed by the Statute Poltrice of the City of London at 3s per bird. At this time the best capon sold for 2½d, a goose for 5d, and a pheasant for 4d, so it is obvious what a supreme position swans held as food. In 1370 the price of a swan was raised to 4s, but it was reduced to 3s 4d in 1388, and remained stable until 1418 when it apparently became uncontrolled, varying from 3s 6d to 6s 8d.

Swans were reared to grace the tables of kings; also to be used as gifts, sometimes between nobility, and sometimes as gifts to corporations. They were also used as bribes: when the Council of Lydd defended the Burgesses of Lydd in 1447 for opening a love-letter of a former priest, they sent presents of swans to various men of authority, including the Archbishop of Canterbury, to 'secure friendship'. Noblemen owned swans to grace their waters as a status symbol and sold them among themselves to increase their stock. A heavier duty was placed on swans than on any other commodity; its levy was 6s 8d, double its value as an article of food at that time. Large numbers of swans were supplied to royalty. Henry III issued requisitions for 40 swans to be served at his Christmas feast at Winchester in 1247, and two years later for 104 swans. In 1251 he excelled himself by calling for over 125 swans from as far north as Northumberland down to Lincoln.

As with all prized possessions, swans were a target for unscrupulous men, and swan-stealing became rife. Raids were made on the estates of the nobility, and disputes arose regarding ownership, damage to property, and an owner's rights. After the fifteenth century, unwritten customs and regulations concerning the keeping of swans were written out and adopted in various districts by justices sitting in Courts of Swanmote. In the only existing code of ordinance, the Witham Ordinances, drawn up in 1524 at Lincoln Swancourt, no one was allowed to throw anything noxious into running waters nor to disturb the vegetation within 40ft of a stream where swans were nesting—a rule that would have great pertinence in these days of pollution and vandalism. Swanherds were ordered under pain of paying a 40s fine to keep their birds in an enclosure within 20ft of a common stream, or the King's Highway, so that they could be on public view. Later, all enclosed swan-pits had to be inspected.

In various districts Deputy Swanherds were appointed, and they were all subject to the King's Swanmaster, an appointment that had been in operation during the thirteenth century. Thomas de Russhams was the first mentioned swanmaster in 1361. Both the swanmaster and his deputies received a salary, a custom that continues to this day. It was the privilege of the Royal Swanmaster to keep the swan book, containing swan-marks, the names of the swanherds, their masters, every swan marked, and every owner.

One of the swanmaster's duties was to seize all strays and swans of doubtful ownership and to bring all offenders against the Swan Laws to Swanmote Courts. He had to inspect the weirs to make sure they were fitted with grates to prevent cygnets being swept over and drowned, and make sure swans were protected, watered, and fed during freeze-ups and floods. The sale of unmarked cygnets, interference with marks, and sales by unauthorised persons all came under his jurisdiction.

The annual swan-upping was his responsibility as it is today. He instructed a swanherd to read the proclamation in the market town of his area, giving the exact place and time of the upping. He hired the fishermen, boat-owners and boats, rowers and waders. He arranged the place for the swan-upping company's dinner and supper, collected the money, and paid the bills. He, or his deputy, supervised the upping, recording all the cygnets and their particulars in the swan-upping book. There had to be a roll-call of the owners, deputies had to be appointed for absentees, and a watch made on swanherds to see they were not acting for more than the permitted number of masters.

After ordering the cygnets to be rounded up the swanmaster had to witness the pinioning and marking, satisfying himself about the ownership of the parent birds. The custom was that if the cob and pen had marks of different owners half the cygnets went to the owner of the cob and half to the owner of the pen. If there was an odd cygnet it went to the cob's owner. This ancient rule applies in swan-upping today. After the upping, the birds were set loose by order of the swanmaster, but not before the owner of each parent bird had plucked feathers from the back of the bird's head to show it had been marked. Then a roll-call of the swanherds was made and if any man had left before the end he was fined.

So closely were swans protected that three proclamations were issued in the reign of Elizabeth I, and another in the reign of James I; and the Royal Swanmaster of Charles I issued a set of Orders in 1632 with a swan drawn on the title page. Among the 35 clauses in these Orders were penalties of imprisonment, fines and ransoms for stealing swans or their eggs, killing swans, driving swans from their breeding ground, and hunting ducks with dogs during the swans' nesting season. The last set of Orders was published in 1664. These old ordinances still applied until 1831 when all these Acts were repealed under the provision of the Game Act and the fine was altered to 5s for every egg stolen. Today it is a crime to steal a swan's egg—they can only be taken for breeding purposes and the maximum penalty for taking or killing a Mute Swan is £5.

Swan-marks were also protected by laws. Drawings of all the marks were kept in the swan-rolls of each area. The oldest swan-roll dates back to 1482 and is in the Public Record Office. Swan-marks were scars made by cutting through the skin of a swan's beak with a sharp penknife and stripping off the skin between the incision. More elaborate designs were made with a branding-iron. All swans had to be marked on the upper part of their bills; there were also marks made on the lower bill; the leg and foot; and the wings by pinioning. Pinioning is done by cutting a small knuckle from the right wing where the wingtip feathers grow. The birds cannot fly more than a few miles in the lop-sided fashion caused by the loss of five flight feathers and they soon content themselves with swimming.

Simple and complicated designs were made on the upper surface of the bird's bill. The simple designs consisted mostly of up to eight triangular notches, or 'gaps', cut in the bill along the lateral margin or margins. Surrey had elaborate marks with the owner's initials branded on the bill. The 'ticks' on the lower bill were only used in the Fenland: they were triangular notches cut on the edges of the lower bill. Leg and foot markings were also used in the Fenland. They consisted of designs cut on the flattened surface of the leg; notches cut on the edge of the

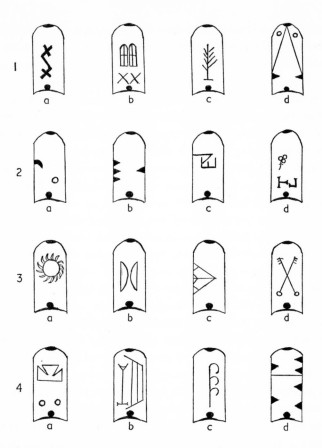

Swan marks. 1 *Oldest marks:* a *mark of Sir Richard de Totesham, the earliest dated mark, 1370;* b *mark of Sir John Golafre, in use before 1400;* c *Sir John Steward of Narford, near Swaffham, Norfolk, in use from 1436 to 1629;* d *mark of David Selby, citizen and Vintner of London, Master of the Vintner's Company 1439 to 1440;* 2 *Simple marks:* a *mark of Robert Ratcliffe of Attleborough, Norfolk, 1509;* b *mark of the Bishop of Norwich, retained until 1843; initial marks:* c *Sir Edward North of Kirtling, Cambs, 1554;* d *Sir Lawrence Tanfield, swan-master of the Thames, 1614;* 3 *Armorial bearings:* a *Sir Thomas Dereham of Norfolk;* b *Sir William Bowes; Church:* c *The Abbot of Croyland, the Scourge of St Guthlac;* d *the Archbishop of York, the Keys of St Peter;* 4 *Marks with colloquial names:* a *St Anthony's Cross, belonging to Robert Adams, Lincs, 1627;* b *boat and rudder, Thomas Adams, Cambs; marks on lower bill;* c *Sir William Willoughby, 1503 to 1525; foot and leg marks:* d *Bishop of Ely*

webs of the feet; two parallel slits cut in the webs; holes punched into the webs; and sometimes the hind toes were cut off or the claws removed.

There was a large assortment of swan-marks. Some marks depicted an object derived from the owner's name, as the two bows of Sir William Bowes. Others had their origin from the owner's calling such as a scourge owned by the Abbots of Croyland, which was a symbol of the scourge being given to St Guthlac (the patron saint of Guthlac Abbey) in a vision. There were marks such as keys, knives, arrows, cross-bows, pikes, swords, spears, oars and anchors. Other marks were crosses, crescents, trefoils, knots and the like.

Some swan-marks were in use for over two centuries. The Vintners Company, who continue to own swans on the Thames today, received their swan-mark from the Crown in 1472. The mark was a $\wedge$ from the nail of the upper bill to a nick each side of the upper jaw $\frac{3}{16}$ in deep. The $\wedge$ was omitted in 1863 and the two nicks have been the Vintners' mark ever since. Their emblem is known as the 'swan with two nicks', but this has been corrupted to the 'swan with two necks', and used as an inn sign. The Dyers Company received their mark by royal grant in 1473 and still use one nick on the right side of the upper bill as their mark for the cygnets they own on the Thames.

During the eighteenth century the custom of marking gradually died out, and it is only observed now by the Worshipful Companies of the Dyers and Vintners. The royal swans of today are unmarked. To this day the Queen's Swan Keeper, Mr F. John Turk, and the Dyers and Vintners Companies, meet for the swan-upping ceremony at the Temple Steps, Blackfriars, at approximately 9.30 a.m., on the Monday of the third week of July. The Queen's party heads the colourful little pageant; they are gaily dressed in scarlet jerseys and white trousers. The Royal Swan Keeper wears a scarlet coat with the royal coat of arms on the left sleeve, and the gold button is embossed with ER. He also sports a white naval cap with the royal crown decorating the front. The two royal skiffs have two flags: one is the royal flag which is white with a crown above and the letters ER in the centre, and the other is a red flag with a white swan in the centre and a crown in the top hoist.

The Worshipful Companies of Dyers and Vintners wear blue

jerseys and white trousers, and white jerseys and white trousers respectively. The Dyers' bargemaster wears a white swan's feather across the front of his dark-blue naval cap. Their skiff bears a dark-blue flag with a white swan in the centre and the arms of the company above. Green is the colour of the Vintners. Their bargemaster has a dark-green, naval cap with an identical white feather. A red flag is hoisted on the skiff with the arms of the Vintners Company above. The full dress of the Dyers' and Vintners' bargemen are blue jackets and green jackets respectively. Inside the skiffs are poles with hooks at the top to capture the cygnets for marking.

Marking and establishing the ownership of all the swans on the Thames takes four days. Every bird has to be caught and cygnets marked according to the mark of their parents as in years gone by. Young swans' wings also have to be pinioned so that they do not fly too far away. The first stop of the voyage is Hampton Court, on the next day the party sail as far as Staines, and the third day they anchor at Cookham, arriving at Henley, the last stage of their journey, on the fourth day. Mr F. John Turk, who succeeded his father as the Royal Swan Keeper in 1963, has to submit a quarterly report on the royal swans to the Lord Chamberlain and a special report to the Queen after swan-upping week.

One of the highest recorded numbers of swans on the Thames was in 1956, when 1,311 were upped. In 1972 there were approximately 700 swans on the river and 90 cygnets were upped. This number was divided between the Queen's swans, which were slightly in the majority, and the Dyers and Vintners Companies. Less swans nest along the Thames than previously—they now fly to the refuge of disused gravel pits to rear their broods, returning to the river for the winter. The mechanically-propelled river traffic has deprived them of their grassy banks and secluded reed beds, besides disturbing the natural weed growth upon which they feed. Also diesel oil has polluted the water. Efforts are made to protect them—before Henley Regatta the resident swans were moved to safer waters. But never again will a visitor to London be able to extol, as the secretary of the Venetian Ambassador Capello did in a letter to his master in 1496: 'The beautiful sight of one or two thousand tame swans upon the River Thames.'

CHAPTER FOUR

The Trumpeter Swan

(*Cygnus cygnus buccinator*)

———◆———

Some of the most spectacular sights of the northern skies are the great flocks of gleaming white swans migrating to and from their breeding grounds. In flight the Northern Swans resemble the Mute Swan but the rushing sound of their wings is not nearly as audible as the deep throb of the Mute's flight. They call loudly when flying, in order to keep their flocks together during their long and hazardous migrations. With the exception of the Trumpeter Swan, the Northern Swans' breeding grounds stretch across the Arctic tundra of the Northern Hemisphere, and as they come from some of the most remote regions of the world they have little contact with man and are the most wild of the swans.

The two species of Northern Swans, *Cygnus cygnus* and *Cygnus columbianus*, are most easily distinguished by their size as they are not consistent either in habitat or in the colour of their bills, although all of them have high bills, angular and flattened near the forehead and with nostrils nearer the tip than the base.

The pure-white plumage of these swans is sometimes stained a rusty colour on the head, neck and underparts owing to their habit of feeding by dipping their heads in water which contains iron or decaying vegetation. On the water they are less graceful than the Mute Swan; they hold their necks erect, often bending them sharply back for a distance and then turning them up, only curving them when feeding or annoyed. They rarely arch their wings but when they are angry they lift their half-open wings and wave them, at the same time pumping their heads up and down. This pumping movement of the head and neck is adopted by all the Northern Swans before they take flight; they call at the same time and sometimes shake their heads from side to side.

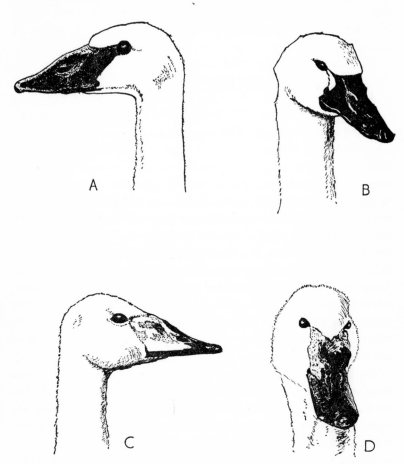

Swans' heads: A the Trumpeter Swan; B the Whistling Swan; C the Whooper Swan; D the Bewick's Swan

On land they have an advantage over their southerly cousin, the Mute, for their legs are higher and they walk with far less effort and much more briskly.

As most of their names suggest, these swans have strong vocal powers by reason of the long coiled windpipes inside the breastbone. They are sociable among themselves and have strong family ties, and their voices are lowered to a conversational tone when they are in flocks on the ground or gathered in families. The non-breeders keep in their flocks for most of the year but the breeding pairs retreat to an isolated territory.

The Trumpeter Swan is the most magnificent of all the Northern Swans and the largest of all waterfowl. Unlike the others of its group it does not breed in the Arctic and does not make long migratory flights southwards from its breeding ground. Its entire range is now confined to the west side of North America between 40° and 65° N. The Trumpeter has the tallest and most statuesque form of all the swans, carrying its long, slender neck erect from its large, white body which is set on high black legs. Its range overlaps with that of the Whistling Swan in western North America, and it is often mistaken for the smaller, shorter bird. A distinguishing feature is the Trumpeter's massive black bill with a narrow red border along the edge of the lower mandible. There is a concave depression each side of its ridge. It is comparatively longer and wider near the tip, and thicker and straighter along the ridge than with the bill of the Whistling Swan, while the nostrils are farther away (50mm—2in) from the tip. The Trumpeter's forehead is flatter.

In voice the two swans vary. The deep, resonant, horn-like call of the Trumpeter distinguishes it from the high-pitched whistling bark of its neighbour. The Trumpeter has the loudest voice of all the swans because its windpipe is greatly elongated with a high upward loop to the back as it enters the breastbone, and a partition of bone separates a section of its convolution within the breastbone; the Whistling Swan's windpipe has no such partition. The vertical loop in the Trumpeter's windpipe develops more rapidly than the horizontal loop and this method of identification is of particular value in identifying two juveniles. The bronchi (the two main divisions at the end of the windpipe of waterfowl) are generally simple and symmetrical, but in the Trumpeter and Whooper Swans this is not the case—they are bony and have interconnections here and there so that the bronchi have the appearance of a basket-like structure, swollen at the bronchial ends.

Trumpeters make good use of their strong voices, expressing their feelings vocally. The name 'buccinator' is derived from the Latin *buccinare* (blow the trumpet). The Kootenai Indians named the swan's call 'Ko—Hoh', which when pronounced gutturally is very descrip-

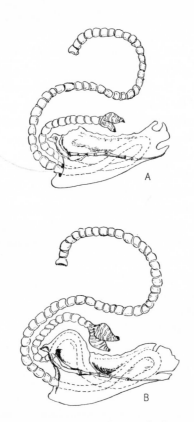

Windpipes: A the Whistling Swan—this merely loops on itself within the breastbone; B the Trumpeter Swan—a partition of bone separates a section of the fold of the windpipe within the breastbone

tive. It certainly has a horn-like quality over a wide vocal range; sometimes it is repetitive and at others it calls after long intervals.

In March and April when the swans are about to claim their territory their voices reach a climax. During their mating display they give

Swans in flight: A *the Whooper Swan;* B *the Whistling Swan;* C *the
Bewick's Swan;* D *the Trumpeter Swan*

voice conversationally at first, then other swans join in and they reach
a crescendo which trails off in a long, wailing note. The females have a
slightly higher-pitched call than their mates. Both swans are fairly
silent when nesting but when the chicks are hatched they give sharp,
tense warning notes; they also have decoy calls which are longer and
repeated frequently. If they are cornered during their flightless period
they hiss.

There is no more beautiful and stirring a sight in the whole waterfowl kingdom than a flight of Trumpeters cleaving through the air

against a setting of rugged rocky mountains and dark conifers. Their flight is firm; with the powerful thrust of their wings their long necks undulate slightly, and the clatter of their great flight quills rises above the rushing sound of their wings flailing the air. On local flights they fly low but when migrating they reach higher altitudes, straining their great bodies upwards with considerable effort. An exceptionally strong male Trumpeter is acknowledged as the head of the pecking order and heads the flock which flies in irregular formation, sometimes in an informal staggered line, often angular, and sometimes nearly abreast. A large flock sometimes adopts a V formation. The swans tuck their legs and feet under the tail in normal flight but in bitter weather they fold them forward, carrying them buried in a 'muff' of thick feathers. They are known to fly at a mile a minute but with a strong tailwind they can probably achieve 80mph, passing directly to their destination by the shortest possible route, and always choosing a large expanse of water for landing to give them a long runway. They calculate the force of the wind then descend with a roar of cupped wings, finally thrusting their huge, webbed feet forward to brake as they skim along the water to a swimming position.

The Trumpeter's breeding range once extended from Arctic Canada westwards to coastal Alaska, and southwards through the forests of the lower Mackenzie Basin into its greatest breeding zone, the Grand Prairie region of north-west Alberta. It also bred through Alberta eastwards to the numerous lakes among the pine forests of Minnesota, and further south-east as far as Indiana. Few of its prime breeding grounds extended into the United States. But with the encroachment of man, the Trumpeter's breeding grounds are now restricted to the western part of Canada and to small localities in the north-west United States. They breed as far south as they can find solitude, and they are very choosy and only accept a limited variety of breeding grounds, favouring the still, quiet waters of shallow lakes, marshes or swamps. Some 35 pairs have bred for some time in the Grande Prairie district of north-west Alberta, and there are possibly some 500 birds scattered over the unfrozen water in the interior of British Columbia and in the Kenai Moore range of the Kenai Peninsula in Alaska. Considerable numbers also nest among the small, shallow lakes in Alaska where the River Brenner broadens into a wide, flat

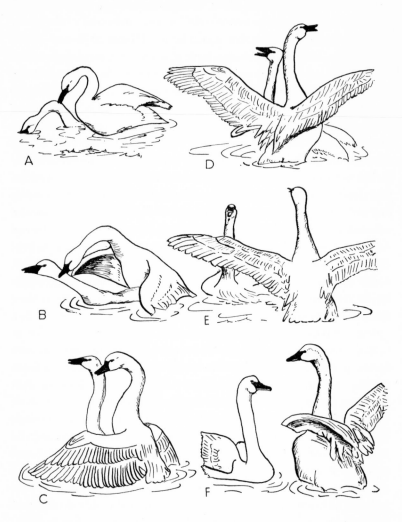

The Trumpeter Swan, mating display and nesting: A copulation—male tread-ing female and grasping her neck; B female starts to call as treading is completed and male extends his wings; C both birds rise in water after copulation, female calls and the male releases the female and joins in the calling; D and E both birds calling while turning in small circle and treading water; F at the end of the postcopulatory display the female is the first to settle back in the water

valley, and in the Tasnuna Basin, both rivers being tributaries of the Copper River.

In their northern breeding grounds the Trumpeter Swans arrive earlier than most of the Arctic birds and they are the last to leave. They fly to the musk-rat houses protruding above the snow while the ice is still fast on the semi-floating sedge bog-mats upon which the houses are built. They choose houses that have been built among bullrush beds and that are surrounded by water, and claim them as their territory and observation posts. They leave at night until April —when the ice has melted—and then settle on them permanently.

The swans in the United States are even more sedentary. They are saved long and dangerous migrations down heavily gunned flyways by the proximity of their winter and summer habitats. They winter in the shallow-water lakes, and streams and ponds of Idaho, Montana and Wyoming which are fed by hot springs and do not freeze over entirely during the long, cold winters. They breed mostly in the Red Rock Lakes of south-western Montana in the Centennial Valley, and in the great Yellowstone National Park, southern Montana, flying to these breeding grounds as early as February and returning to their hot, spring-fed ponds and streams to feed.

Trumpeters mate for the first time during their third year and seem to resent the intrusion of any other swan. They mate for life and begin nesting any time from their fourth to sixth year. In choosing their territory, mating pairs claim a nesting ground where food is available and where there are defences in the shape of small bays on the shore far from other nesting pairs. They have a preference for islands on lakes of some sixteen acres, ignoring straight shorelines and any stretches of water under nine acres that impede their flight take-off and defence against intruders. They return to their original nest year after year, repairing it or building another nearby if the old one has been destroyed.

Aggression in the Trumpeter Swan begins with claiming a territory, reaches its height during nesting and early breeding, and gradually subsides as the cygnets mature. Opposing swans rush together with loud staccato trumpeting, their quivering wings outstretched and their heads and necks extended. Other swans join in, and the tempo and intensity increase, the water being alive with great wings flapping and heads bobbing. For a few minutes the two combatants strike each other with their wings and grab at each other's feathers, then the intruder beats a retreat. Sometimes mated swans will take to the air in pursuit of a swan invading their territory, and the male will overtake it and follow its almost perpendicular flight until it is chased away. Triumphant, the breeding pair return to the water, trumpeting in staccato ecstasy and meet breast to breast with their wings outstretched, finally dipping their heads in the water with prolonged wailing notes. Nesting Trumpeters are also intolerant of Whistling Swans, geese, and other large birds, but they do not attack man or large mammals.

When they are on the ground these swans are more alarmed at the proximity of man than any other living creature: they hold their necks stiffly erect at his approach and give terse, trumpet-like warning notes, nervously pumping their necks. But when they take to the air they appear to lose this wariness and coast the shore, often passing a hunter's hide at low altitude. If they are pursued on water they sink low, and will dive if their flight is impeded. They can subside by compressing their feathers and air sacs thus forcing out air. In common with most birds Trumpeters can retain visual images, they are alert to events and recall detail well, and their hearing is equally well developed. Anything that has frightened them becomes deeply imprinted on their consciousness and if they are captured they are very elusive after release.

There is no graceful preening and head-turning in the Trumpeters' mating. Their display consists entirely of head-dipping which is performed synchronously, with their wings raised and extended. This only lasts 10–15 seconds before the male mounts the female, grasps her neck and begins treading. After copulation the male spreads his wings and the female begins to call. The birds rise in the water, calling in unison, and turn in a partial circle before settling back to bathe.

There is much activity when the swans are building their nest. The nest is made of reeds, grasses, sedges and leaves of willow or mountain bog birch, and reinforced with twigs and rushes. The female is the more active, finally lining the nest with tender leaves and stems and the nibbled down from her brood patches. The nests measure 5–6ft in width at the bottom, and the total height is about 3ft, with the top protruding 22in above the water-line. The swans choose water no deeper than 4ft for their nest sites and seek willow and birch trees for protection until the sedges grow tall enough to hide them.

During the first two weeks of May the female lays one of the 4–6 off-white eggs every other day. These elongated oval eggs are somewhat granular in texture, they measure 111 by 72mm (4·37 by 2·80in) in diameter and weigh 325g (11·50z). The shells are very strong, averaging 1mm in thickness, but in spite of their strength only about 65 per cent hatch successfully. Ravens have been seen extracting their embryo, and bears and otters cause damage to both nest and eggs. Other causes are infertility, fatal chilling of the embryo, flooding, and the pen abandoning the nest. Human intrusion is, however, the greatest cause of egg failure in the nature parks of Montana.

After the incubation period of 33–40 days the 7oz chicks hatch out. They are white, with head and neck mouse-grey and the backs of their bodies grey; the down is very short and dense and their feet and bills are flesh-coloured. As with the Mute Swan chicks there is a rare white phase when the entire plumage is white with the feet yellowish and the bill flesh-coloured. Some 13 per cent of the cygnets in Yellowstone Park were of the white phase in 1937, and there is a record of a white phase occurring in Icehouse Reserve, Idaho.

As soon as the cygnets are hatched the mother starts to moult and is flightless for a month or more. The cob moults after his mate. For the first few days the mother keeps the cygnets under her warm down, but during the first week of their lives they are subject to most hazards, such as being trampled on by their parents, or becoming entangled in plants and drowning when they venture to feed for the first time on their own. The parents' close supervision mostly prevents predators harming them, but even so their mortality averages 50 per cent and is heaviest among newly hatched cygnets. The close family unit cannot always prevent gulls, otters and mink attacking the young. Eagles and ravens were the greatest menace to cygnets at one time but now the increased range of the coyote has made it a greater danger. Cyanide 'coyote-getters' and other trapping devices have been installed in breeding areas to curb the coyote's carnage. Another protection is an artificial nest with eggs treated with strychnine to trap skunks, racoons and other ground-hunting predators. The swans are protected against human predators by the Royal Mounties in Canada, and they are under seasonal observation by the Canadian Wildlife Service in the Grande Prairie district of Alberta.

The parents' aggression is at its height when the chicks are very young, the female being even fiercer than the male. Intruding swans are driven away, but should man encroach upon their nesting site, the parents try to hide their brood under dense undergrowth before deserting them.

The chicks can run about and swim after a day or two, but they are fed by their parents for some time; they snap eagerly at the aquatic beetles, insects and crustaceans which cling to their diet of white, tender, basal parts of sedge. Some 95 per cent of animal matter has been found in the cygnets' droppings for the first three weeks of their lives. The stomach of a four-week-old cygnet contained freshwater fairy shrimp, sedges, mussgrass and sandgrit. After about three weeks they up-end in deeper water and plant life gradually replaces animal matter so that by two to three months the cygnets' diet is nearly the same as the parents.

Trumpeters' powerful legs, large webs, and prominent toes stir up the soft mud of their shallow marsh environment to dig up the tubers and rhizomes, and they pull out roots and shoots from the shores and river banks. In the fields around their lakes they eat grain and other vegetation and are not averse to insects and snails. Their overall food consists of *Myriophyllum exalbesceus* (water milfoil); *Potamogeton pectinatus* (sago pondweed); and *Ranunculus* (white water buttercup); they also greatly enjoy the wild celery they pluck from the bottom of the Alberta lakes. In winter they add to their diet leafy pondweed, clasping-leaf pondweed, mare's tail water moss, *Glyceria elata* (mannagrass) and various seeds. Their summer diet is augmented with algae, *Characeae* (stoneworts), *Nuphar polysepala* (yellow pond lilies), *Sagittaria* (arrowhead); waterweed, duckweed, and tules; the seeds of *Nymphaea polysepala* (spatterdocks), *Sparganium augustifolium* (bur-reeds), and mosses.

The long daylight of the short summer assists the young to mature rapidly and by 29 days they show aggression. The first feathers appear in the sixth week and by early October they weigh 19lb and have reached the grey phase. Their head, neck and upper back are by then brownish-grey and the underparts a lighter grey. The forehead,

Chicks, cygnets and nests: 1 the Trumpeter Swan: a chick's head; b chick; c cygnet; 2 the Whooper Swan: a chick's head; b chick; c cygnet; 3 the Trumpeter Swan and nest; 4 the Whooper Swan's nest in Iceland

crown, back of head, nape and upper cheeks have become a light, reddish-brown and the wings consist of white feathers with dark shafts. Their feet and legs are now greyish fleshy-pink, later turning to a yellowish or olive grey-black before becoming completely black. Their bills are still fleshy-pink at the middle portion of the ridge and the rest is the first to turn black; at this stage the edge of the lower mandible is a dull flesh-colour. The cygnets have more yellow on their feet than those of the Whistling Swan and their underparts are less pale. In the white phase the chick's down is replaced immediately by white feathers and the feet and bill are the same as in the grey phase.

The immature birds have a voice like a toy whistle, high-pitched and wavering. Gradually the windpipe grows longer and by January the birds have a hoarse off-key imitation of their parents, but they do not achieve their full voice until they are a year old when the windpipe has fully developed and the looping within the breastbone is complete. By four months old the cygnets are fully fledged. Those bred in Alaska are able to fly at 84 days but in Wyoming and Montana it takes them 100 to 120 days to fly. They rise directly from the water into the air and fly without any effort. They are very active on the water and dive with great ease. An early freeze-up at this stage can cause starvation among the cygnets and they can be injured when attempting their first flights. The parents are now spreading their great wings, with a span of over 6ft in the pen and 8–10ft in the cob, and they take exploratory flights with their cygnets in preparation for migration. If the nesting area is on a small lake the cygnets may tire and fall to the ground, injuring themselves so that they are unable to regain flight.

Eventually, head-bobbing and calling heralds migration from the fast-freezing lakes. With their long necks curved in the effort of taking-off the family take to the air, calling loudly. The Trumpeters which breed in Alaska fly to the wilds of British Columbia and around 1,000 visit Vancouver Island during the winter. In the United States the most important wintering areas are the Island Park area in Idaho where some 300 swans winter at Henry's Fork on the Snake River which is fed with abundant warm water from the Osborne, Harriman, Elk and Big Spring; and the warm springs on the Red Rock Lakes which also provide some 100–200 swans with the only wintering habitat they have in that area. The famous Firehole River and the Madison River are kept free from ice in Yellowstone Park by warm water from various geysers and springs, which makes this area suitable wintering habitat near to the Trumpeter Swans' breeding grounds. Several warm springs on the National Elk Refuge, near Jackson, Wyoming, keep Flat Creek open during the winter and the number of swans there is continually increasing. Through the fall and winter seasons most of the swans are gathered loosely into large flocks and they give voice both individually and in synchronised flock calls, which are audible for several miles. The immature birds are sociable and the cygnets of the same brood often stay together when their parents have left for the next breeding season. During this second summer their feathers turn white and by the winter they have only a few grey neck and body feathers, with brown on their crown and wings.

Since the last half of the nineteenth century the swans' winter habitats have diminished greatly. Before then they wintered in Washington, Oregon and California in the Pacific flyway; Montana, Wyoming, North Dakota, Nebraska, Wisconsin, Iowa, Illinois, Missouri and Louisiana in the Mississippi region; and Maryland, Virginia and North Carolina along the Atlantic flyway. Now all these regions are settled in and much of it is shot over, which has sadly reduced the population of the spectacular Trumpeter Swan. Although the Migratory Bird Treaty of 1918 prohibited the shooting of swans in the United States and Canada, there is an annual loss of both species of swan due to unscrupulous and uninformed hunters. The large Trumpeter Swans travel in small groups and are much tamer than the smaller Whistling Swans whose great flocks pitch out in the middle of the larger waters and rarely come inshore except at night. The Trumpeter's incautious habit accounts for its disappearance from all but the western coast of North America, for in the United States more Trumpeter Swans die from shooting and lead-poisoning than from any other cause. Illegal shooting has occurred chiefly during the open waterfowl season in Idaho on the Snake River and its tributaries, and in Montana and Wyoming. A new United States Fish and Wildlife Service enforcement agent was appointed in eastern Idaho in 1956 to cope with the illegal shooting, and there has been increased publicity via radio, TV, newspapers and posters to help protect the Trumpeter Swan.

Lead-poisoning affects the swans when they feed in the water that has been shot over. Even though hunting has been banned from some places in the Red Rock Lakes Refuge Feeding Grounds swans have still been found dead from lead-poisoning. There have also been casualties in British Columbia and Vancouver Island, where in 1946, in each stomach of 13 dead swans, 2–29 lead pellets were found, while one Trumpeter Swan in British Columbia had 451 pellets in its stomach.

Starvation accounts for many deaths. In the more northern habitats Trumpeter Swans die when ice remains over their feeding grounds for a long period. They become so weak that they are unable to struggle free from the frozen water and sometimes their wings become iced up in the slush-ice. Non-breeding swans have difficulty in finding anywhere to feed during the summer—if they land any distance within the vicinity of a breeding pair their presence will not be tolerated.

Few diseases have been reported in the wild Trumpeter Swans, but cases have been found of *Pasteurella multocida* (fowl cholera); *Trematodes* (flukes) enter their bowels, and such parasites as *Hymenolepis* (tapeworm), and *Sarconema euryurea* (filarial worms). *Mallphaga* (feather lice) have been found in their plumage. Leeches are only a nuisance to mature swans but they can be lethal to cygnets. Cygnets are also subject to foot deformities, which prevent them from standing. Captive Trumpeter Swans have been found to suffer from avian tuberculosis; *Aspergillosis*, a fungus disease, and *Botulism* (poisoning by *Clostridium botulinum*).

As with most swans one of the greatest hazards to Trumpeters in flight is civilisation with its pylons, telegraph cables and fence wires.

Records of this swan's longevity are few. One lived in Philadelphia Zoological Gardens for 29 years and another was noted by F. H. Kortwright of the Wildlife Management Institute of Canada to live for 32½ years.

The Trumpeter was discovered on the Merrimack River in Massachusetts, New England, in 1632, by Thomas Morton, a New Englander; he recorded their flesh as not being popular, but their skins as being greatly in demand for feathers and quills. The Indians of those days took them for food, but valued them even more for their decorative and symbolic value. They used their feathers for head-dresses, their leg bones for making implements and cut other bones into beads. In at least four ancient Indian village sites in Ohio these bones have been found among kitchen midden material.

The first time the Trumpeter Swan is mentioned by name is in 1709, when John Lawson, the Surveyor General of North Carolina, reported two species of swans in his country. One species was named the 'Trumpeter' because of the great trumpeting noise it made. These swans came in great flocks to the fresh rivers in the winter and stayed until February when they flew to the lakes to breed. Young Trumpeter cygnets were hunted at this time after the white man had discovered their flesh was more palatable than the adult swans.

The swan suffered near extermination from the hunters' and traders' greed during the nineteenth century. The Hudson's Bay Company traded in swan skins as far back as 1769, and their plumage remained an article of frontier commerce for over a hundred years, eventually reaching the London fur market by the thousands of skins. Besides taking them for food the Hudson Bay Indians made a living from hunting swans and selling them to fur companies. The swans were still abundant on the Mississippi in the early part of the nineteenth century. John Audubon, the American ornithologist wrote: 'As I gazed over the icebound river, flock after flock could be seen coming from afar and in various directions alighting towards the middle of the stream.' But the great flights of Trumpeters became a rare occurrence on the Atlantic seaboard and almost disappeared from the Pacific coast where they had been abundant in Oregon, Washington and California. In 1806 the Hudson's Bay Company exported 396 swan skins, and the Canadian company's sales reached 800 in 1818. Some 5,072 skins were sold to London in 1828, and 4,263 the next year. These skins were used as swansdown for the manufacture of powder-puffs and for the adornment of women's clothes. The quills made excellent pens. Live Trumpeters were also shipped abroad. By 1838 the Trumpeters of the eastern seaboard appear to have been exterminated. At the end of October 1838 the lower Ohio River froze and the swans flew southwards, to be caught when they reached Texas and sold in the markets of New Orleans. By the end of the century the trade in swan skins no longer flourished.

At the same time, the Trumpeter Swans breeding within the Arctic Circle were dwindling in numbers, but the traffic in wild swans still continued into the twentieth century. Their eggs were also sold. In a

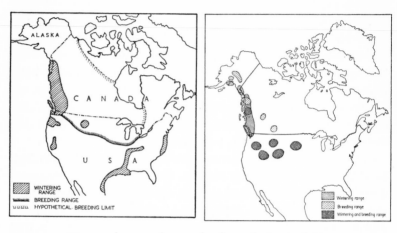

Trumpeter's past and present breeding and wintering habitat

catalogue of North American Birds' Eggs, 1892, the price of a Trumpeter's egg was $4, and that of a Whistling Swan was $2.50. Young cygnets were sold to zoos, municipal gardens, and to those interested in their propagation and exhibition. At one period a pair of Trumpeters was priced at $50. Later, between 1927 and 1931, F. E. Blaauw, the Dutch ornithologist, who reared swans, sold around ten young Trumpeters to Kellogg Bird Sanctuary, Michigan, for about $500 apiece, they were so rare. He also helped to stock the American National Parks to propagate the species.

The United States National Park Service had already become fully aware of the danger of this magnificent bird's extinction and a survey was started in 1929 which received the co-operation of the Fish and Wildlife Service in 1931. From this, only 35 birds and 15 cygnets were found in the United States and little was known about the more northern populations. The Trumpeter's extermination was accounted for not only by the hunters' and traders' greed, but by its range being diminished by agriculture and human settlement. It was placed on the list of endangered species in the Red Data Book of ICUN's Survival Service Commission.

The United States and Canada both made strenuous efforts to preserve the remaining Trumpeters and to propagate the species. Canada attempted to make reserves of their winter waters but they would not be confined, and their breeding habitat was too scattered to be protected from predators. In 1929 the Migratory Bird Conservation Act authorising the acquisition of land for waterfowl refuges was passed by Congress. The United States made refuges of the Red Rock Lakes (Montana) and the lakes of Yellowstone National Park (Wyoming), and the swans increased from 1935 at a constant annual rate of 10 per cent until 1954. Mated pairs were found to be more numerous than non-breeders during the early years of the swan census, but by 1950-4 the reverse was the case. This was caused by the older mated pairs refusing to concede their territories to the younger birds, and consequently mated pairs increased at a slightly lower rate than immature and non-breeding groups, resulting in a decline in cygnet production. This inversity is characteristic of many animal populations. By 1955 the total swan population in the United States was nearly 600, and the Canadian and Alaskan stock was estimated to be close to 1,000 birds. By 1971 the Red Data Book removed the Trumpeter Swan from the list of endangered species when their numbers totalled around 5,000. The United States and Canadian governments are to be congratulated for this remarkable increase which was brought about by vigorous protection and the discovery of new breeding groups.

In spite of this recovery the Trumpeter's shimmering white flocks are no longer seen in the central and southern parts of North America, nor do they frequent the shores of the Great Lakes. But it has accustomed itself well to man-made surroundings, and has been introduced to many new breeding habitats in North America, such as the Delta Waterfowl Research Station in Manitoba, Canada; The National Elk Refuge, Wyoming; Malheur National Wildlife Refuge, Oregon; Ruby Lake National Wildlife Refuge, Nevada, and Lacreek National Wildlife Refuge, South Dakota. The United States has established the Clarence Rhode National Wildlife Range in Alaska, and there are now 4,000 swans in that country besides other refuges in the nesting areas of the Canadian North. Taking as an example the recovery since World War II of the population of the Mute Swan in Europe, there seems no reason why the Trumpeter Swan should not respond to a sound programme of transplanting. Although it lays a smaller clutch of eggs than the Mute, and is more vulnerable to shooting, there is cause for optimism if the hunting losses can be eliminated.

The Canadian Government sent three pairs of Trumpeters to England as a present to the Queen, who placed them with the Wildfowl Trust. They have since bred both at Slimbridge and the trust's grounds at Peakirk.

CHAPTER FIVE

The Whooper Swan

(*Cygnus cygnus cygnus*)

The Whooper Swan is the Eurasian cousin of the Trumpeter Swan and is the second largest of the Northern Swans. It breeds from Iceland across northern Eurasia as far east as Kamchatka, Sakhalin, and the Commander Islands, and as far south as central Asia. Of all the swans, its range extends the furthest, covering almost the entire central part of Eurasia, with its non-breeding habitat extending from the British Isles to the western border of China, and reappearing again on the Pacific coastline.

In form, the Whooper Swan resembles the Trumpeter. It has the same elongated shape, the long, erect neck, high, black legs, and a long bill with a concave depression each side of its high ridge. The bill is quite distinct from the Trumpeter's in colour pattern—the base and lores are yellow, triangular, and extend forward each side of the bill half-way down the base of the nostrils. The rest of the bill is black.

On the water the Whooper Swan can be distinguished from the Mute by its erect carriage, and the smoothly closed wings and downward curve of the tail. The Whoopers are the most goose-like and generalised of the swans; they possess a strong, alert personality and are highly social among themselves. They bear an aloof and wary look, and express themselves with much wing-flapping and calling.

The windpipe of the Whooper Swan has a small upward loop inside the breastbone—similar to the Trumpeter Swan, but it is not so elongated and is not separated by a partition of bone. The bronchi are bony with interconnections here and there similar to those of the Trumpeter. These swans are very noisy, their call consisting of a double bugle-like note, often repeated after a short pause. Brendan Lehane, who went on an Icelandic swan-survey, described their call as 'Whooperese' and gave a very descriptive example of the sounds:

> ahng-ha
> oglank oklang ONK ONK
> Loo-ang A klooang ok ok ok
> Whoop—aaa.

It also has a high-pitched, weaker, and shorter variety of conversational notes. Pairs often call in duet: they make a great and prolonged noise, their heads and necks bobbing up and down and their wings waving in a semi-open position. The male has a shriller call than his mate. They bring their bugling to a finale with their necks rigidly outstretched. In alarm they give a loud, harsh 'Kwock', and they have a low, turkey-like gobble when impatient. At the first hint of danger— such as the approach of man—every swan in a flock will raise its head. The leader will give a loud, warning yelp and the others will join in, at first querulously, and then with their voices rising and falling until they swell to a climax. Next come the pre-flight movements. Heads pump up and down as they call, sometimes they shake them from side to side, and then the entire flock runs forward into the wind and is quickly airborne.

Compared with the Mute Swan's arduous efforts to take to the air the Whooper can take off easily in a fairly confined space, although in its breeding grounds in northern Sweden its wariness prevails upon it to establish an escape distance of 1,500m (nearly a mile). It is a swift and agile flyer, reaching greater heights than the Mute, and carrying its neck in the characteristic, stiffly upright manner of all swans, with its black feet trailing behind its slightly rounded tail. A flock of Whoopers' wings produces only a slight whistling sound, but their presence is proclaimed by a musical clarion of 'Whoop—eh' on a rising cadence in time with their wing-beats; this sound gave them their name.

When the mild weather starts around the end of February the Whoopers become strangely restless in their winter habitat. They begin to bugle and indulge in extravagant courtship displays, facing their mates with their wings outstretched and raising and lowering their heads with a sinuous pumping up and down of their necks while calling at the top of their voices. Courtship is infectious, and soon the entire party is bobbing about and crying with high-pitched, doleful voices. When an amorous Whooper is really aroused its wailing is continuous, drawn-out, and full of haunting strains; it reveals the yearning to depart for their northern breeding grounds on some secluded lake or river. They leave towards the end of April, bugling as they head northwards. A few birds may linger until June. Flocks of Whoopers fly in wedge formation with small bodies of them in a line. On migration to their breeding grounds, the leading swan steers them northwards over the Norwegian fjords, coniferous forests, and ice-capped mountains, to northern Scandinavia and the taiga of the Soviet Union, south of the tundra. Quite large numbers nest in northern Mongolia where the temperature reaches 10–20° C (50–68° F) during the summer. The Whooper used to breed in Britain, and they were still breeding in the Orkneys until the eighteenth century. They still breed occasionally on the remote lochs of Sutherland and the Western Isles, and a few breeders may still nest in southern Greenland.

The longest non-stop flight undertaken by any of the swans is the Whoopers' migration from the British Isles to Iceland—they travel 700 miles with nothing but a great expanse of sea below them. Their numerous vocal signals help them to keep their families and flocks in formation on their 14–15 hours' flight through the night and most of the day, at a speed of around 50mph. Without these signals many would perish in the changeable and stormy weather they have to contend with during their passage.

Some 5,000–6,000 Whoopers pass Iceland's wild, stony uninhabited coast to where the ground is flat and muddy, and grassy tussocks intersperse with the low tidal creeks. When they land they relax their tired muscles by wing-fanning, and rest by lowering their necks and laying them straight back. When mating couples meet on land they greet one another effusively, breasts swelling towards each other, wings open and beating close together in a whirl of reciprocatory pleasure. Then they lower themselves, thrusting their heads forward and back in rhythmic sequence. They swim, preen and carry out their courtship displays among the creeks, feeding on the abundant algae and grazing among the grassy tussocks.

Whoopers mate spasmodically during this time, they are mono-gamous but not above flirting, and they change partners more often than the Mute and the other Northern Swans. Rivals for a female will fight savagely, standing breast to breast and belabouring each other with their wings. Sometimes they hiss and lift their wings, waving them vigorously in a partially open position while repeatedly bending and extending their necks and calling with their bills pointing upwards. Sometimes this ends in ground-staring when the bird opens its wings and bends its head so that its beak touches the ground. Should the swans continue aggression in flight they lose altitude and skim the surface of the water, the victor landing amidst a foam of spray as the loser makes his escape. A strange form of threat display involves submerging their heads in water prior to confronting each other.

Eventually, mated couples fly into the interior of Iceland to nest in the shallows of lakes and tarns, or on the islets of rivers racing down from glaciers. Their trumpeting resounds clearly in the crystalline air of the remote, lake-scattered tundra and snowy mountains. The late spring sun sets for only a short period, and polar winds sweep across the ice-crusted land, some years retarding the melting snow and ice until as late as June. Although the Gulf Stream brings warm spells to the coasts of north-west Europe the interior of Iceland remains cool.

The swans now start the natural cycle of all their species—finding a territory, defending it, and building a nest. Both sexes build the mas-sive 3ft high heap of twigs, grass, leaves, reeds, lichen, moss, mud or whatever their environment provides. Inside the nest the depression, with a covering of down, is so deep that the brooding pen's neck is all that is visible, and the nest is so well camouflaged among reeds, tus-socks, or dwarf willow trees, that a man could be unaware of its presence from 10ft away.

Mating is now performed in earnest with sinuous up and down movements of the swans' heads and necks; the female is somewhat unresponsive before she finally flattens herself, splaying her tail feathers and sinking low into the water. Copulation is performed in the same manner as the other Northern Swans; afterwards the female calls

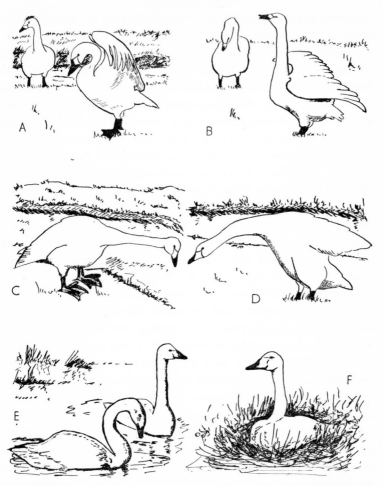

The Whooper Swan, posture, display and nesting: A and B triumph ceremony (male right); C threatening posture while calling with neck rigidly outstretched; D male performing general shake-down during threat display; E courtship; F female nesting

and is joined by the male who spreads his wings to meet her as she rises to face him breast to breast. As with the Trumpeter the pair turn in a semicircle and then bathe.

So it is, in the middle of April, that the pen settles in her nest and a day later drops her first egg into the naturally heated incubator. Where migration has only been a short distance such as from the south to the north of Sweden. The pen lays 6 creamy-white, elongate eggs weighing 331g (11·7oz) and measuring 112·5 by 72·6mm (4 by 3in). But in Iceland, where the pen's energy has been expended on a long migration, the clutch is only about 4 eggs, weighing around 328g (11·6oz) and measuring 111·8 by 82·3mm. Incubation takes 31 days. The brooding pen spends her time pulling grasses up around her nest and standing up at intervals to turn the great eggs completely over. She leaves the nest at the warmest time of the day and covers the eggs with nesting material, wriggling it off again on her return before settling down. While she is incubating she begins her moult and regains her plumage in about a month. The male is on guard nearby throughout incubation, and is a savage and jealous protector and will attack any human or animal that approaches the nest. When frightened he is likely to become bewildered and resort to nest-building movements or pretence at drinking. At the approach of another swan alighting on his lake he takes flight and flaps towards it, whooping formidably.

The Whooper Swan chicks resemble the Trumpeter's young in shape, and weigh 210g (7·4oz) on hatching. They have pale, greyish-white down above, and white below, and their crown, nape, shoulders and rump are a slightly darker grey. Their feet are fleshy-yellow in common with their bill, which is feathered in a point to the nostrils. They remain under the protection of their mother's wings for the first day or two but are soon swimming about and picking up the food their parents dig up, snapping eagerly at the glittering insects and larvae. During their intense care of their young the parents are extremely close, greeting each other with enthusiasm when the male returns from any excursion. They fly together, demonstrating their pleasure by flaying the air and water with their wings, and when afloat coiling their necks and crossing their heads from side to side with honks of excitement.

The cygnets' lives are a race to grow strong enough for the strenuous autumn migration. They grow quickly and can soon feed themselves, reaching the aquatic plants below the shallow water and sorting them out with their serrated bills. They are powerful swimmers and can run very fast. By two months they have grown a full plumage and start to fly. Their feathers are now brownish-grey above, and whitish below,

Page 101 (*above*) The Whistling Swan; (*below*) Bewick's Swans at Welney
Marsh, The Wildfowl Trust Reserve in Norfolk

Page 102   (*above*) A Black Swan and chicks; (*below*) female Black-necked Swan with chick

with white around the eyes. The bill becomes flesh-coloured or pink, edged and tipped with black, and the legs and feet are a pale, fleshy-grey. They still have wavering, high-pitched voices, for their wind-pipes have not yet fully developed. The cygnets which have survived predation by eagles, gyrfalcons, Arctic foxes, and even pike, in their first two months, have little to fear for the rest of their sojourn in their nursery ground, having outgrown most of their Arctic enemies. Although very young chicks have no fear of man—by the time they are 2–4 weeks old they will feign death at his approach. The parents bestow upon them a cocoon of care, and the cob, having moulted after the pen, will detract attention if man invades their territory when they are small chicks, by flying ahead of him and then walking in the opposite direction to the nest.

The greatest hazards for both the swans and the cygnets are now approaching. They have to absorb as much food as possible in preparation for the winter trek southwards. The parent swans look exceptionally large because of their great intake of food during the month or so when they are grounded. They eat by day and night. As summer advances the days grow longer, until for a few weeks the sun does not set. Throughout its life the Whooper Swan feeds for over three-quarters of its waking hours, but the food it swallows only remains an hour and a half in its gut and it is therefore vitally necessary for it to extract enough nutrition. During the summer, vegetation flourishes in these Arctic breeding grounds, the fields are carpeted with brightly coloured flowers and the dwarf birch and mountain willow burst into leaf. The waters are full of algae and plant life, and the swans can up-end from anything from 3–4ft down and remain submerged for 10–20 seconds, while the 7–8-month-old cygnets can up-end for a maximum of 10 seconds. The swans feed on algae, *Ranunculus tricho-phyllus* (water crowfoot), the seeds of *Eriophorum* (cotton grass) and *Empetrum* berries, reeds and grasses, and small quantities of worms and snails attached to the plants. In Iceland the heads and necks of the swans become stained a red ochre from the iron oxide in the water.

The moment at last arrives for which the swans have been preparing. On evenings in October and November the cygnets gather with their parents in family groups or flocks of thirty or so, and range themselves in lines against the wind, in tense, quavering excitement. Then suddenly with a united flapping of wings and squelching of great webbed feet across the shallow marshes, they take to the air. Some swans remain; it is estimated 1,000–1,500 birds spend their winter in Iceland. When the migrating flocks have left the mountains and the fields behind and venture upon the great flight over the expanse of ocean, many of the first-year cygnets fall exhausted into the sea, or lose their parents and consequently perish. The only resting place from Iceland to the British Isles is the Faroes, a small group of islands, easily missed in the swans' south-east passage. Even when the cygnets reach their winter habitat many of the six-month-old birds will die before they reach their second year. In their inexperience of the built-up areas of the temperate zone they are victims of electric wires, flying into aircraft, or being sucked into jets. Foxes also account for their deaths, taking advantage of their bewilderment when they wander away from their parents.

The winter habitat of the Whooper Swan stretches as far westward as the British Isles, where in Scotland their population numbers 2,000

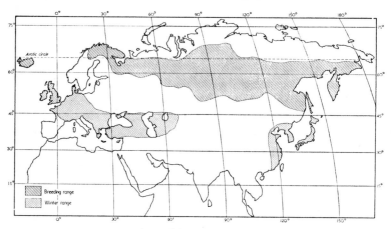

Habitat of the Whooper Swan

and they outnumber the Mute Swan in many districts. Large flocks of 300–400 winter in Aberdeenshire where they feed mostly on spilled grain, turnips, and waste potatoes from the farmlands, and towards the spring they wander far from water to partake of the grass and growing cereals, much to the annoyance of the farmers. They are also to be found on Loch Leven, and in the Hogganfield Loch on the outskirts of Glasgow in parties of 20-30; they arrive shortly after the end of the boating season and depart, it would seem instinctively, just before it is about to begin in the following spring. During the winter of 1970 there were 75 Whooper Swans wintering around Eastpark Refuge at Caerlaverock. In spite of their wariness some birds settle on stretches of water in industrial areas, and in northern and central Scotland some linger until June (mostly because they are injured and immature, and incapable of undertaking the long sea-crossing). It is estimated about 500 of these swans winter in northern and eastern England, the majority favouring the Wash and the Welney Marshes in Norfolk. During severe ice and snow they may fly further south taking refuge on Radipole Lake, Weymouth, and Swan Lake, Slimbridge. Up to 2,000 Whooper Swans winter in Ireland, favouring the lakes of Ulster and Connaught.

In 1968 there were 10,000 recorded wintering in Denmark, 1,500 in Sweden, and 1,200 in Germany; they occasionally land in the region of Lake Neusiedl in Austria. There are small numbers in Poland, the Baltic Republics, Norway and the Netherlands. Further south they frequent the Caspian Sea and great flocks of some 25,000 swans winter south-west of the Black Sea between Crimea and the Danube Delta. Greece had 400 swans land on the Evros Delta in 1969, and great flocks of 1,663 have been reported wintering in Iran. Eastwards, up to 1,000 winter in the area between the Aral Sea and Western China. A few remain in Mongolia; during the winter of 1967-8 several dozen died on the frozen northern part of the Khirgis Nur lake.

Whooper Swans, formerly abundant in Japan, were almost exterminated by hunting before being protected in 1925. Just as their numbers were increasing they fell prey to poachers during World War II, but now, when Siberia becomes locked in ice and snow, skeins of swans head southwards for Japan. They fly hundreds of miles from Siberia via Sakhalin or the overland route over Korea. More than half of them settle in Hokkaido on Lake Furen; they also winter in Honshu, Shikoku and Kiushiu, but they rarely frequent south-west Japan. On the west coast of the main island, Honshu, there is a rectangular, 300-year-old reservoir named Hyoko (Lake Hyo), in the little-known town of Suibara, in Niigata Prefecture. Facing the sea of Japan this has a warmer climate (10° C or 50° F), than the northern island, although the snowfall is exceedingly heavy. The Whoopers begin to arrive there in their hundreds in January when Suibara and the neighbouring mountains are blanketed in deep snow. Now, thanks to the love and solicitude of a farmer named Jusabura Yoshikawa, and on his death, his son, Shigeo Yoshikawa, great hosts of Whoopers have been persuaded to take up their winter residence on this sanctuary. In all some 11,000 Whooper Swans winter in Japan. Other wintering quarters for these swans on the Pacific coast are Korea and the Chinese coast around the Yellow Sea.

During the winter the Whoopers spend their time up-ending in shallow lochs and bays, dredging up slivers of water weeds such as *Zostera, Ruppia, Potamogeton, Elodea canadensis*; and roots and rhizomes such as *Glyceria maxima* (reed grass), and *Glyceria fluitans* (flote-grass). In Germany they graze among the clover. If food grows scarce, families move away from their wintering flocks and discover new feeding grounds. During severe frosts the swans swim backwards and forwards day and night to keep a channel open for food. When the frosts hold they take to the estuaries or the open shores, and in the new year the flocks generally shift from one inland loch to another. And so they feed, preen and doze without raising their voices until the milder weather alerts them and towards the end of February they migrate northwards. The parents leave their year-old cygnets in the flocks and return to their breeding grounds. By this time the young birds have become whiter, but still remain mostly grey above, blotched with white. The base of the bill turns first white and then yellow, and the feet and legs become black. They remain in flocks together for two or three years, migrating to and from their summer and winter habitats, and learning to adapt themselves to the pecking order of their flocks. By reason of their size and lesser strength they are subdued at first, but as the older birds suffer disability or die the cygnets gradually ascend the scale. With mated pairs, a female will quickly climb into the position of her deceased, high-status mate. A young swan practises display and aggression and has flirtatious attachments with a succession of females, but it is not mature enough to hold a territory or to retain a mate, until its fourth year, when, garbed in all white plumage, it has reached maturity. A pair of young swans strengthen their mating bond through the winter, their display growing ever stronger in ardour and eloquence, until the hormone changes in their bodies incite them to fly to the breeding grounds in search of a permanent nesting site.

A succession of yearly cycles of breeding and migration then begins. Having survived their first years the swans will probably live some 15–20 years. A good, long life could be around 40 years. In captivity a Whooper lived for 25 years. Whooper Swans breeding in Iceland and wintering in Britain have a mortality of about 17 per cent, including losses of young birds. In Scotland 30–40 swans were found dead with traces of mercury which they had probably ingested from wheat seeds that had been treated with agricultural chemicals before sowing. This poison probably accounted for other deaths of Whoopers in Scotland. Other diseases recorded in Whooper Swans are *Trematodes* (flukes); *Acanthocephala* (thorny-headed worms) of which two genera infect Whoopers: *Polymorphus boschadis*, a small reddish-brown worm which can cause anaemia, wasting and death; and *Fillicollis Anatis*, a slightly larger worm, which, as in the former, spends part of its life in crustacea upon which the swans feed. *Ectoparasites* (feather lice) can affect the swans for a good part of their lives but it is only when they are too weak to preen that it proves fatal. A Whooper's swan-song, in common with the Whistling Swan's, is quite musical—when it dies its lungs collapse and its windpipe emits a feeble, flute-like, and strangely melancholy sound.

The tradition of hunting Whooper Swans in Iceland stems from the Viking times, and it is only a hundred years ago that huntsmen on horseback chased them across the snow with hounds yapping at their plunging white wings, trying to capture them before their frantic efforts to lift clear bore them to safety. Tribes in northern Russia hunted them for their flesh and down; some used dogs of the Laika group and others chased them in boats, using nets for their capture. Iran also netted them on their wintering grounds. They are now protected both in Russia and Iceland and all European countries. The sight of a white flock of Whoopers once sent huntsmen grabbing their guns in eager expectancy, but now that same whiteness acts as a curb to the poacher's gun because they are protected birds, and in Britain there is a fine of £25 for killing one.

It has been found from fossils that Whooper Swans frequented

Britain and Europe since the Pleistocene period, but the first reference to the two distinct species of swans in Britain is found in the Anglo-Saxon vocabulary of Archbishop AElfric in the tenth century, when he mentions the names *Cygnus* and *Olor* as two distinct Latin words for swans. This gives reason to suppose that since the two sexes of both the

St Hugh of Lincoln, taken from a photograph of a sculpture

Whooper and the Mute Swan are alike, the Anglo-Saxons recognised the difference in the bills of the two species and gave them separate names. In the Lincoln Treatises of 1186, Giraldus Cambrensis describes how a swan 'such as had never been seen before, being much larger than the other swans, and without the knob and black colour on its bill' flew down into the Manor of Bishop Hugh (later Saint Hugh), who had just been enthroned at Lincoln. This swan overwhelmed and slew the great number of swans on the lake, saving only one female, apparently for a mate, although the aggressive bird appeared to have little need for one of its kind because it attached itself to Bishop Hugh, a kindly man with a great gift for taming wild birds. So attracted was the swan to the bishop that it kept company with him, welcoming him with great display, feeding from his hand, and attacking anyone who approached the holy man at mealtimes. It is thought this bird must have been a very large Whooper Swan, although it certainly acted out of character, Whoopers being too wild to become domesticated like Mute Swans. The swan's devotion certainly gives credence for the bishop's influence over birds.

Although the Whooper Swan's life has been hard and dangerous, it has been surrounded by legend in common with the Mute. In the past Icelanders revered it, believing it to have supernatural powers; and until migration was understood, they believed these swans returned to a mountainous Valhalla or flew to the moon during winter.

Whooper Swans have been kept in captivity on ornamental waters for many centuries. They bred at the London Zoo in 1839 and repeated their nesting in the years following. They have also bred at Vincennes Zoo, and the Kellogg Sanctuary, Battle Creek, Michigan. Breeding successes of recent years have been at Slimbridge and Whipsnade, but Whooper Swans on the whole do not take kindly to breeding in captivity. Breeding pairs need to be isolated as they are instinctively aggressive. If Whoopers are placed upon the same waters as Mute Swans they dominate the more sedate, ostentatious Mutes by reason of their quick, active form of attack. They are by no means as graceful either in shape or posture as the Mute but they have alert, vigorous characteristics, and their clear, bugle-like voices bear a haunting reminiscence of the mysteries of the remote Arctic regions of their birth.

CHAPTER SIX

The Whistling Swan

(*Cygnus columbianus columbianus: Olor columbianus*)

The Whistling Swan is the common and more abundant swan of North America, and ranks second only to the Trumpeter among the continent's waterfowl. In contrast to its larger and more statuesque neighbour it migrates great distances from the Arctic tundra of North America to as far south as 35° N, mostly on the coastal regions of Maryland and North Carolina on the eastern seaboard, and in California on the Pacific coast.

The Whistling and the Trumpeter Swans, both having white plumage, black legs and feet, and a black bill, are often mistaken for each other. The Whistling Swan has the shorter body, averaging 1·3 metres (4ft 3in) in length, and has the more rounded head typical of the species *Cygnus columbianus*. In comparison with the Trumpeter Swan's great weight of some 20–30lb, a Whistling Swan's maximum weight is 18lb. A young swan weighing 6,123g (13lb 7oz) was found to have 25,216 feathers, weighing a total of 2,621g (5lb 12oz), with 80 per cent of the feathers belonging to the head and neck. The bill, on close inspection, is an aid to identification, the Whistling Swan's being shorter and more depressed in the middle of the upper mandible, with no red border on the lower mandible. Usually it can also be distinguished by a narrow, yellow patch—rarely more than 20mm (0·79in) in length—on the naked lores in front of the eye, but sometimes this is minute, or completely lacking. Two other somewhat variable points of identification are the position of the nostrils which, in the Whistling

Swan, are nearer the tip of the bill. Also, although of no practical use for quick recognition, the Whistling Swan's tail has 20 tail feathers in comparison with the Trumpeter's 24.

By far the best criterion is the relationship of the windpipe to the breastbone in the two species. The shorter windpipe of the Whistling Swan has no bony partition separating its loop as it passes in and out of the breastbone, but simply folds on itself, giving the Whistling Swan's voice a higher-pitched note. The voice is a positive distinguishing feature between the two North American swans, but as both species are usually silent on the water and mainly quietly conversational in flocks, this means of identification is only effective in flight. The notes of the Whistling Swan are sometimes loud and striking while at other times they make soft trumpetings like musical laughter, or a high-pitched whistling sound. They also give a high-pitched, whistling bark—'Wow-wow-wow'—heavily accented on the middle note and terminating in a round full note, louder at the end. Other variations are long whoops or clucking sounds; repeated 'Who-who's'; high-flageolot-like notes, and sometimes various high and low murmurings.

In posture the Trumpeter and the Whistling Swans are very similar, both carrying their necks erect and their bills horizontally, with their wings held close to their bodies. The Whistling Swan's actions are slightly faster and more excitable than those of the Trumpeter. In common with the Whooper Swan it sometimes threatens with the head submerged in water but otherwise there is no marked difference in the two North American swans' aggressive display. It is greatly to their advantage that they are far more wary and shy of man than their more vulnerable neighbour, although at times they suffer from lapses owing to their alert and inquisitive natures.

With the first signs of spring, around the end of March, the Whistling Swans acquire their species' inherent restlessness to leave their winter quarters on the coasts bordering the north Atlantic and Pacific oceans and head for their breeding grounds. They gather in large flocks and preen vigorously in accompaniment to a constant flow of loud noises as though discussing the time, period, and method of their departure. Finally, after much pumping of the head and neck, and with loud 'Who-who's' they run along the surface of the water for

15–20ft, flapping their wings and beating the water with their feet alternately, until having gained sufficient headway, they rise into the air with surprising swiftness in the face of the wind. Flock after flock follow in quick succession, branching out into V formation in order to resist the strong, northern air, as the leader 'breaks the trail', until they are well on their way and rapidly gaining height when he will slow down to allow another leader to take over. These swans are strong and powerful flyers, and the beating of their hundreds of wings sounds like the roar of a mighty surf as they fly up to 100mph before a heavy wind. They fly faster than ducks or geese but are reluctant fliers when resting and rarely reach 1,000ft during local flights. On migration they reach much higher altitudes in an attempt to avoid the bad weather. Fortunately for them, unlike the Whoopers' migration over the north Atlantic, they fly over land, and have a chance to rest at various waterways on their northern journey.

Platoons of Whistling Swans are one of the great ornithological spectacles of North America. Their great, snow-white forms, with the large black feet protruding beyond their tails, their long, triangular, slow-moving wings, the slender line of their outstretched necks which occupy more than half their entire length, make them easily recognisable from ducks and geese.

The Whistling Swan's breeding grounds stretch from the Yukon-Kuskokwim Delta along the Bering Sea coast in the vicinity of St Michael's and St Lawrence Island, between 60° and 63° N, with a small concentration along the west tundra of the Kotzebue Sound on the Arctic Circle. The temperature in these regions reaches 10° C (50° F) in the summer and is wetter than the swans' other nesting grounds above the Arctic Circle lying between 70° and 71° N, where, to the north of the Brooks Range, the rolling hills blend into uneven uplands and spread out into a flat plain crossed near the coast by some fifty streams and rivers. Although this terrain resembles the treeless tundra of the swans' breeding ground in the Yukon Delta, the climate is drier and colder and sea ice is often visible from the shore during the entire nesting season. There is a permanent frost underneath Alaska's sparse vegetation and only the few inches of top soil thaws during the short summer, the rest remaining frozen. The frozen soil produces poor drainage and with the low evaporation rate the surface

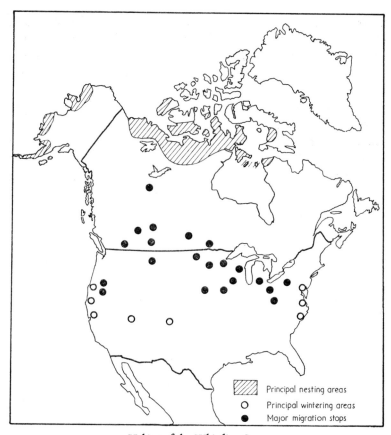

Habitat of the Whistling Swan

is boggy. During the short summer there are long hours of daylight and lush meadows of sedge, *Carex* and *Eriophorum*, with shrubby willows and alders growing along the streams.

The waterfowl habitat of the Arctic Slope is smaller than the Yukon Delta by 3,000 miles, and consequently the swan population is smaller; but surveys have been carried out by amphibious aircraft and in 1966 it was estimated there was a population of around 800 birds and a mean brood size of 2·2 in comparison with 3·4 for an average year in the Yukon Delta. The lower production in the Arctic may be compensated for by less predators.

The density of Whistling Swans' nests in northern Canada is

greatest along the coastal strip from the west side of the Mackenzie Delta to the east side of the Anderson Delta. They also nest regularly on Banks Island and Prince of Wales Island. The southernmost limit of their breeding range is near the Thelon River in the northern Canadian barrens. This swan continues breeding across the Arctic coast and the associated islands to Baffin Island, but it rarely frequents the rugged, rock-ribbed areas in central and eastern Arctic Canada, and only ventures inland where tundra replaces rocky barrens. Occasionally it nests on Cape Churchill in the Hudson Bay.

Mating takes place in the third year of the Whistling Swan's life but breeding is withheld until the fourth or fifth year. The swans mate for life; their loyalty has been witnessed on the lower Detroit River where a pair of nesting swans lingered too long during migration and the female became frozen in the ice. She was rescued by conservation officers and for a month her mate remained on the icy waters while she was nursed back to health. He eluded capture and swam forlornly to and fro to keep enough water open for food. When his mate recovered and was released, the pair gazed at each other and swam blissfully out of sight.

During the first weeks of May the swans arrive at their breeding grounds singly, in pairs, or small parties, and pitch into the icy waters gracefully, without a splash and without extending their feet in front. There is still much snow and ice in these remote tundra regions and a late spring can prove fatal to breeding, the icy ground offering no nesting sites. Nature here has to be speeded up, for the scene changes so rapidly that delay in breeding exposes the young cygnets to an icing up of their habitat before they are able to fly. Nest building takes place almost as soon as they land. They choose a variety of nesting sites, mostly at the water's edge but sometimes on the top of low hills half a mile from water. Their preference is for small islands in shallow tundra ponds.

Mating is accompanied by much calling and displaying: the swans walk about with arched necks and outstretched wings and bow to each other with their extended necks bobbing up and down. Each nest is separated from its neighbour by 130–320 hectares ($1-1\frac{1}{2}$ square miles). It is composed of moss or sedge, dried grass and down, and stands 1–2ft, well hidden by a mound of dried grass or dwarf willows and alders. A captive pair of Whistling Swans were observed while mating and the male did all the work, bringing sticks and moss and throwing them over his flanks in the characteristic manner. He mounted the nest and helped to shape it, taking 4–5 days in all to complete his task. The female took no part in the building, but this may have been due to her being a much younger bird than her mate and cannot be accepted as the general procedure.

The Whistling Swan's copulatory display is very similar to the Trumpeter's. It takes place towards the end of May and the pregnant female will lay 2–7 creamy-white eggs, the number being influenced by the weather and the habitat: less eggs are laid in a cold, late spring. On average the eggs weigh 280g (9·9oz) and are 107 by 68mm (4·2 by 2·7in) in size. Incubation takes around 32 days. From observations made with the captive breeding pairs the male changed places with the female on the nest every 15 minutes when the weather was hot, but never when it was cold, so it can be assumed that under arctic conditions the female performs most of the incubation. By the 1 July the young are hatched. They resemble young Whoopers with their white down tinged with pale grey above, although their weight, averaging 179g (6·3oz) is some 20g less than a Whooper's. The bill is flesh-pink, with grey at the tip and along the sides, and the down does not extend as far along it as in the Whooper's. Their feet are fleshy-pink. After they have left the nest and swum about they sometimes become buffy-yellow on their head, neck and breast from the iron content of the water. Early in July their parents lead them to the vicinity of a large lake or stream in a secluded spot in order that the adult birds can moult in peace and be free from the threat of predators in their flightless state. The female begins her moult when the chicks are two weeks old and the male moults when she has regained her plumage. The cygnet's growth is much faster than in the Trumpeter chicks—they eat a great many insects with the plants their parents pull up for them, and after 70–75 days they show a three-fold increase in weight.

During the short summer the swans eat enormously, lining their bodies with fat to sustain them on their southerly migration; but it has been found from a few husks of seed discovered in the stomach of a southerly migrating Whistling Swan, that they do not eat in the period immediately preceding migration. They are chiefly vegetarians but

The Whistling Swan, postures: A *threatening posture with head submerged;* B *threatening with the wings extended and the bird calling (also triumph ceremony);* C *threatening with wings held out from body without waving;* D *calling without extending wings;* E *taking flight*

they do eat small insects, molluscs and particularly snails. Their diet varies according to their habitat. They show a preference for roots and tubers such as *Potamogeton* (pondweed), and *Sagittaria* (arrowhead). They also eat the leaves, stems and seeds of pondweeds, *Characeae* (stoneworts); *Ruppia* (wigeon grass) and *Vallisneria* (wild celery), and the leaves of *Typha* (reedmace); *Scirpus* (club rush); *Equisetum* (horsetail) and *Polygonum* (persicaria).

In spite of the parental care enjoyed by the cygnets, they are prey to coyotes which have spread from the western part of North America as far north as Alaska. Arctic foxes and golden eagles are other predators of the young and immature cygnets. Young chicks have no fear of man but, similar to the Whoopers, from two to four months old they will feign death when handled, drooping their necks in a lifeless posture. The parents are not always endowed with sufficient courage to protect their young—some remain with them in danger but others fly away several yards.

By the end of September the cygnets have lost their first brownish-grey feathers and their entire plumage is a pale, ashy-grey, darker on the head and lighter on the breast and belly; here again the iron in the water may turn their plumage from plumbeous, to sooty-brown. The bill changes to a reddish or purplish colour with the tip dusky red. Unlike the Trumpeter cygnets young Whistling Swans' feet do not have a yellowish tinge but change from flesh-coloured to dusky-pink. Even after 2 years their mature white plumage may have a few stray grey feathers. A yearling cygnet is about one-third the size of an adult bird and it takes 3–5 years for it to assume its full size and maturity. The flight feathers are complete by the middle of September, and their parents—also in full plumage—prepare their young for their migratory flight of 2,500–3,000 miles southward. At this stage a late spring and early start to winter will take toll of the cygnets, who will still be flightless by the freeze-up, and even if they can find food until they can fly, malnutrition and exhaustion together with the departure of the main flocks, will beat them on migration. Many of the young never live to gain flight under these conditions.

The winter migration is more leisurely than the great flight northwards in the spring, and the swans start to leave their breeding grounds in the middle of September. Some of the swans from northern Alaska cross the Rocky Mountains in the Arctic region to join the Canadian population flying southwards through the interior of Canada. At the beginning of October large flocks rest and feed in the small lakes east of the Mackenzie River, and concentrations of 25,000 build up on Lakes Claire and Richardson, located at the delta of Lake Athabasca in north-eastern Alberta. Populations separate after resting, some, heading over the Prairies of Canada south-eastwards, refreshing themselves on the Great Lakes before reaching their winter quarters on the Atlantic seaboard. Others travel south-westerly, some wintering in British Columbia, where a population varying from 150 to 225 birds occupy the South Thompson River near Kamloops, and others visit the lower mainland region of the Fraser River, Lonesome Lake, and Queen Charlotte Islands.

All along the states of the Pacific flyway the Whistling Swan is the latest to arrive in the fall and the first to leave for the north in the spring. During the second week of October most of the United States Pacific population of Whistling Swans arrive at the Bear River Delta in northern Utah, and by the end of November between 10,000 and 20,000 swans congregate there, some of them wintering on the State Federal waterfowl refuges if the weather is not too severe. The centre of their wintering habitat is in the large marshes of the Great Basin and the Klamath Basin, and in the Sacramento Valley in California, where they eat grain and waste potato from arable land. Small numbers pass the winter in Washington and Idaho. The central United States is mainly a resting place for the swans wintering in the Pacific flyway or flying eastwards. Flocks pass through Freezeout Lake in Montana and some land on the lakes of the Wind River Indian Reservation and the Big Horn Basin in Wyoming. Family groups migrating eastward pass through north-east Dakota where their presence causes concern because it is thought they destroy aquatic duck foods. The west coast population from 1952–6 averaged 86,000 swans.

Bird watchers travel long distances to see the great gatherings of Whistling Swans in Chesapeake Bay. Over one half of their entire population spend winter on the estuaries of the Chesapeake Bay and Currituck Sound in Maryland, Virginia, and North Carolina, and the number is increasing. In January 1967 Chesapeake Bay alone had over 52,000 birds. In the upper portions of the bay there are extensive areas

Page 119   (*above*) A pair of Coscoroba Swans; (*below*) Swan-upping at
Maidenhead, England

Page 120
Leda and the Swan, by
Michelangelo

of shallow, fresh and brackish estuarine waters which make ideal habitats. In the fresh waters great beds of submerged aquatic plants such as wild celery, widgeon grass, sago pondweed, and, to a lesser extent, clasping leaf pondweed, together with an abundance of shelled molluscs, such as long clam and baltic macoma, furnish an ample food supply. In the bay's brackish waters the swans eat mostly widgeon grass, with small amounts of sago pondweed and clasping leaf pondweed, but in the salty estuarine waters further out to sea they avoid the increased salinity of widgeon grass.

These great gatherings of swans on the Chesapeake Bay caused concern to the local shellfish gatherers who claimed that these birds took the commercially valuable long (soft-shelled) clams, and they demanded that an open hunting season should be introduced. To discover whether there were any grounds for this complaint, aerial surveys were carried out by personnel of the Branch of Game Management and the Bureau of Sport, Fisheries and Wildlife, both belonging to the Fish and Wildlife Service. Field studies of the swans' environment and laboratory analysis of the food they ate were conducted by Robert E. Stewart and Joseph Manning, and this valuable clam was found in only 14 birds, constituting approximately 8 per cent of their food, which, it was agreed, did not merit any action to reduce the swan population.

Small numbers of swans occur in the estuarine marsh ponds in Dorchester County, Maryland, where they adapt themselves to eating root-stalks of emergent marsh plants besides the popular widgeon grass. Great wintering concentrations of swans frequent the brackish estuarine water of the Potomac River on the western side of Chesapeake Bay, and along the bay's eastern shores they are to be found on the Chester River and Eastern Bay.

The only other important wintering ground of the swans along the Atlantic coast is the tidewater area extending from Back Bay, Virginia, to the north shore of Pamlico Sound, North Carolina. Only on very rare occasions has the swan been identified as far south as Louisiana and then during November through to February.

In the Chesapeake Bay area the Whistling Swan lives alongside one of the most rapidly expanding populations in the eastern United States. Migrating swans pass over important airline routes, and in 1962

Chicks, cygnets and nests: 1 *the Whistling Swan:* a *chick's head;* b *chick;*
c *cygnet;* 2 *the Bewick's Swan:* a *chick's head;* b *chick;* c *cygnet;* 3 *the*
Bewick's Swan's nest; 4 *the Whistling Swan's nest*

a Viscount airliner in Maryland was lost and all seventeen people aboard were killed, as a result of a collision with swans. This accident prompted growing awareness of the risk that large waterfowl were to aircraft security, and in 1966, the Air Force Office of Scientific Research emphasised the necessity for biological studies of bird migration involving their nesting and feeding habits in order to avoid further accidents caused by birds.

The Canadian Wildlife Service managed to promote a programme in February 1967 to study the local and migratory movements of the Whistling Swan in the Chesapeake Bay. Their headquarters, the Chesapeake Bay Centre for Field Biology, is on the western shore of the bay. Great attention has also been given to the large concentration of swans on the eastern shore between Eastern Neck Island and St Michael's. A tranquilliser, Diazepan, mixed in bait with an anaesthetic, alpha-Chloralose was experimented upon to trap large numbers of swans by funnel traps, or, during icy weather, by cannon net.

The United States Fish and Wildlife Service uses aluminium bands for identifying the swans; cygnets up to their first winter have them on their left leg, and adult birds on their right leg. On the opposite leg are placed tall, plastic coloured bands 1·5in (38mm) deep, similar to those used on Bewick's Swans by Peter Scott at Britain's Wildfowl Trust. These bands are coloured white for Maryland and Virginia; red for Arctic Canada, and blue for Alaska. For individual identification three $\frac{7}{16}$in (11mm) numbers are printed on them with a letter prefix, all reading upwards and repeated five times around the band. Banding has also been used on swans in their Arctic breeding grounds in the Yukon-Kuskokwim Delta in Alaska, and the Canadian Wildlife Service banded several hundred in the Mackenzie and Anderson river deltas of the North West Territories, Canada. Small numbers have also been banded at Bear River National Wildlife Refuge, Utah, and Shiawaisee National Wildlife Refuge, Michigan.

To observe large flocks of migrating swans, the swans were dyed yellow, black or purple. The swans in Chesapeake Bay and Arctic Canada are dyed yellow, and black in Alaska. The swans in Chesapeake Bay were painted on the lower part of the neck as well as parts of the back and wings, and in the same manner swans were dyed black in Back Bay, North West Territory, and Virginia; but the Arctic

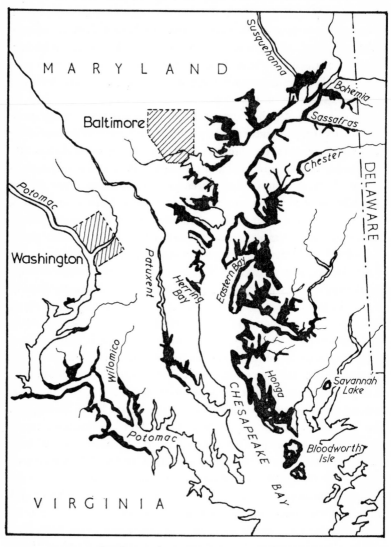

Winter distribution of Whistling Swans in Chesapeake Bay

swans were only dyed on the top half of the neck. These dyes do not harm the birds—they lose the colour when they moult and regain normal plumage within 5 months. The colour change does not appear to alter their behaviour pattern in any way (see supplement at end of this chapter).

These investigations have shown that swans cannot always forecast weather conditions before they start on migration. Large numbers of swans left Chesapeake Bay in March 1968 in ideal conditions but flew north-west into rain and fog. They circled the State College at Philadelphia in confusion and landed in small ponds and fields during the night, many of them returning to Chesapeake Bay for the summer.

The large flocks of migrating Whistling Swans leaving their winter habitat at fairly predictable times have proved excellent subjects for radar. They produce large echoes on the screen and their speed of flight should enable them to be differentiated from other large birds. Biotelemetry is being used to obtain information on individual birds. Transmitters weighing about ninety grammes were harnessed to eight swans in March 1968, and, using portable receiving equipment in a truck and aeroplane, it was found the average speed of one swan was 45mph.

From the surveys carried out by the Fish and Wildlife Service it was found that the wintering populations of the Whistling Swan in Chesapeake Bay fluctuated from year to year. From 1952 to 1956 the average population was 41,000, it soared to 71,000 in 1955, and dropped to 20,000 in 1956. When this decrease occurred in Chesapeake Bay there was a marked increase in the western populations and a considerable increase over the rest of the Atlantic coast. Annual censuses have been made of the entire population of the Whistling Swan for many years, and the average for 1964–9 was 103,000.

Many hazards have to be faced by swans on their migration to and from their breeding grounds. Although they have little contact with man on their Arctic breeding grounds, on migration southwards they have to pass over areas such as Lake Erie, that are highly polluted, and any swan seeking rest on such waters would be in danger of death from poisonous algae. During some seasons on Idaho's lower Coeur d'Alene River, the swans, stopping on migration, have suffered heavy losses from a form of metallic poisoning similar to lead-poisoning.

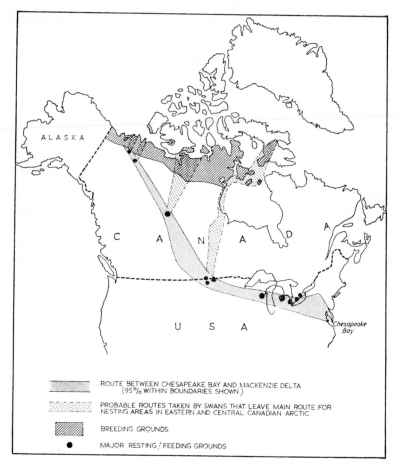

ROUTE BETWEEN CHESAPEAKE BAY AND MACKENZIE DELTA
(95% WITHIN BOUNDARIES SHOWN)

PROBABLE ROUTES TAKEN BY SWANS THAT LEAVE MAIN ROUTE FOR
NESTING AREAS IN EASTERN AND CENTRAL CANADIAN ARCTIC

BREEDING GROUNDS

● MAJOR RESTING / FEEDING GROUNDS

Migration route followed by Whistling Swans

On one of their migratory flights south early this century disaster
faced them when they wheeled down to their only resting place for
150 miles, the Klamath Basin, which had formerly been rich in food
for migrating birds in its marshlands and lakes. This expanse of fertile
upland, hemmed in by high mountains, forest, and desert, between the
Californian-Oregon border, had had four shallow lakes and the
surrounding marshland drained since the swans' previous yearly visit,
and barley and potato were growing in abundance. Further drainage,

irrigation, and power projects reduced the bird refuges so that there were insufficient resting places and food for the hosts of swans. It was not until they were starving and riddled with disease that they ravaged the farmlands. An enormous amount of money was spent trying to drive them off the land. Blank shells blazed at them, aeroplanes buzzed them, and searchlights flashed as keep-off warnings. A solution to these costly operations was reached in 1948 when the American Congress appropriated $500,000 for the development of the Lower Klamath and Tule Lake National Wildlife Refuges. A great deal has since been done to provide dykes, marshes and islands for the migrating birds, including pumping stations to keep the water-level adequate for the growth of aquatic vegetation. The birds soon found this area fulfilled all their needs and no longer worried the farmers.

One of the greatest reasons for mortality in Whistling Swans, as in the Trumpeter, has been lead-poisoning. Some 6,000 tons of spent shot are deposited on waterfowl habitat each year, and although most of it settles in deep water, some of it falls on the river beds where the swans feed. In autumn 1966 the Sporting Arms and Ammunition Manufacturing Institute and the Bureau of Sport, Fisheries and Wildlife, initiated a co-operative research effort to try to solve the problem. They financed a $100,000 two-year study by Illinois Institute of Technology to try to develop a suitable substitute for lead shot. Although some progress has been made, industry is still trying to resolve this problem. Swans have also been found to have died from toxic levels of copper and zinc when they frequented a river polluted by mine washings.

In the Chesapeake Bay an infection of heartworm (*Sarconema eurycerca*) is common among Whistling Swans. In California, wintering swans have been subject to outbreaks of fowl cholera, an infection caused by a tiny bacterium *Pasteurella multocida*, which must invade the tissues of its host to bring about ill-effects. Some strains of the organism cause an acute, rapidly fatal infection while others bring about a more chronic form of the disease.

Post mortems have been carried out on Whistling Swans, and they have been diagnosed as dying from *Aspergillosis* (fungus disease); tuberculosis; pneumonia; silicosis; dropsy; and parasites such as lice infestation around the fluff of the vent, gizzard worm and common poultry roundworm. Some species of protozoal diseases have been reported in Whistling Swans: *Haemoproteus* (avian malaria) the most common malarial parasite found in birds; *Trypanosomiasis*, parasites transmitted by mosquitoes; and *Tyzzerria anseris* a species of *Coccidiosis*, which has been found in a swan's intestine. Two other cases of *Coccidiosis*, one fatal, have occurred.

The Niagara Falls have proved a hazard to migrating swans—more than 100 Whistling Swans were caught in the rapids and swept to their death among the rocks.

Except for two open seasons on Whistling Swans in the State of Utah, these swans have been protected since the Migratory Bird Treaty with Great Britain in 1918. A 90-day open season was introduced in Utah in 1962 and 1963 when a thousand one-bird permits were issued, resulting in 320 and 392 swans being bagged consecutively. In 1969 an 86-day permit was issued to 2,500 sportsmen when 1,290 swans were bagged and a further 1,217 were hit without being retrieved. There is an annual loss of Whistlers as well as Trumpeters due to unscrupulous shooting by uncaring and uninformed hunters. But the Whistling Swan has many advantages over its less common cousin. It breeds in wild, remote tundra seldom trespassed upon by man, and in spite of its migration in great flocks, which fly far out to sea and at a great height, the swan's wariness instinctively keeps it out of the reach of man even when it lands at its winter habitat.

In the past these swans were taken for food and plumage by the Indians and early settlers in North America in the same way that the Trumpeter was, but being less vulnerable they survived. In spite of this they have been exterminated from their wintering grounds on the Texas Gulf Coast, and the great flocks of the lower Columbia River have disappeared from the vast wapato marshes, where, in 1806, the explorers Lewis and Clark found them in abundance at Fort Clatsop, near the Chilluckittequaw Indians. It was here the explorers observed two distinct species of swans, the Whistling Swan exceeding the Trumpeter by five to one. They discovered the Whistling Swan's voice was very different from that of the Trumpeter. 'It begins,' they stated, 'with a kind of whistling sound and terminates in a round, full note, louder at the end, but at no time as loud as the Trumpeter's.' Before this time, in 1714, a surveyor-naturalist wrote of the two swans in his book, *History of North Carolina*. He mentioned the smaller swan as being called a 'Hooper'. Since 1815 it has been known as *Cygnus columbianus* after the River Columbia where it was found by Lewis and Clark, who also gave it the English name of the 'Whistling Swan' because of its individual sound. The Alaskan Indian names for the swan are 'Boopers', 'Tohwah', and 'White Swan'.

In Arctic Canada, Eskimos in kayaks and canoes pursued the moulting swans, and the young Eskimos competed for the honour of capturing a bird single-handed. The swans deserted the Perry River in Arctic Canada because of hunting. Further west the trader and naturalist, MacFarlane, recorded Whistling Swans nesting on the coast and islands of the Liverpool and Franklin bays on the Arctic coast of the Yukon in 1891.

Whistling Swans are not generally kept as ornamental birds because they are less picturesque, wilder, and rarely breed anywhere but in their native breeding grounds. They were introduced to the London Zoo in 1903 but without any breeding success. Until quite recently they have not bred in captivity in North America: after mating a Whistling Swan with both Mute and Whooper Swans on a farm in Connecticut, a Canadian farmer, Mr John Gebauer, had a breeding success with a pair of Whistling Swans on one of his large ponds near Winnipeg.

It is to be hoped the future of these spartan species of Arctic swans is assured. Much of their habitat has been ditched, drained, and ploughed, and exploration and development in the Arctic regions has been expanding, but both the United States and Canadian Wildlife agencies are endeavouring to protect some of their habitat. Twelve sanctuaries have been established in waterfowl nesting areas in northern Canada, and the Whistling Swan's breeding grounds in the Yukon-Kuskokwim Delta, in Alaska, have been established as a sanctuary by the United States. A well informed public can do much to protect these hardy, native swans by preventing indiscriminate shooting and the destruction of their breeding habitat.

The legend that before a swan dies it sings a beautiful farewell has been discovered to be true in the case of the Whistling Swan. Dr Daniel Elliott, a great ornithologist, and one of the builders of New York's American Museum of Natural History, shot a Whistling Swan for the museum, and as the bird came sailing down he was amazed to hear a plaintive and musical song, so unlike the call in life, which lasted until the bird reached the water.

(Supplement on migration: from W. J. L. Sladen, Department of Pathobiology, Johns Hopkins University, Baltimore, Md, USA.)

After intensive research the migratory habits of the Whistling Swans were found to be influenced by the birds having obtained adequate food and rest prior to their departure. When the weather was favourable, with light tailwinds occurring during early evening and sometimes early morning, the swans would make exploratory flights in the vicinity of Chesapeake Bay, before undertaking their long migration northwards. They appear to migrate on a fairly narrow front about 100 to 150 miles wide from the Atlantic coast to North Dakota, and then branch north and north-west towards their wide breeding area. The migration is performed in a succession of long flights between 250 and 700 miles each, interspersed with rest periods of 10–20 days. The first stage of their migration between Chesapeake Bay and the Great Lakes consists of great hazards both to the swans and to aircraft, for here the birds encounter maximum aircraft traffic, and also, during adverse weather conditions they have few places to land.

CHAPTER SEVEN

The Bewick's Swan

(*Cygnus columbianus bewickii*)

———————◆———————

The Bewick's Swan shares the vast regions of the tundra with its western cousin, the Whistling Swan, breeding along the northern coasts of Eurasia above the Arctic Circle. Part of its habitat overlaps with the Whooper but it does not breed as far west as this swan, and rarely ventures south of the Arctic Circle to nest; its population and distribution are therefore on a smaller scale. In the nineteenth century its migration to the north of the British Isles and Ireland was similar to that of the Whooper's but it was not until 1830 that it was distinguished from the larger species and named by Yarrell, 'The Bewick's Swan', in honour of a fellow ornithologist, Thomas Bewick of Newcastle, who died in 1828. Thomas Bewick was also an engraver and famous illustrator of birds.

This dainty, courageous swan is the smallest of the Northern Swans and resembles the other slightly larger member of its species, the Whistling Swan, in size and shape, having a shorter, more rounded body and a more rounded head on a shorter neck. The ridge of its bill is depressed in the middle as in the Whistling Swan, but the yellow rounded patch of the Bewick's is much larger and never missing as is sometimes the case in the North American bird. These yellow markings vary on individual Bewick's and each one has a pattern of its own. In common with all the Northern Swans its eyes are brown, and it has a narrow yellow ring around them.

The two Eurasian Arctic swans may often be seen frequenting the same waters during winter. They are easily distinguishable from each other, the Bewick's being roughly a third smaller than the Whooper and weighing one-third less. Both swans carry their necks stiffly, but the Bewick's neck is slightly more relaxed and is shorter than its body, whereas the Whooper's rigid neck is sometimes longer than its body. Although the basal half of both swans' bills is yellow and the tips black, the Bewick's bill is shorter, and the yellow, rounded patch is less uniform and does not extend to the nostrils as in the Whooper.

The windpipe of the Bewick's Swan is long and convoluted as in all the northern species, but it is not as long as in *Cygnus cygnus*. The Bewick's voice is similar to the Whistling Swan, but softer and lower pitched with a pleasantly musical tone. Its voice has been described as a 'musical babbling' when it is at rest on the water. It also gives a 'Hoo' or 'Ho' note and makes a loud honking signal resembling 'Tong, tong, tong', when in flight.

In behaviour this swan is similar to the other Northern Swans but it is quicker and more excitable than the larger species. It is also more gregarious and strictly maritime; and, contrary to the Whooper, favours brackish waters on the coast and in estuaries rather than waters further inland. Although much of its range overlaps the Whooper's the two species have never been known to hybridise. In temperament it is wild, but less aloof and distrustful of man than the Whooper, except on its breeding grounds where it becomes very disturbed at the approach of man. During the winter it accepts close vicinity with civilisation, mainly in north-west Europe. It gathers in flocks near human habitation and becomes quite tame if it is befriended by man. Thunderstorms and strong winds cause panic among flocks and the swans will either huddle together in the water or take off, exerting all their strength to reach the safety of their nesting grounds among reeds and marshes.

During mid-March when the climate in the Bewick's wintering quarters in north-west Europe becomes mild, the swans start calling and bending and stretching their necks in the characteristic pre-flight manner of their species. They become airborne without any great difficulty, rising from a confined space and forming themselves into flocks—from as many as 100 to an average of 35 birds. Nature has endowed them with great flight wings, comparatively longer than those of the Mute Swan, and these are vital for their 2,600 mile migration north-east to the Arctic tundra of northern Russia. They fly close together in wedge formation or straight lines with their necks erect, and reach great heights over the pine forests of Sweden, the lake-studded mountains of Lapland, and the great Ural mountains of the Soviet Union. Their breeding grounds stretch from the most north-westerly point in Russia at Pechenga River, eastwards to the Kanin Peninsula, Vaygash Island, and to the southern half of Novaya Zemlya Island. Other flocks fly to the Yamal Peninsula where they nest in the mouths of the great rivers Ob and Yenesei, which rise from the Sayan and Altai mountains and flow into the Arctic forming great tundra marshes bordering the Kara Sea. Further eastwards they nest in the lower reaches of the rivers Lena, Yana and Indigirka, and spread further eastward to the River Kolyma. There have been reports of their nesting in the Anadyr River as far east as the Bering Sea. The swans east of the Lena River are intermingled with the Eastern Bewick's, known as the Jankowski's Swan. During the short summer of these Arctic regions the temperature rarely reaches more than 10° C (50° F), and the climate is dry.

The Bewick's nest under similar conditions to the Whistling Swans. Few men penetrate their breeding grounds, the sea is rarely free of ice-flows and only the surface of the ground thaws out in the short summer to provide growth of moss and lichen.

Although the Bewick's migrate in flocks, the mated swans arrive in pairs at the breeding grounds. They normally breed when they are four years old but some not until a year later. Close study has been made of the Bewick's mating behaviour at Slimbridge, and it has been found that these beautiful little tundra swans are wholly monogamous and no cases of divorce or re-marriage have been observed. Bereaved swans have been known to remain unattached for 3 years, and well mated pairs often meet up again after they have been separated. In March 1969, when the swans were migrating from Slimbridge, one of a pair was injured in a flying accident and was detained for treatment. Its mate waited for it for 5 days before following the other birds. The injured swan was released after 16 days and next November the pair returned to Slimbridge together.

The swans' mating display and copulation follow the pattern of the

Triumph ceremony: A Black-necked Swans with cygnet joining in; B Bewick's Swans

other Northern Swans: they are aggressive while mating and indulge in the triumph ceremonies of their kind. They choose islets in the estuaries and marshes for their nests which are often built fairly close together in colonies. Both parents help to build the large, conical mound out of moss, lichen or dried plants. It has a depression in the centre and is more symmetrical than the Whooper's nest. The swans must mate, build their nest, lay their eggs, incubate them, and raise their young all in the space of 120–30 days when their breeding grounds are ice-free. The pen rarely lays a repeat clutch and if she does so it is because the first clutch has been destroyed, but the clutches have to be laid in quick succession because of the time factor. The second clutch of eggs are small and weigh 9·5 per cent less than the first eggs. In captivity Bewick's produce a second clutch around two weeks after the first if it has been taken from them for artificial incubation. On two occasions at Slimbridge the Bewick's pen failed to hatch her eggs after a full incubation period and then re-nested and successfully hatched a second clutch; this was quite a remarkable feat in a high Arctic species which would have inadequate time to undertake a full-time double clutch in its natural habitat.

The Bewick's 4–5 creamy-white eggs are laid late in May and measure 103·0 by 67mm (4·0 by 2·6in) on average, weighing 260g (9·1oz), which is 4·6 per cent in proportion to the mother's body weight. Although the Bewick's Swan is the smallest of the Northern Swans, it lays the largest egg and, inversely, has the smallest clutch size. This is a feature of the *Anatidae* family; the clutch size evolved by each species is a compromise between counteracting factors which relate to the availability of food for the laying female and newly hatched chick. There are hazards in the cool, Arctic summer, and weather conditions can cause a partial or even a complete breeding failure either when the adults are laying and need food close at hand, or when the cygnets have just hatched. The Wildfowl Trust at Slimbridge has made a close research of the Bewick's Swan and it is now possible to identify individual swans and ascertain whether the species has had a good or bad breeding season. In the winters 1965–6 and 1966–7, some 29 per cent of the Bewick's Swans visiting Slimbridge were young birds whereas during the following two winters it fell to only 9 per cent. This is thought to be due to the bad weather conditions on the breeding grounds. The percentage of young birds fell to 7 per cent in 1969–70 but the brood size was relatively high and this indicated that weather conditions were worse in some areas than others. In 1970–1 there was a rise to 18 per cent in the cygnets but the brood size remained the same.

As the Bewick's eggs are comparatively large, they have bigger food reserves than the smaller swan eggs and this gives the chicks a greater chance of survival for the first critical week of its life. Incubation is undertaken by the female but the male may sit on the eggs while she is feeding. The incubation period of 29–30 days is the shortest period for all the swans and the embryo has a higher metabolic rate which enables it to develop faster. So in every respect the Bewick's cygnet's life is quickened to enable it to keep pace with the short summer which breaks by September, when the freezing temperature once again covers the tundra pools with ice. The chicks are similar to the Whistling and Whooper chicks but they are slightly smaller and rounder; the down is a pale greyish-white with an indeterminate darker pattern, and is lighter in colour than in the Trumpeter chick. Unlike the Whooper the down does not extend so far down the base of the bill. The feet are orange. These chicks, weighing 184·5g (6·5oz), which is relatively heavy for the smaller Bewick's Swan, hatch by the end of June when the Arctic waters are normally rich in plankton, which contains vast amounts of algae to nourish them and strengthen their muscles for their first winter migration.

The food of the Bewick's Swan is much the same as that of the rest of the species. It partakes of the leaves and stems of *Potamogeton* (pondweed); *Characeae* (stoneworts); *Myriophyllum* (milfoil) and *Zannichellia* (horned pondweed). Both pasture grasses, reed and flote-grasses and salt-marsh grass are a part of its diet. It also eats the tubers and rhizomes of *Potamogeton*, *Zostera*, *Scirpus* (club rush), reed grass and white clover, and enjoys grazing on *Trifolium* (clover). It eats various seeds including those of *Eleocharis* (spike-rush), and insects clinging to plants. It eagerly receives grain and bread when it reaches populated areas.

Both parents care for the chicks which mature quickly. By 3 months they have lost their down and have a uniform brown-grey plumage with a flesh-coloured bill; the lores from the base of the bill to the cygnet's eyes are still feathered but the legs change to grey. By this time the parents, who moult together, have grown their new plumage, their flight feathers being replaced earlier than in the other species.

Nesting swans, and those with young, guard their nest and family jealously. Their chief predators on their breeding grounds are the Arctic fox, the marten, stoat, and the gyrfalcon, which steals the eggs of shore birds, and, should the vigilance of the parents be distracted, carries away the young chicks. The protective instinct of a Bewick's parent was witnessed at the Dumbles, Slimbridge, when a falcon, carrying a teal it had caught, landed near the flock. One of the adult swans which had cygnets, advanced slowly toward the falcon with head drawn back and held very low, its wings spread and 'shoulders' hunched. As the two birds faced each other the swan made a lunge at the falcon, knocking it off its kill, then both birds fought until a blow from the swan's wing temporarily knocked the falcon down. Returning to his mate and family, the swan called loudly and performed the triumph ceremony.

These swans have a very closely-knit family life. They not only take their three-month-old young on their migration flights, but some of the cygnets of their second, and even third year join up with them, often accompanied by their mates, which may make a party of up to fifteen birds. The pecking order is well observed, and different families are aggressive towards each other. If a cygnet's parents are powerful and top of the pecking order the cygnet can intimidate another adult or even a pair of less aggressive swans. By the time the swans are preparing to return from their winter habitat to their breeding grounds the following March the cygnet's grey plumage is intermingled with white, the basal part of the bill is white, and the legs and feet have become blackish. At a year and a half a young Bewick's Swan is similar to an adult except for a few grey feathers on the neck.

In September the Bewick's begin their long flight southwards over sea, snow-capped mountains and pine forests. They arrive by late October and early November in Denmark, Holland, Germany, the British Isles and occasionally France. Small numbers migrate to the southern seaboard of the Caspian Sea in northern Iran, where 843 were sighted in 1967. They have also been recorded further east on the Aral Sea, and as birds of passage as far east as Mongolia. South-east Europe is

Postures: A Bewick's Swan in aggressive posture; B Mute Swan preening and showing large, webbed foot

outside their normal range but they have occasionally been reported on the Evros Delta in Greece, and in other coastal regions of the Mediterranean, some reaching Algeria. Vagrants have been seen in northwest India as far south as the Gulf of Kutch.

Usually the Bewick's Swans return year after year to their familiar wintering habitat, but their southwestern migration route from the wasteland of Siberia has changed dramatically within living

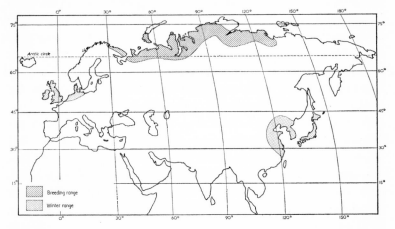

Habitat of the Bewick's Swan

memory. Besides severe winters accounting for their movement further south, their former route straight to the west of Scotland en route to their winter quarters in Ireland has been re-directed to Holland where the damming of the Zuyder Zee, and its conversion into a freshwater lake, has attracted these swans in their quest for rest and nourishment. They are to be found on the shallow, flooded areas along the Yssel, between Kampen and Zwolle, where they gather in flocks of 300. They also concentrate along the Veluweener on the shore of the east Polder just south of Elburg. Once the rivers become flooded and are too deep for them to obtain food, they move to shallower districts, sometimes flying to the fields a mile away from water and grazing in pastures near Nyjkerk. They also gather on the Dutch coast, spending their time sleeping, preening, and feeding with their necks below water, occasionally up-ending and at times showing aggression. Many feed close to human habitation, some frequenting the river beside the main traffic bridge across the Yssel in Zwolle; and much to farmers' consternation they establish themselves near farms; one farmer says they eat as much grass as three cows. Altogether their population in the Netherlands numbers 3,000.

Bewick's are more plentiful in Denmark in the autumn. They concentrate in their largest numbers at the reserve, Vejlerne, in Jutland, where there are three shallow lakes. They also frequent the shores of the large fjords, the Ringkøbing, Bøvling and Limfjorden, and favour river mouths such as the River Tudea in west Zealand or any place where there is shallow water, even settling on small pools; they appear to vary their habitat from year to year and seek areas away from human habitation. Some 700 Bewick's settle in Denmark for the winter, and another 300 frequent West Germany.

Formerly some 1,500–2,000 Bewick's used to winter in Ireland, but now there are less than a thousand; this decrease is caused, not only because of the change of route but also by loss of habitat due to land development. A flock of 420 were seen on Wexford Slobs in March 1971, and large numbers are to be found at the Wildfowl Refuge at Kilcolman Marsh, County Cork. A few still revisit their old haunts in Scotland and Wales, but they are no longer seen in great numbers in the Shetlands and the Outer Hebrides.

Until 1938 Bewick's were scarce in Norfolk and less common than the Whooper, but since 1950 this position has reversed owing to the swans crossing the Channel route. They now congregate in herds of 60–70 along the Norfolk coast. The Washes supply an ideal habitat for them during the winter months. These shallow waters stretch 21 miles across the Fens from Earith in Cambridgeshire to Denver Sluice in Norfolk. This fen district was an inhospitable tract of marsh, almost permanently under water until, in 1629, the Earl of Bedford commissioned Cornelius Vermuyden, a Dutchman, to reclaim them. It was not until 1651 that the Wash became a flood-plain and now it is the largest inland area of regularly flooded, grazed grassland in Great Britain. Cattle, a few sheep, and horses, graze on them from April to early November, then when winter rains exceed the capacity of the drainage rivers, the surplus water is released on the Washes and the flood builds slowly across from the north-west. The river authority also floods them at any time during heavy rainfall. While the water remains shallow there is rich feeding for swans, the grassland is free from herbicides, and there are 16 species of the pondweed *Potamogeton*. They are therefore of immense ornithological importance. In January 1970, some 41,000 wildfowl were counted there, and that same winter 938 Bewick's Swans, 394 Mute, and 46 Whoopers, were reported in the area. As voluntary bodies have bought up more and more land the wildfowl have been largely protected against shooting.

The Bewick's Swans winter on the Ouse Washes twenty miles from Denver Sluice through the Norfolk and Cambridgeshire fens. Their numbers fluctuate, but an unprecedented influx of Bewick's flew in from their continental habitats during the severe winters of 1954–5 and 1955–6. There was a population of 705 Bewick's in this district during the winter of 1955–6, and also 50 along the north coast of Norfolk from east of Blakeney to Hunstanton where herds of 60–70 birds are now regular features. In the winter of 1970–1 there were 1,500 Bewick's wintering on the Ouse Washes in Huntingdonshire, Cambridgeshire and Norfolk. The number wintering at the Wildfowl Trust's Welney Reserve has increased enormously from 17 Bewick's in 1950–1 to 400 in January 1971. They have been successfully decoyed into the lagoon in front of the observatory, and underwater agitators have been installed to keep the water from freezing in severe weather. Even the observatory floodlights do not deter the 300 Bewick's from remaining on the lagoon after dark.

There were no regular migrating Bewick's wintering on the Severn Estuary until a Bewick's cob, probably attracted by a Whistling Swan installed on one of the ponds of the Wildfowl Trust at Slimbridge, flew down on the pond in November 1948. The Bewick's was captured and a mate was procured for it from Holland, which resulted in the unique achievement of the pair breeding in captivity. These wild swans do not take kindly to nesting away from their breeding grounds but the pair at Slimbridge still breed irregularly. Other Bewick's passing over on their migration to Ireland were attracted by their species swimming on the pond, and by 1963 some twenty Bewick's visited it. The family of Bewick's were moved to the pool in front of Peter Scott's house, and wild Bewick's were lured there with barrow-loads of wheat scattered around the pool twice a day. Soon, twenty-four Bewick's took advantage of the food and peaceful water and the Trust set about making a detailed study of their species.

By the winter 1970-1 a record of 626 swans had been counted in the pool which only measured 120 by 60yd. By reason of this increasing number of Bewick's Swans that wintered there it earned the name of 'Swan Lake'. Now, as though predestined, Thomas Bewick's telescope, fashioned in 1794, has been installed to assist the public in watching the swans.

Great interest was aroused when it was found that individual swans could be recognised by the variable black and yellow patterns on their bills: by 1969-70 names had been given to 1,073 birds and each bird was given a dossier listing its family connections, arrival and departure dates, and included a drawing of its bill pattern. Some of the swans' bills changed from year to year, and to help identification further, white plastic rings with a large space for numbers that could be read through binoculars, were fitted to the swans' legs. Even ringing proved inadequate when trying to identify the swans on their migratory routes, and in the winter 1970-1 the Wildfowl Trust made 114 swans recognisable by dyeing their tails, scapulars and wingtips yellow. Since then dyed birds have been recorded from Archangel, Soviet Union; Latvia; East Germany; West Germany; Denmark; the Netherlands; southern Sweden, and the Baltic Republic of Estonia.

Many Bewick's Swans gather on the Severn Estuary and frequent the Dumbles, a salt-marsh lying between the estuary and the Wildfowl Trust. They also feed regularly in a wet field called the Moors, a mile from the Trust, and they are to be found at Walmore Common and Ashleworth Ham in Gloucestershire. In Somerset 300 swans have been observed on the Levels near Langport, and also at Sedgemoor and Chew reservoirs. At Abberton Ringing Station they attract much attention by grazing near the roadway. Others alight at unexpected waters such as the River Cherwell Floods in Oxfordshire; Caldicott Moor, Monmouth; the Reservoir at Bough Beech, Kent, where a family of four were seen in winter 1972; and occasionally at Eastpark Refuge, Caerlaverick, in Scotland. It is estimated that the average population of Bewick's wintering in the British Isles is 2,500. Their total population in north-west Europe is believed to number around 6,000-7,000.

The Wildfowl Trust at Slimbridge thoroughly examines all Bewick's Swans that alight on Swan Lake. The swans are measured, weighed, photographed, have blood samples taken, and are X-rayed. From the X-rays it has been found that 24 per cent of the birds examined carried lead shot; some birds carried as many as 4–5 pellets. At Welney a dead swan was found to have been poisoned by ingested lead shot. It is apparent that although all swans are protected in all the countries they pass through on migration, the law is being disregarded somewhere along their route.

The Bewick's mortality is affected by the hazards common to the other swans. They fly into trees, telephone wires and television aerials during strong winds, and oil accounts for many deaths. In January 1970 some 30 Bewick's arrived badly oiled at Welney Marshes. They had come from Holland where a fuel tanker containing 8,000 tons of crude oil had collapsed into the waters of the Biesbosch near Durdrecht.

Some diseases similar to those found in Whooper Swans affect Bewick's; such as thorny-headed worms (*Acanthocephala*), parasites of the small intestine; feather lice (ectoparasites); thickening and hardening of the arterial wall (atherosclerosis), and *Staphylococcosis*, a bacteria which gains access through cracked or calloused feet and spreads to other parts of the body. Other diseases are Tuberculosis, roundworms and filarial worms in the coronary blood vessels.

This hardy little swan's life span in the wild has not yet been determined—it is thought to be somewhere in the region of twenty years, but can possibly live from forty to sixty years in captivity. The mortality rate among Bewick's wintering at Slimbridge is estimated at around 15 per cent.

The tundra is so remote and mysterious that these northernmost swans have had little to fear from man in their most inaccessible breeding grounds. Apart from occasional ships' crews, the only people who venture into their wild territory are the more primitive of the Lapps, who remain nomadic and move northwards from their forest dwellings during the summer, ever seeking lichen, the reindeer's food, known as 'reindeer moss', which grows beneath the crust of ice. Reindeer are the Lapps' livelihood and the two are inseparable. Dogs of the Laiki breed also accompany them, and for years have aided in hunting the swans over the snow. Further east, with the Samoyed

tribe, the Samoyed dogs—the most beautiful of the Laiki group—
accompany the men in capturing the swans along the banks of the
River Yenesei and around the basin of the River Taz. In the nineteenth century, swans were hunted, not only for their meat, but for their
beautiful down which was sold to make boas and other trimmings for
ladies' clothes. The tough texture of their skins was also valued by the
Russians for making caps and jackets, and the Bewick's were still being
hunted in Russia in 1940.

It is to be hoped that the protection now afforded these endearing
tundra swans will be recognised by even the most primitive of hunters
as they become more closely linked with their better-informed and
more southerly countrymen, and that the Bewick's relatively small
population will be allowed to remain stable in the seclusion of its
breeding territory.

JANKOWSKI'S SWAN (Eastern Bewick's)
(*Cygnus columbianus jankowskii*)

There is some difference of opinion among taxonomists regarding the
status of the Eastern Bewick's Swan, which breeds from the Lena Delta
eastwards as far as the Anadyr River on the Bering Sea. According to
the Russian ornithologist, A. J. Tougarinov (1941), the Eastern
Bewick's, named by some ornithologists the Jankowski's Swan, cannot
be recognised as being a distinct species from the Bewick's Swan.
Tougarinov does concede with Jean Delacour's statement that in the
eastern part of Siberia the larger-billed specimens are more numerous,
although there are swans with an intermediate bill size throughout the
range. Jean Delacour found that all Eastern Bewick's studied by western
ornithologists have a distinctly higher and straighter ridge to their bill,
more angular near the base and with a longer yellow patch, similar to
the Whooper Swan but shorter.

In every respect the Jankowski's Swan is similar to its close relative,
the Bewick's, except in bill and habitat. The bill is definitely longer,
broader near the tip and higher near the base than the Western
Bewick's; also the yellow patch is brighter and extends a little nearer
the nostrils, not being so bluntly truncated. With no distinct region

between them the two swans' habitats overlap, but the Eastern Bewick's Swan is definitely more to the east. The population breeding on the Lena Delta is very mixed, the Western Bewick's, the Eastern Bewick's and the intermediate species are to be found there.

Twice a year these Eastern Bewick's pass through the northern provinces of China, where they are more abundant than the Whooper Swans. They appear in March on the north-eastern coast of China and frequent the marshes and rivers in considerable numbers. During the winter they migrate southwards passing Kamchatka, the Kuril Islands and Sakhalin. They fly to the mouth of the lower Yangtze River and are seen in large numbers on the Poyang lake. Some of the swans have been reported as far south as the Fukien and Kwangtung provinces, and exceptionally they reach northern India. Other Eastern Bewick's winter in Japan where they are known by the name of 'Hakucho' to distinguish them from the hundreds of Ohakucho (Whoopers) that flock to Japan. A recent survey reported 540 Eastern Bewick's Swans on Japanese waters. They mix with the Whooper Swans at Hyoko, and are treated with the same care and respect by Shigeo Yoshikawa, the swan-father of Hyoko.

CHAPTER EIGHT

The Black Swan

(*Cygnus atratus*)

———◆———

The Black Swan of Australia presents a strange and beautiful sight gliding on lagoons, estuaries, and large expanses of fresh or brackish water, either with its mate, in a family party, or in very large flocks. It was once thought to be sedentary but close study has found its movements to be nomadic and erratic. Its presence has been reported from all over the continent with the exception of Cape York Peninsula.

It is among the smallest of the swans and it can be distinguished easily by its black silhouette and long neck. Its dark plumage is relieved by a red iris glinting keenly from a slightly rounded head, and by the crimson-red to orange bill which lacks a frontal knob but which is high and thick at the base with a broad, white band near the tip and an off-white nail at its extremity. The swan's plumage is not true black but often has a brownish-grey tinge, with the breast and abdomen paler than the rest of the body. On the back the feathers have a greyish border, which, together with the bird's long, sinuous neck give it a somewhat snake-like appearance; but this is slightly modified by the attractively ruffled appearance of the greater wing coverts which are broadened and wavy. The silhouette of this swan in flight is impressive. Its neck, proportionately longer than any of the other swans', is conspicuously longer than its short-tailed body, and its white pinions strike an attractive contrast to its dark form. The first 10 primaries, the primary coverts, the last 2 feathers of the alula, and 3–6 secondaries, are entirely white, while the remaining secondaries, their contour feathers and the first 2 feathers of the alula are partially white. All these feathers are hidden when they are tucked under the remaining black contour feathers when the bird is resting.

The male is slightly larger than the female and has a longer neck and head with a straighter, more deeply coloured bill. His iris is also generally deeper in colour. He holds his head higher and his neck more erect than his mate. With an abundance of nutritious food these birds' weights may increase considerably and both male and female may exceed 9kg (19·8lb).

Although the Black Swan is very different from the Mute in appearance, the two swans resemble each other in much of their posture and behaviour. They have the same methods of feeding, taking flight, display and courtship. In common with the Mute, the Black Swan raises its shoulders in anger, but it holds its greatly ruffled neck more erect, only sharply curving the upper part, close to the head, and pointing the bill slightly downwards. Its blackish-grey legs and feet are set back on its body in a similar position to the Mute's, giving it the same aquatic efficiency and the disadvantage of a clumsy walk. Also it shares the Mute's habit of foot-drying. During the breeding season it possesses the same fierce and jealous temper as the Mute, and it can become savage towards human beings, striking out with its wings, but it is neither as strong nor powerful as the Mute Swan and can do little harm. On the other hand it *can* dominate other species of swans, and during its breeding season in Kew Gardens it becomes very aggressive to Canadian geese which have black necks and dark plumage. There are rarely any casualties and the Black Swan is considered to be a peaceable bird on the whole.

Another similarity between the Mute and Black Swan is their difficulty in taking flight. The Black Swan has no pre-flight movements and needs forty or fifty yards take-off distance; this handicaps it in thick vegetation, among timber or in rough water. Once in the air its flight is powerful, but slow, undulating and graceful, and is accompanied by the strong humming of its white pinions.

Flocks of Black Swans fly in long skeins or V formations, unlike other Australian waterfowl. They can fly at great heights and have been reported striking aircraft at altitudes of about 1,000ft. When they are flying over the Great Dividing Range in New South Wales they must reach 4,000–8,000ft. They are also capable of sustained flight, having appeared on desert water-holes more than 400 miles from the nearest water. They fly about the lakes and wetlands during the day, but their

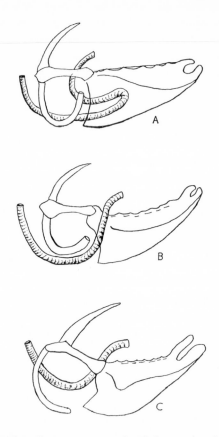

Windpipes: A *the Whooper Swan;* B *the Black Swan;* C *the Black-necked Swan*

long flights are undertaken in the evening and are announced with much bugling.

In comparison with the Northern Swans the Black Swan's voice is relatively weak, for although its windpipe forms a sharp angle, it does not have the length and convolutions of its northern cousins. It has a stronger voice than the Mute Swan, its windpipe being compressed from back to front—rather than sideways at the syrinx, as in the Mute —and its syrinx and bronchi are both smaller than in the Mute. In different situations its high-pitched, musical bugle varies in tone and intensity, and it bows its head when crying. When swimming it stretches its neck right out on the surface of the water and produces a trumpeting noise. Mating pairs call repeatedly in duet.

Mated birds nest in very close colonies, each pair defending a territory of no more than 5ft from their neighbour. They flock in thousands and are usually scattered over large bodies of water.

The breeding and distribution of this swan in Australia depends largely on the weather conditions of the continent's 3 million square mile land-mass which extends from far into the tropics to the southern mid-temperate region. In spite of its large range of climate, Australia supports less waterfowl than any other continent. This is because it has few lofty mountains to become snow-laden or induce rainfall on the slopes, and consequently has few permanent swamps. The north coast has monsoonal rainfall in the summer and the southern districts receive rain from the winter depressions from the Southern Ocean. The interior, with a very low rainfall and a high evaporation rate, is arid. The flow of surface water in most of the country is limited to periods immediately after heavy rain and the whole continent's average annual run-off corresponds to a depth of only $1\frac{1}{3}$in ($3\cdot4$cm) of water in comparison with $9\frac{3}{4}$in ($24\cdot8$cm) for all other land surfaces.

The timing of the breeding season of the Black Swan varies from place to place and it is able to breed at any time of the year under favourable conditions, which are dependent upon sufficient rainfall providing availability of a firm nest foundation in or near water, and an increased and nutritious food supply. Resident populations of swans are found in the better-watered coastal and southern regions of Australia where there is a stable habitat and they can have a regular breeding season during winter and early spring. Water-level largely influences the sexual activity in breeding swans. This is generally high in May and the males produce sperm in June and July, but if there is a high water-level in March the male's testis rehabilitation is complete and they produce sperm in April. Even if there is a high water-level in December they have been known to produce sperm, but normally the

Mating, display and nesting. The Black Swan: **A** *and* **B** *Swan performing wing-flapping threat display while calling;* **C** *and* **D** *nest-building behaviour;* **E** *swan on nest;* **F** *start of nest relieving ceremony*

water-level decreases as spring advances and the swans' sperm gradually declines and ceases by September. The sexual cycle of the female is similar but occurs later and egg-laying is completed normally at the end of August.

The largest concentration of swans is found in the Coorong, a lagoon and long stretch of land on the west coast of Victoria, where, to the west, there are numerous swamps, potholes, and lakes that provide suitable breeding habitat. The Murray-Darling river system spreading across nearly half a million square miles of country is another favourite breeding habitat. The rivers rise in the Eastern Highlands and before joining the Murray River fall to flood-plains across which they meander for hundreds of miles developing extensive systems of billabongs, swamps, and effluent streams which attract large populations of breeding swans. South-western Australia is isolated from the rest of the continent by great deserts—the summer drought dries up many of the numerous small streams and some of the swamps are not permanent, while others have been drained for agricultural purposes. But there are permanent and semi-permanent swamps near the coast, such as at Benger, Western Australia, where the swamps are flooded during the winter and the swans breed abundantly in June.

In the north the Black Swan breeds up as far as Bowen, north-east Queensland, and North West Cape, Western Australia. Their range extends around 1,000 miles inland on the east coast, and 500 miles inland on the west. In north-east Queensland, with a summer wet-season, breeding occurs from February to May, in reed beds, on islands, in salt-pans and samphire flats, which are usually flooded in December and January. The swans are vagrants in this region because sometimes there is insufficient rainfall to flood the area to a suitable depth and nests are deserted or the broods that hatch perish. In recent years the swans have invaded brackish waters and swamps of coastal club rush (*Scirpus littoralis*) on impounded salt-pans, but sometimes their attempts at breeding have been destroyed by flooding. Other nomads are attracted to the arid inland zone when there is a sudden heavy rainfall which enables the pasture plants to grow quickly and supplies the swans with food. The birds will occupy any creek or depression, and if water remains they will nest all the year round.

In lignum creeks and swamps west of Booligal, New South Wales, nests have been found nearly all the year round, and as far inland as Cunnamulla, central Queensland in April. Regular breeding takes place in the permanent swamps near Ivanhoe, New South Wales, but pairs of swans have been found nesting nearby in a half-acre depression in an arid salt-bush plain that had been filled in by a storm. In the permanent swamps there was an additional burst of sexual activity in December 1964, which coincided with a massive growth of the annual species of pondweed, *Potamogeton*, upon which the swans fed exclusively. A similar event occurred at Lake George where there was an unusual growth of algae bloom.

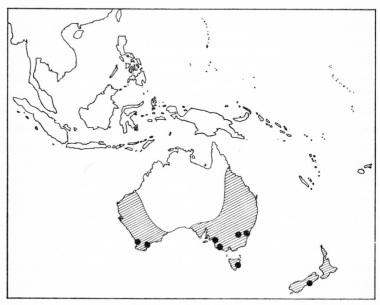

Habitat of the Black Swan

Rudimentary attempts at nest building, indicating the first inclination to breed, are apparent in one-year-old swans, but none of them actually mates or produces eggs while retaining juvenile plumage. Under favourable conditions swans in their second year, attempt and are quite successful at breeding, but others may fail to breed in five years. Some mated couples have a strong pair-bond similar to the

Mute, and maintain a strict territory around their nest site; they will even attempt to breed in a drought year, and attack any intruder that may venture near their small swamp or pond. But strongly bonded pairs comprise a very small percentage of breeding birds in a good year; these swans have a much more casual attitude towards breeding than the Mute, particularly among the younger birds who are promiscuous and even form homosexual associations.

All concentrations of swans in the breeding season contain a very large number of non-breeders. In 1963 only 400 clutches were begun in Lake George, near Canberra, although there was a population of 2,000–3,000 swans. This was probably accounted for by a shortage of nesting sites and large numbers of immature birds.

Mating of Black Swans follows much the same pattern as that of the Mute. As the male Mute Swan's knob becomes enlarged during mating, so, sometimes, during the sexual cycle the male Black Swan's iris turns white. The pre-copulatory display begins with a spell of chasing, followed by mutual head-dipping alternating with the erect posture. Much serpentine entwining of necks takes place under water when they are up-ending, and as they rise they emit a short, faint, whistling note. They do not indulge in the customary preening of the Mute Swan, but coition is similar. The cob rises after copulation, flaps his wings, and with his neck outstretched utters a single, muted, trumpet-note of triumph in which the pen joins. Then, holding their necks outstretched to the utmost angle and pointing their bills downward at a right angle to the neck, they swim around in a circle before bathing.

Nest building takes place 1½–2 hours before sunset with displays by the male who stretches out his neck in front, partly opening his wings, and fanning out his tail feathers. Birds with strong pair-bonds often refurnish their old nests. The male brings the material and drops it at the nest site for the female to build, sometimes helping himself, and the couple rest in the nest together. The pen usually picks up the material brought to her and heaps it about her, finally lining the cup of the nest with white down extracted from her brood patches. Sometimes the first egg may be laid before the nest has been started, but usually some attempt at building is made. Birds nesting on islands sometimes lay eggs on the ground and surround them with a low bank of material;

as the swans have the ground to protect the clutch, and water is accessible for escape from predators, abundant material is not so important on islands. Nests built on the ground consist of such available material as sedges, windswept algae, grass, wheat in flooded wheat fields, or twigs up to an inch or so thick in flooded billabongs. The completed nests are 2–3ft (61–91·4cm) in diameter and a foot (30·48cm) high. When the swans breed on islands the first birds to arrive build their nests on banks of water-swept algae in the shallows, or at the water's edge; the later breeders are obliged to move inland until the whole island is covered. In other places nests are found among swamp vegetation, tops of flooded stumps, in bases of trees, and in floating masses of debris.

Nests that are built in water are sheltered by dense vegetation; thick clumps of cumbungi provide abundant, easily collected bulk. A nest is a 5ft (152·4cm) wide heap of vegetation with 1ft (30·48cm) of its 3–4ft (91·4–121·9cm) depth protruding above water-level. Some swans nest in isolated clumps of cane grass (*Eragrostis australasica*) and prefer it to be between 5 and 20ft (1·5 and 6·1m) in diameter. The water around them is 16–24in (406–610mm) deep, and the cane grass varies in height from 50 to 58in (1,270 to 1,290mm) and may be of any density from 500 to 3,000 stems per square yard. With this material for protection from predators the swans can nest far from the shore.

There may be more than a hundred nests on an island of less than an acre—this occurs with birds lacking strong pair-bonds who appear to have little territorial aggression. Material here is in short supply and the birds pilfer each others' nests, dislodging eggs which they often roll up the sides of their own nests, so that clutches of eight or more are probably produced by more than one pen. Any swan with a desire to nest will take another's eggs—and even the whole clutch and the nest, if left unattended. Pens without a strong pair-bond remain on their nests alone without the males in attendance. On the other hand a strongly mated pair both remain near their nest, and either sex may retrieve eggs that roll from the nest. All the swans start laying at the same time with the first sign of the rainy season. The eggs are laid on down and left uncovered. The first three eggs are laid at intervals of about 36 hours and then laying is increased to about one every 24 hours. They are laid by day and night. The eggs weigh 260g (9·1oz), and have an average length of 104mm (4·09in) and breadth of 67mm (2·6in). They are oval with a pale-green, slightly lustrous, coarse-grained shell. The clutch sizes range from 4 to 8 eggs.

In clutches of 4 and 5, incubation begins after the third egg is laid, after the fourth egg in clutches of 6, and after the fifth egg in clutches of 7 or more. The incubation period averages from 35 to 45 days and when there is a strong pair-bond both parents participate in incubation, the male Black Swan being unique among swans in possessing brood patches as well as the pen. There is an elaborate ceremony when the pair relieve each other from incubation. The pen usually incubates at night and the male stands guard, but in the morning the pen moves away from the nest in a slinking, submissive posture, and the male assumes incubation duties after repeated head-lifting and simultaneous calling. After about eight hours the female relieves her mate, greeting him by lowering her head and up-ending with the head in a sloping position and emitting a short, faint whistling. Both birds sit on the nest together for a time, then the male leaves, passing a few sticks or grasses for the nest over his flank. If there should be a swan nearby he will leave quicker, warding the intruder off his territory with short, aggressive rushes and wings arched.

Hatching of the brood extends over 24–48 hours, the last laid egg being the last to hatch. Should the first clutch be lost before incubation is well established, and providing the pen is still laying, she can re-nest after a period of 3–4 weeks, and as many as five clutches may be laid in as many months. If, however, the eggs have been incubated for 2 weeks or more and are destroyed, the female will not have the ability to lay any more that season.

Eggs fail to hatch because they are addled, infertile or broken. Also the nest may be abandoned because of aggressive encounters between birds that have to nest too close together. Eggs are stolen by such predators as the Australian raven, the swamp harrier, the yellow-bellied swamp rat, the common rat, hawks and the sea eagle. But the greatest hazard to eggs is flooding. When the swans are faced with this disaster, or any serious disturbance, they slip off the nest and swim away quickly with their heads held very low.

Strongly bonded parents both care for their young. When all the chicks are hatched the mother leads them to the water. Their long, fluffy down is a light, brownish-grey above, and white below. They have dark, grey-black bills with light-grey tips, about 22mm (0·9in) long, and their tiny immature wings measure on average 44mm (1·8in); their legs and feet are dark grey and their irises grey-brown. They weigh 125–215g (4·4–7·5oz). They are very precocious and as soon as they leave the nest they are capable of swimming strongly. Under good conditions an average of four cygnets hatch from each clutch, and of these, approximately three survive to fledging. Under adverse conditions as few as eight cygnets have been known to fledge from a total of 189 clutches. But few die on their nesting area, and with strongly bonded parents who only have one brood a year they have a good chance of survival. As with the Mute and Black-necked Swans, the mother carries her young on her back when they are in need of succour.

Cygnets of parents with a weak pair-bond have to contend with chaotic hatching conditions. The female, having to bear the brunt of incubation sometimes obtains help from another friendly swan, which, if a female, may lay eggs in the same nest. In a large colony of swans there is always a shortage of nesting material and many eggs are wasted, but if there is suitable food the chicks that hatch have a chance of survival. Single-parent cygnets remain with their mother for the first few weeks, but as she is likely to mate again and have two or three clutches during the year, the cygnets only roost with her, and attach themselves to a friendly neighbour during the day, so that all the broods form one large family with little parental discipline.

There is a colour phase among Black Swans. The cygnets are white with pink legs and bills. Contrary to the Mute and Trumpeter leucistic swans, the lack of pigmentation becomes more noticeable with age, the plumage being light-brown and sometimes almost white, which proves a barrier to the swan's mating chances.

After the cygnets have completed their 2–3 weeks' brooding on the nest with their mother, the strongly bonded parents take them to a sheltered place in the shallows. Up to this point they have been nourished by the succulent aquatic plants, fresh green herbs, grasses, sedges, rushes and seeds, found in the shallows around the edge of their breeding habitat, or if they are living in deeper water they rely on their parents to uproot such bottom-growing plants as pondweeds.

They grow slowly, increasing to only twenty-seven times their birth weight in 180 days. When they leave the nesting ground they become prey to swamp harriers, native cats, the sea eagle, and gulls and terns which kill them on the water. They gradually lose their down: first the head loses its nestling feathers, then the breast, the back near the head, and then the belly. The tail becomes noticeable, but the wings are still feeble, and the rump is the last part to lose its down. The bill turns to reddish-purple, and the eye changes to a light or dark brown with a black pupil. Gradually the plumage darkens to a mottled grey-brown and black. The wings and pinions are the last to develop—the power of flight is attained slowly and the cygnets do not fly until they are six months old. By then they weigh 4,000–5,000g (8·8–11lb). The juveniles are lighter and browner than the adult, their necks still retain a few nestling feathers, and they are often bi-coloured with the upper, light portion separated from the lower, dark part by a sharp demarcation line. By the time of fledging the wings are black-tipped, and, with the exception of their major flight feathers, and also that they are smaller, young swans of six months are almost indistinguishable from their parents. It is not until they reach two years that they have the same plumage as their parents.

The parents' annual moult lasts about four months and occurs in October and November when the cygnets are still unable to fly. The swans seek the large and safe water areas such as permanent lakes and estuaries in the Coorong, and along the Murray River where they can keep far from the shore. They are very vulnerable and their cygnets' independence grows as the parents lose a certain amount of interest in them. By the time the parents have regained their plumage the young are fully fledged, and, contrary to the close relationship of the Northern Swans, they reject their offspring and drive them away. Later in the year they leave their moulting refuges for the return to their breeding grounds.

Unlike the majority of swans which moult at a regular time annually, Black Swans are to be found in moult at all times of the year owing to the unpredictable rainy seasons. The non-breeders moult before the parent birds and often undertake moult migrations.

Weather dictates the sedentary or migratory habits of the Black Swan. During the advent of heavy rainfall it deserts permanent refuges to seek the new green foods that spring to life. It is vegetarian and only swallows molluscs, insects or snails adhering to the plants. Although cropless, this swan's large gizzard crushes food beyond recognition. It feeds mostly on the water, reaching downwards with its long neck and up-ending in deep water. It can only reach food about 3ft below the surface, and for this reason it is essential that abundant vegetation should be growing up to this level to support a permanent population. It also dabbles along the surface of the water for duckweed and floating plants. Its food is largely dictated by the changes in the water-level of the lake or swamp where it feeds. When the water-level is high its main food is floating plants, and plants that grow on the boggy edges of swamps, such as barley grass (*Hordeum*), hornwort (*Ceratophyllum demersum*), smartweeds (*Polygonaceae*), sedges such as *Cyperaceae* and *Juncus*, and shallow-water plants growing less than 18in down such as waterfern (*Azolla*), stoneworts (*Characeae*), algae (*Chlorophyceae*), water-couch grass (*Paspalum disctichum*), *Zostera* and water milfoil (*Myriophyllum*). But when the water-level is lower it will readily up-end for such deep-water plants as naiad (*Najas*), wild celery (*Vallisneria*), pondweeds (*Potamogeton*) and *Phragmites*. On cumbungi swamps such as the Barrenbox Swamp near Griffith, New South Wales, the swan feeds on the tender young leaves and new shoots of the reedmace cumbungi (*Typha angustifolia*), while the large population inhabiting the southern coastal permanent lakes and estuaries feed mostly on widgeon grass (*Ruppia*), and during the winter makes use of the seeds of club rush (*Scirpus*) and spike-rush (*Eleocharis dulcis*).

During extensive flooding the swan resorts to grazing on pasture plants, and in the Wimmera district of Victoria it has gained notoriety for foraging among cereal crops, which caused the government to allow a short, controlled shooting season in recent years to reduce the swan's numbers and endeavour to scare it away. There is also seasonal and controlled shooting in parts of Queensland. Apart from this the Black Swan is not mercilessly persecuted; it is protected by law, and both the shooting and taking of eggs is controlled. Fortunately it is highly esteemed by the public and there have been sustained public objections when the state authorities have needed to reduce the local overpopulation. In some districts fishermen complain that large swan concentrations on coastal lagoons deplete the fish population by feeding on their food and cover. But no action has been permitted against the swans on these grounds.

Adult Black Swans are practically immune from predators and water pollution, although botulism has been reported. They carry large and varied parasite burdens such as endo-parasitic *Trematoda*, known as flukes, and suffer from worms (*Drepanidotacinia bisacculina*). Small leeches (*Theromyzon*) attach themselves to the nostrils and move up into the sinuses. According to E. R. Guiler in his paper 'Breeding of the Black Swan in Tasmania', their main diseases are fatty degeneration of the liver and cirrhosis of the liver. Swans on Lake Ellesmere in New Zealand have been badly affected by *Aspergillosis fumigatus*, a fungi disease affecting the respiratory system, caused by overcrowding and flooding, which prevented them obtaining enough food. Avian malaria, transmitted by culicine mosquitoes, has been reported in the Black Swan and it affects the bird for life.

The mortality of Black Swans in the wild is only 3–6 years, but in captivity they can live for at least 20 years, and have been known to live for 33 years.

Their population has not been fully assessed in Australia, but concentrations of 2,000–5,000 are common on many lakes, and sometimes exceed 30,000. H. J. Frith, chief of the Division of Wildlife Research, and officer in charge of the Australian Bird-banding Scheme, estimated 50,000 swans in the Coorong in 1957, and similar numbers eastwards on Lake Albert. These banded birds have been found to fly long distances in a very short time, and although individual swans in flocks come and go, the size of the population may remain constant. In south-eastern New South Wales an aerial count showed Lake George supported up to 5,000 birds, and a further 5,000 were counted along the south coast of New South Wales. Many large lakes in New South Wales, such as Lakes Cowal and Yanga, support up to 15,000 birds.

Black Swans are found on lakes and ponds throughout Tasmania both in small numbers and flocks of hundreds. The majority gather on Moulting Lagoon on the east side of the island, where there is food in plenty, and eleven islands offer important breeding sites, rich in submerged aquatic plants such as *Chara* and *Nitella*, widgeon grass and glasswort (*Salicornia*). The Apsley Marshes have a dense coverage of tea-tree (*Leptospernium*) in very low swampy ground, and the upper part of the marsh is covered with rushes. In late July and in August the swans build nests about 70cm (27·5in) in height between closely grown tea-trees. If the material is scarce the nests can be only 14·76cm (5·8in) high with the basal width 94·3cm (37in) and the cup diameter 14·8cm (5·8in). The nests are made of bark, rushes, twigs, leaves and flood debris, flood damage being their greatest hazard. The eggs are larger than on the mainland, weighing 300g (10·6oz), but the swans usually only lay 5 eggs. The chicks also weigh more than those on the mainland. Poaching of eggs is controlled by policing, and egg management is practised. Any eggs found on the ground are placed in nests where clutches are not yet under incubation. The greatest predator of the chicks is the Tasmanian devil. Other breeding grounds are Duck River on the north-west coast, Port Davey on the south-west, and Flinders Island off the north-east coast. In the greater salinity of brackish waters *Zostera* and *Cymodecea* abound. Banding was started at Moulting Lake in 1961, and 4,415 swans had been banded by 1965. A population count on the lagoon totalled 4,150 swans, and 1,390 were counted around Port Davey.

Black Swans were introduced into New Zealand by the Canterbury Acclimatisation Society in 1864. They were first released on the Avon River in Christchurch in the hope of controlling watercress on the river. Seventy birds were liberated in the Southland and Otago districts and within a few years thousands of swans were reported in the great lagoon at the entrance to the Opawa River, in Otago, and on the west coast of South Island. Swans were also liberated by the Auckland Acclimatisation Society, some being released on Kawau Island, North Island. Breeding now takes place in the swamps and lakes of the Waikato River where water-levels are established in the valley by hydro-dams and reach their peak in June. They are maintained well into the summer, encouraging swans to breed from June to January.

By 1900 swans were common in New Zealand, and there has been breeding since 1867. Large flocks settled in South Island on Lakes Ellesmere and Whangape, in extensive harbours such as Kaipara and Tauranga in North Island, and in small coastal lagoons. Lake Ellesmere became the swans most favoured breeding region. This shallow lake with about 80 per cent of its bed just below sea-level, lies on the coast to the south of Banks Peninsula in South Island. It is 14 miles long and 7½ miles wide and its immense indented margin stretches approximately 58 miles. Sea-water enters it through a drainage tunnel during high tides, and this, together with water interchange during tide cycles and storms, maintains the lake's salinity. Fresh water enters through the rivers and canals and the swans are nourished by weed beds of widgeon grass (*Ruppia spiralis*), and water milfoil (*Myriophyllum elatinoides*) in the more freshwater beds. The water reaches a height of between 3·5 and 4ft (107–121·9cm) above sea-level about three times a year and the swans breed after the final winter peak. By the end of July most of the swans go ashore to Birdling's Flat and find ample material to build their nests from wind-driven widgeon grass, but further inland material is sparse and they make low nests of Australian glasswort (*Salicornia australis*), robbing the ground of every available stem. Rushes, tussocks and shrubs are the only barriers between the nests which are often no more than 2ft (61cm) apart. The pens begin laying in the first week in August and close on 20,000 cygnets are hatched annually. The only significant predator, the black-necked gull, preys on nests during floods.

The swans increased to such an extent in the excellent conditions in New Zealand that although they had been shot as game from 1875, the North Canterbury Acclimatisation Society was granted statutory authority to collect their eggs in 1915. Both these practices remain to this day and it is now the policy of the society to limit the number of cygnets hatching on the lake to an average of 20,000 per year. Swan's eggs are sold for 50p (a dollar) a dozen, and before farmers objected they were used for making a malt chocolate drink. They are now used for cooking, and feeding race-horses. The present population around Lake Ellesmere is 40,000–50,000 and at times may rise to 100,000.

Before the coming of the white man, small tribes of Australian Aborigines took the swans' eggs and flesh extensively for food. Besides being hunted the swans had to contend with irregular rainfall and so they bred during floods, wandering in search of available water when there was a drought. In this way they maintained a delicately balanced population which unfortunately was disturbed by the coming of European man in 1788, after Captain Cook discovered New South Wales in 1770.

Nearly a hundred years earlier, in January 1697, a Dutch navigator William Vlaming, discovered the Black Swan on his arrival in Western Australia with a Dutch expedition. The sailors could not believe their eyes when they saw the black, long-necked fowl swimming on the tributary of what is now the Swan River. At first the bird was given the name of *Anas atrata* (goose clothed in black), but it has since been classed with the swans. Today in the city of Perth, situated at the mouth of the Swan River, there is a small lake where Black Swans breed continuously. Western Australia has made the Black Swan their emblem, and it is venerated by Australia by having a place on the Arms of the Australian Commonwealth.

In the late eighteenth century the European settlers discovered the swans made good eating and shot them in their large, moulting flocks. The settlers invaded Australia, floating down inland rivers, breeding sheep which trampled over the lagoons and billabongs, and destroying floating plants and sedges growing along the borders. Much of the waterfowl habitat was destroyed by burning, clearing of land, and large-scale drainage. Rivers were dammed and their flow controlled to divert vast volumes of water to irrigate crops. Levées were built to protect great low-lying areas from flooding, and the rivers' flow was reduced to reticulate water across the plains for stock. The swans had always bred in the lagoons, billabongs, swamps and creeks which formed as the rivers twisted and wound across the endless flat plains before reaching the sea or disappearing in the sand and depressions. Until the heavy rain fell or the snow melted hundreds of miles to the east, to send water coursing down into the rivers, the depressions were parched and the billabongs only consisted of a few inches of muddy water. These breeding sites of the Black Swan were greatly diminished in the Murray-Darling system—their most important breeding range —when man reduced the flow of water and checked the floods.

Fortunately, in most cases inland lagoons were not entirely drained and inland refuges still existed in a few permanent swamps such as the artificial lakes at Menindee, New South Wales, the Cumbungi swamps of the Murrumbidgee River, and also the land-locked water of the Murray River west of Balranald, New South Wales. But with so much deprivation, the waterfowl were in need of the coastal refuges stretching from Adelaide, South Australia, across the lakes of western

Victoria to the valleys of the northern rivers of New South Wales and the coastal plain of the Burdekin River in north Queensland; but, here again, drainage to cater for the thriving agricultural region, has reduced the wetland. Fortunately the creation of dams and lakes has offset the loss of some of the swans' moulting refuges. The authorities have become aware that much of the land drained in the nineteenth century served no useful purpose for agriculture and could be restored to waterfowl habitat.

As a result of hunting and interference with their habitat the Black Swan population, in common with other Australian waterfowl, was in danger of becoming decimated by the end of the nineteenth century. Some fifty years ago protection was found to be necessary and now the swan is protected by law all over Australia, and even the natives have been prevailed upon to limit the taking of eggs. Since 1962 the Black Swan has been a subject of intensive study by the Council of Scientific and Industrial Research, and it has been found that the species has shown remarkable adaptation to the constantly changing Australian environment and has utilised the man-altered surroundings. It is now abundant in suitable regions and its conservation is secure.

This swan's adaptability has been apparent under various alien climatic conditions. The first two Black Swans to be transported alive from Australia reached Djakarta (Batavia), Java, in 1746. The birds survived in an environment only 5° from the Equator with a continuous high temperature, heavy summer rain and dry winters. They reached Europe about 1791 and bred in England for the first time in the Earl of Derby's menagerie at Knowsley. Their strange exotic beauty attracted the Empress Josephine, and before the end of the eighteenth century she had several Black Swans on ponds at Malmaison, and the Dauphine also kept some at Villeneuve l'Etang, near Paris. Since then they have been reared in Swedish parks and gardens, and are well known in the United States as ornamental birds. They lay almost any month of the year from January to April and again from August to October, and are immensely popular throughout the world in zoological gardens and parks.

Japan introduced the Black Swan into her zoos and parks after World War II. It was noticed that although the swans first attempted to breed during the winter, some pairs bred earlier each following year until the first clutch was laid in the high autumn rainfall. The Southern Swans advanced their laying time slowly from winter to autumn, and did not delay laying to synchronise with the northern season, which indicated that the breeding rhythm was maintained, and could imply that there are changes in the swan's responsiveness to environment which can control breeding activities. The clutch size and time of laying varied very little from the normal.

From the historical standpoint the most famous Black Swans in England are those at Chartwell, Kent, the home of the late Sir Winston Churchill. Before World War II Australia sent him a pair of Black Swans and he became very fond of the birds. Sir Winston's delight at the hatching of six eggs turned to distress when crows took the day-old cygnets. Since then the swans have had seven cygnets but only two survived, the others being caught by foxes. After the brood was augmented they were gradually lost by disease and predation, and the Black Swans now on the lake were procured after Churchill's death. A wire fence has been put round the lake in such a way that it is impossible for the foxes to dig their way through. Mr Vincent, the head gardener at Chartwell, finds the swans very hardy—they attempt to nest as early as the end of February with snow on the ground, but of late, their breeding attempts have been unsuccessful. He finds them good parents but they do not appear to suspect crows of being predators. They are aggressive to dogs, and rather bad-tempered, spending a good deal of time fighting among themselves in a non-violent manner; an odd swan, however, suffered such persecution that it had to be destroyed.

Black Swans have been reared recently in England, both at the Wildfowl Trust's reserves at Slimbridge and Peakirk, Peterborough, and in 1972 five chicks were hatched and successfully reared at Kew Gardens.

CHAPTER NINE

The Black-necked Swan

(*Cygnus melanocoryphus*)

The remarkable Black-necked Swan is the only member of the genus *Cygnus* in South America. Although it may be found in most regions south of the Tropic of Capricorn, it mostly frequents open lakes, marshes and brackish lagoons south of latitude 30° where it gathers in flocks in the states of Brazil, Uruguay, Paraguay, Chile; and Argentina, south to Tierra del Fuego and the Falkland Islands.

Although it is the largest of the waterfowl in South America, it is the smallest and most distinctive of the swans, with its long, narrow white body and comparatively short black neck, which has 24 cervical vertibrae in comparison with the Mute Swan's 25. Its singular appearance is enhanced by a thin, white streak running from the side of its black, velvety forehead through its dark-brown eyes to its nape; its chin is also white. Unlike any of the other swans its bill is leaden blue with a conspicuous scarlet base which carries a very large, fleshy, double-lobed, frontal caruncle which is also scarlet. The male's bill is darker than the female's in most cases, with minute black spots near the pink nail which is often seen to be a fleshy-grey from foraging in muddy water. The female is distinctly smaller than the male with a considerably shorter neck; her caruncle varies from being as red and large as the male's to being less pronounced.

This swan's pale, flesh-coloured legs are very short and handicap it on land, making it an even more awkward walker than the Mute. Although it resembles the Mute and Black Swans more than the Northern Swans, it is unique in many respects and not very closely related to any of the species. Its wings are short in comparison with its body, and it flaps a good deal before taking off, but once it is airborne it flies strongly and is capable of covering long distances. It has occasionally been found as far off the coast of Chile as the Juan Fernandez Islands, and a stray bird was captured in the Atacama Desert. They fly rapidly, their short wings producing a loud rustling sound, which, together with low honking calls, rather resembling those of geese, helps to keep the flocks in close contact.

The windpipe of the Black-necked Swan, in common with the Mute and Black Swans is unconvoluted—it shows only a slight bend—and the syrinx is small and of distinctive shape with narrow and bony bronchi. Its voice is a high-pitched whistle, rather like the sound of a toy trumpet, quickly repeated, with up-and-down movements of the head and neck. When it is in flight, or excited or alarmed, it gives voice frequently. Its low, honking calls in flight resemble a sound like 'kaum', by which name it is known in Tierra del Fuego. The mother bird hisses in aggression.

Many of the habits and displays of this swan resemble the Mute. It up-ends, and sometimes carries its legs on its back like the Mute and Black Swans, but unlike these birds it keeps its wings close to its body during threat and attack, although it curves its neck and thrusts it forward. Its aggression is mainly confined to the breeding season when it jealously guards its nesting area. It rears up in the water, flapping its wings formidably several times, then suddenly stops when near its enemy, with wings outstretched, neck bent, and bill pointed towards its opponent. Sometimes it lowers its head so that it is just above the water, this being a sign of appeasement. When it fights, it beats its opponent with its wings, and after chasing off an intruder the male always returns to its mate in triumph, calling continuously and lifting its chin up and down as it does in the threat display. The female replies in the same manner, the two birds giving high-pitched calls with their heads only a few inches apart and their bills almost touching. If young birds are present they will join in. Their mating behaviour resembles that of the Mute and Black Swans they both dip their heads rhythmically into the water and then stretch their necks upwards, and also swim around each other moving their heads up and down. There is no conspicuous display after copulation except the habitual bathing.

The Black-necked Swan: A male threat display, chin-lifting and calling (also triumph ceremony used by both sexes); B attack by male; C the swan partially submerging head in water after attack; D another form of threat display by male swan—the feathers on the bent head are erected; E threat display with outstretched, flapping wings; F female swan carrying young on her back

When wintering in large flocks this swan is sociable and gregarious and it spends most of its time on water in proximity to the coast, swimming with buoyant grace and elegance. It is wary, hiding among the reeds and rushes and avoiding human contact. It only attacks larger fowl than itself (except in captivity when it shows a distinct hatred for the European shelduck which is similar in plumage to the swan, having a black head and neck and much white plumage on the body).

This swan breeds as far north as Santiago in southern Brazil, and in Uruguay. Within a 400 mile radius of Buenos Aires, the Argentine Pampas is studded with hundreds of small lakes, and the swans are found in the marshes and lakes to the south and east of Buenos Aires in a belt of freshwater rush-marshes of *Scirpus californicus*. Large numbers are also present in Cape San Antonio during the summer and remain in the winter to nest from July to October. Another ideal Argentine breeding habitat are the marshes bordering the Bay of Samborombon, covered with marsh samphire (*Salicornia peruviana*), and a few low trees and bushes. In all these regions the climate is moderate and there is a fairly even rainfall. The swans reach their maximum density beyond the valley of the Rio Negro in Patagonia, south into Santa Cruz, almost to the Straits of Magellan, and to the base of the Andes in the west, where there are numerous lakes with patches of permanent green vegetation. The climate is more austere than in the Argentine Pampas. The high winds blowing from the west sweep with them cold air currents from the Andean snows, and snow and ice are regular features of the prolonged winter.

Thriving populations of Black-necked Swans frequent the Chilean coast in the provinces of Valdivia and Curico, and further south, past the island of Chiloe, where the coast has been called 'the Norway of the South'. Here the Andes decrease in altitude and split into numerous islands, submerged valleys, glacier-fed lakes and picturesque fjords, while further eastwards Chile is isolated from Patagonia by ice-fields. Between Chile and Tierra del Fuego in the wet, cool region on the Magellanic coast, the swans reach their greatest abundance, and many travel further south into Tierra del Fuego, to breed in the brackish lakes and lagoons of north-western Isla Grande, as far south as Lago Faguano. They have been recorded on the island in January, April,

September and November. The climate is bleak in the winter—reminiscent of the Scottish Highlands—being only 650 miles from Antarctica, and the majority of the swans migrate northwards.

The hardiness of these swans requires no greater proof than their presence on the Falkland Islands, where they endure cool summers and cold winters with winds blowing almost unceasingly, and rain falling every two days out of three, for every month of the year. The swans are mostly resident on the eastern side of the islands and they nest there from August to September.

In captivity Black-necked Swans have been found to nest when they are two years old, which is no doubt the normal age in the wild. July to November is their regular breeding season; in the central provinces incubation starts either in July or August, but further south it is at least a month later. From observations various pairs have been found in Isla Grande with young in November, and 20 per cent of these pairs have been found to have young of all sizes in April, so it is assumed the swans have two clutches during the breeding season.

Each pair claims a territory of 18m which is much closer than with the Northern Swans. The nest is almost always placed in thick reed beds around the edges of lakes or lagoons, or, when possible, on small islets. The Black-necked Swan brings material to the nest site; such vegetation as rushes and aquatic plants are used to build the large, bulky structure, which is loosely packed and partly floating and partly dry. It is neither as big nor as neat as the nest of the Black Swan. A nest built in captivity was found to have material weighing 15lb (6,810g). The pen lays on average 5 eggs at the rate of one every 1½ days. The cream-coloured eggs are nearer the conventional egg shape than those of other swans, having one blunt and one pointed pole. They have thin shells and measure 101 by 66·5mm (4 by 2·6in) when laid by a mature swan, with a weight of 245g (8·6oz); the eggs increase in weight and size as the swans grow older. A Black-necked Swan's egg is relatively larger in size than the Mute's, but the Mute Swan has a larger clutch.

The female incubates for about 36 days and the male is always in attendance and sometimes sits on the slope of the nest; he also stands guard while his pen leaves to feed, and never deserts the nest except for an occasional meal or to chase off an intruder with a great rush of aggression. In captivity the pen leaves her eggs uncovered when she feeds, but in the wild she covers them to protect them from predators such as gulls and the rat opossum. She will sit on her nest for 2–3 days without leaving to feed, and then feeds mostly in the evening.

The newly hatched chicks are whiter than any of the other cygnets, and with faint pale-grey on top and their abundance of fluffy down they are very pretty. They weigh 150g (5·3oz). The base of the bluish-grey bill is covered with white down as far as the nostrils, and the legs and feet are also bluish grey. They give light, fairly high-pitched cheeps and before stumbling out of the nest into the water they remain with their mother for 48 hours; most of their time for the first two or three weeks is spent under the wings of their parents' backs, because, having very short legs, moving around on their own is slow and diffi-cult. The cob, as well as the pen, does his share in carrying them, and sometimes takes over the duty entirely. The chicks only leave their parents' protective cradle to feed, returning quickly if they are dis-turbed. In the Magellanes, southern Chile, the manager of a sheep farm reported that on several occasions he has seen the parents actually fly from one lagoon to another with the cygnets clearly visible among the feathers on their backs. The parents certainly give their brood excellent care: they are shy and cautious during the breeding season, keeping well in the shelter of reeds and rushes, rarely coming ashore to feed, and spending more time on the water than the Northern Swans. Predators such as gulls and the great condor have little chance to swoop on unprotected chicks because the parents never leave them.

The Black-necked Swans are vegetarians, but are not averse to insects and fish-spawn. The young eat the same food as their parents, pecking at the leaves and stems of the submerged and floating plants that their parents pull up for them. Having their chicks on their backs, the parents never up-end but only dip their heads below water. Other additions to their diet are leaves of emergent plants, occasional seeds, and in Tierra del Fuego, kelp and algae that they find along the coast.

The swans' moulting period takes place from November to March, and by March the cygnets are able to fly northwards with their parents. For the first year a cygnet's head and neck are brownish-black and flecked with pale grey, the white body feathers have rusty-grey tips on the upper parts and sides, and the ends of the primaries are broadly edged, and spotted with blackish grey. During the second year the

Chicks and cygnets: 1 the Coscoroba: a chick's head; b chick; c cygnet; 2 the Black Swan: a chick's head; b chick; c cygnet; 3 the Black-necked Swan: a chick's head; b chick; c cygnet

body becomes pure white, with a black head and neck, but a little black remains at the tip of the primaries. The frontal caruncle does not grow into its full prominence until the swan is in its third or fourth year, and the base of the immature's bill is dull red.

There are exceptions to the swans that migrate northwards around March. In some places, such as the Falkland Islands and the warmer

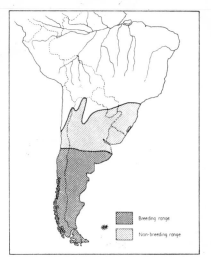

Habitat of the Black-necked Swan

zone around the Rio de la Plata, they remain on their breeding grounds all the year round. The majority fly northwards to winter in large flocks, which are greater in number than those of the Coscoroba. Many reach as far north as the Tropic of Capricorn. In the tropical area of north-east Argentina there is the vast plain of Gran Chaco where the winters are warm and there is a regular rainfall. Both the Gran Chaco and the Pampas further south are studded with hundreds of small lakes. In the vicinity of Resistencia, the capital of the Territory of Chaco, there is a limited area of marsh, small lagoons, fields and pastures to accommodate the wintering swans.

The South American swans are not extensively shot—their size and distinctive plumage make them recognisable and there is no excuse for the hunter who deliberately shoots them. The standards of waterfowl hunting are not as popular in South America as in the Northern Hemisphere, but it is favoured by the Anglo-Argentine and American businessmen, who organise safaris. As the standard of living increases, outdoor activities also increase and hunting becomes more popular, but so far there is a lack of pressure for shooting sites, and hunting methods are simple. Each of the twenty-two provinces of Argentina is able to set seasons on all game without federal influence and some provinces have specific shooting seasons and bag limits. Besides having some measure of protection, the Black-necked Swan does not make pleasant eating and it is not often to be found in the hunter's bag.

Black-necked Swans are hardy birds and can stand sub-zero temperatures as long as open water is available. There have been no reports of lead-poisoning among them. They do, however, suffer from various diseases common to other swans. Culicine mosquitoes transmit avian malaria into their bloodstream and it is thought this can infect them for life. One of the gape-worms, *Cyathostoma bronchialis* has been recorded in their respiratory tract; young birds particularly are affected and can contract pneumonia. In common with most swans *Mallaphaga*, feather lice, also troubles them. In captivity young swans have been known to be affected by the crustacean daphnia which carries the roundworm larva *Echinuria uncinata*.

There is no record of this swan's life expectancy in the wild as no ringing has taken place, and its range is so wide and scattered that it would be impossible to estimate its numbers, which are considerably larger than the Coscoroba. In captivity its mortality is on average some 6 years, but Black-necked Swans have been known to live for 20 years.

The two swans of South America are the least known of the species. The Black-necked Swan was first seen by a European in August 1670, when an English naval commander, Sir John Marlborough, observed them while he was sailing towards the Straits of Magellan. Previous to the Europeans settling in South America the swans were hunted, and in some cases, revered, by the natives. Their range stretched to those regions frequented by various races of Indians. In the sixteenth century, the Argentine Pampas, inhabited by Pampas Indians, was overrun by the fierce, nomadic tribe called the Araucanians, who hunted the swans under the name of 'Thula'. Northern Patagonia was inhabited by the Guenaquen tribe, while further south the Patagonians built their tents from the skins of the guanocos, and other tribes from eastern Patagonia migrated southwards to the undulating plain of cold and windy grassland in eastern Isla Grande. These tribes lived almost entirely on the guanaco and snared the birds of the region. Here, and on the wetter parts of Tierra del Fuego, the Black Swan was among the natives' prey, while the Canoe Indians travelled long distances in their bark canoes, searching for their main food—edible mussel, fish, seal, and water-birds and their eggs.

In 1872, European settlers began to occupy the northern part of Isla Grande and their large sheep farms deprived the natives of the food on their old hunting grounds. The natives became riddled with European diseases and are now practically extinct. But there was no respite for the swans from man's pursuit. In the latter part of the nineteenth century, Europeans captured them to sell their skins for making powder-puffs, in the same way as the Trumpeter was exploited in North America. Thousands of their skins were stored in the Argentine, awaiting shipment abroad, the price of a pelt being 25 cents.

Alexander Wetmore, the ornithologist, recorded seeing swans near Lavalle, Buenos Aires in 1920, and in 1921 they were found in large numbers at the Laguna Castillos, near San Vincente, Rocha in Uruguay. They were also formerly resident on Lake Budi, Vichuquen, Chile, and certain lakes in Santiago, but persistent persecution drove them away. Recently, thanks to a measure of protection, and a greater civic awareness of their value as a source of aesthetic beauty, they have staged a notable comeback, and there are thriving wild populations in northern Chile, and in Santiago, Brazil. Unfortunately their breeding habitat in the large radius of Pampas around Buenos Aires has the highest human population of Argentina, and it is now the major agricultural zone and competition is rife between the farming activities and wildlife resources. Waterfowl destruction is intense. Huge agricultural drainage ditches remove excessive rainwater from the rich rush marshes of eastern Buenos Aires Province. Some of the canals have control structures which allow tidal action to influence marshlands to such an extent that nests are in danger of being flooded. Fortunately the marshes remain essentially fresh water.

There is a serious need for national research and management organisation for wildlife in South America. Juan Daciuk, a conservationist of Argentina, is fully aware of this and advocates systematic study between conservationists and scientists. He writes that the White Lake National Park, in the province of Neuquen, was established in 1945 for the protection of the Black-necked Swan and other waterfowl.

There is still much to learn about the Black-necked Swan in its natural habitat. Being a hardy bird it has been established in Europe since 1846 when some pairs brought to the Antwerp Zoo bred, and one pair produced three clutches and reared fifteen cygnets in a year. Other successful breeders have been M. Maillard in Brittany and F. E. Blaauw at Cleres. The only hatches that have been known to have been laid in North America were at Brookfield Zoo, Chicago, and Mr Sibley's farm in Connecticut. They were the first species of swan to breed at Slimbridge, Gloucester, England, and two pairs continue to breed there regularly. They lay during February when English weather is considerably colder than in their native land. The first egg is produced any time in the 13 weeks following early February. This corresponds with their home breeding season, and the nesting season is spread over a similar period. The chicks are fed on growers' pellets at first, and after 4 days are given cooked grain or rice, and then advanced to soaked grain after 4–5 weeks.

Black-necked Swans have never been known to cross with any other species, which makes them all the more to be valued. This, coupled with their long, elegant shape, moderate size and striking plumage, places them among the most desirable waterfowl for the adornment of ornamental waters. These swans become very tame when they grow accustomed to man and are delightful and interesting to introduce on lakes and private waters.

CHAPTER TEN

The Coscoroba Swan
(Coscoroba coscoroba)

The Coscoroba Swan of South America is the only species of the genus *Coscoroba coscoroba*, and with its conflicting characteristics its exact position within the *Anatidae* family is still somewhat doubtful. By reason of its large size, long neck and white plumage Jean Delacour and other leading ornithologists have placed it among the swan family. In many respects it resembles the whistling ducks of the tribe *Dendrocygnini*: it has the same curved, sloping back and short, rounded tail, the same thick legs and large feet, and has the characteristic pale, rosy-pink colour found in some of their limbs. Its carmine-crimson bill is also similar in shape, being high at the base then sloping suddenly to become deeply depressed and flattened, giving it a slightly concave line. Its bill is extended sideways towards the tip, the upper mandible becoming very broad and the triangular, whitish-pink nail overhanging the lower mandible. With its width, flexibility, and fine, well formed serrations the bill is an effective strainer for the muddy water favoured by the dabbling Coscoroba. Unlike the swans, the Coscoroba's face and lores are completely feathered. Its eyelids are pink, and while the females and immatures have brown irises, the adult males have exceptional, whitish eyes. This swan is more stockily built than the Black-necked Swan and on the water its silhouette resembles to some extent that of the Mute, although its neck is shorter, and it has shorter, broader wings with the six outer primaries tipped with black for about one-third of their length. In common with the other swans

176

it has a small bony knob at the bend of the wing. The female is markedly smaller than the male and the head is less convex.

Another feature which identifies the Coscoroba more with the swans than the ducks is a windpipe without a *bulla*. Its windpipe is unconvoluted and has a syrinx resembling the Mute Swan's. The male's voice is higher pitched than the female's, as in the geese. It has the sound of a smooth, trumpeting croak of four syllables, the first note high and sustained and the latter three short and descending; they can be distinguished as 'Cos-Co-Ro-Va' from which the Swan's name is derived. This call is used in alarm and uttered continuously in the wild at the approach of man or any other danger. It also uses the call in greeting and flicks its bill upwards when calling.

The Coscoroba has an odd variety of behaviour and would appear to assume the role of the droll, endearing clown of the swan family. In many ways it resembles the Mute Swan, raising its wings in aggression and arching its neck as it pushes violently forward with its feet, but it has an individual and rather cheeky habit of moving its head backwards and forwards in fairly quick movements similar to some of the ducks, and no doubt shares with them this method of keeping a close watch on its territory. It stands on one leg when resting like the Mute Swan but it has no pre-flight movements in common with this swan, and it has not been observed performing a triumph ceremony. When feeding on sub-aqueous plants it spreads its wings and up-ends, chopping its legs through the water to maintain its balance. Standing very much on its dignity, it never revels in bathing in deep water as the other swans do but prefers shallow water (although it is a strong swimmer). On land it has an advantage over the Mute Swan, for with its high legs it walks with much greater ease.

With a relatively short wingspan of some 812mm (31·9in), the swan's strong, broad wings enable it to take off easily. In the wild it is very wary of approach by man or beast and usually takes to the air before any of the other birds have even become alarmed. It rises steeply and flies strongly, with a clearly audible whistling of the wings, usually accompanied by its characteristic cry of 'Cos-Co-Ro-Va'.

The temperate zones of South America are the breeding grounds of the Coscoroba. It is not as gregarious as the Black-necked Swan and is local in distribution, favouring lagoons and swampy areas where pairs

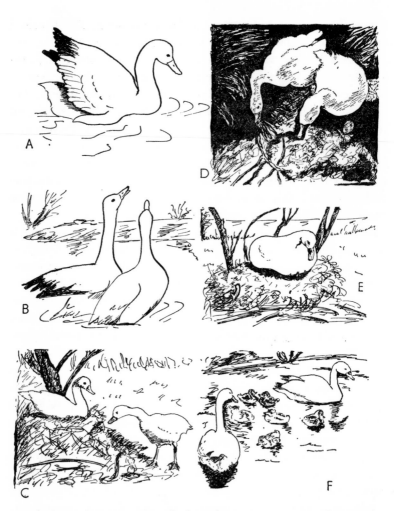

The Coscoroba Swan, mating, display and nesting: A *in posture of territorial aggression;* B *postcopulatory display;* C *during incubation the mated pair will be nervous at the approach of a man. The female will not leave the nest until the last moment of danger but the male approaches the stranger with his neck stretched out in the first stage of the characteristic curve of the attack posture;* D *nesting Coscoroba pair. The female is over the nest; the male curves his body and lifts his wings slightly in the characteristic behaviour pattern during emotion and fear of possible attack;* E *female in brooding posture;* F *nestlings with their parents. Their cry of danger is a signal which keeps the family together until danger is past*

or small groups gather in loose association with the Black-necked Swan and various other species of South American waterfowl; and being less aggressive than the Black-necked Swan, it lives quite peaceably. In other cases the Coscoroba prefers to live on its own, and in some cases one swan will live completely alone. It is resident and a fairly common bird from about 45° S to Cape Horn and the Falkland Islands, but it is a rarer breeder in the latter than the Black-necked Swan. Its maximum concentration is found in the Magellanic region of Chile, and the corresponding latitudes of Argentine Patagonia, chiefly around the valley of the River Chubut. In Tierra del Fuego it prefers the freshwater lakes, lagoons and ponds of the northern, unforested part of Isla Grande. During the austral summer its white plumage makes it very conspicuous as it gathers in these wetlands in large flocks to moult before the winter migration northwards.

In 1970 the Coscoroba was observed in the localities of Bahia, Inutil, East Caleta, Josefina, East China Creek, East Gente Grande, Lago Balmaceda and the Laguna de Los Cisnes. Isolated pairs were seen as far apart as the lagoons in the open country to the north of Porvenir in Tierra del Fuego, and the various lagoons thirty kilometres inland from Rio Grande in Uruguay. In the more northerly districts such as Brazil and Uruguay the swan appears to lose its wariness and forsake the reeds and rushes to gather in flocks. On the water-line of the sandbanks by the Lagoa Mirim, bordering Brazil and Uruguay, they sleep and preen during the day, and fly to the other side of the lagoon when there is a strong wind blowing, to shelter among a small strip of dunes. The swan breeds here twice in succession, on the 'ilhotos' (little islands) in shallow water. It is also to be found, in common with the Black-necked Swan, on the marshes around Buenos Aires. There have been reports of it nesting in northern Argentina and the Paraguayan Chaco.

Breeding takes place during the austral spring. The Coscoroba reaches maturity when it is two years old and it starts breeding at three to four years. A pair of swans will separate from the flock during the summer moult and set up a territory on their own. They favour small islands of floating vegetation where they can have a nesting habitat which is part on water and part on land: they build a nest 2–3m from a river bank near the shelter of large trees or shrubs. Sometimes they choose ant-hills for their nest site. Once established, they keep the same nesting place, building a new nest year by year. They defend their territory fiercely—the male is saucily aggressive during the mating season, rushing forward at the sight of an intruder, calling and bobbing his head excitedly, and should another swan try to seize his territory the two birds will fight, sometimes to the death. The Coscoroba is a solitary nester, but in Argentina it has been found nesting in an area of 370sq m (450sq yd), with some nests only 18m (19·7yd) apart.

The pre-copulatory display of this swan is similar to the Mute's. The male dips his head in the water and then flies up on the female's back, grabbing her nape with his beak; but, contrary to other swans, the Coscoroba copulates standing in the water with the pen's head under water and her neck thrust forward. After treading, the male releases the pen and the two birds stretch their necks and heads vertically, calling in duet, the male raising his folded wings in a fashion similar to the Mute Swan.

The weather has to be cold when the swans start nest building; should it become warm when they have started they will wait for the colder weather to return—they seldom abandon a nest. The building starts between 20 and 30 days before the pen lays the eggs. Both swans help in the building, but the female works the harder, sometimes diving near the bank and pulling up the material which she throws on to the land with a sideways movement of head and neck. Both these swans stand stationary as they build, unlike the active Black-necked Swan. They transport the material to the nest by swivelling round without moving their feet and throwing it as far as they can over their flanks. The nest is made of slender branches, grass stems, dry leaves, straw, sticks, and in some cases, snail shells have been found in the nest's cup. The thick material is used for building first, and when the nest reaches a certain height the female stands in it and throws material over and under her, placing the finer material round the cup. Then she turns round, pressing her chest against one wall and her feet against the other, after which she repeats the whole procedure.

The nest when completed is the shape of a truncated cone. It is only some 50cm (2ft) high, with a 25cm (10in) hollow in the centre and the diameter at the base measuring some 66cm (26in).

Any time between July and October, and according to the location and temperature, the female lays 4–7 eggs at a rate of one every other day. The eggs are dull white, with a slightly rough, granulated shell; they measure 89 by 60mm (3·5 by 2·4in), and weigh 185g (6·5oz). When the temperature rises the pen stops laying until it turns colder again. After the last egg is laid she sheds the down around her brood patches and lines the cup; the Coscoroba uses more down for this than any of the other swans. During this period the pen occupies the nest with the male in close attendance most of the time; before she leaves she covers the eggs with twigs, then she joins the cob to swim and feed. Should one of the swans see an intruder approaching it will warn its mate by emitting a strange cry—nervous, highly-pitched and sharp. This sends them both back to land and the female mounts her nest while the male stands beside it; both arch their necks in the aggressive posture and give strong, high-pitched screams. Should the intruder come close to the nest the male attacks it, using the whole weight of his body and thrashing out furiously with his wings. When the pen returns to the nest in the normal way she drags out the covering of twigs with her feet, then moving clockwise brushes them aside, until the eggs are uncovered ready for her to resume incubation.

During incubation the pen remains on the nest for much longer periods than while egg-laying; she usually leaves for food for about an hour during the morning and afternoon, never deserting her territory. There is no take-over ceremony, but the male guards the nest in her absence, mounting it if she is away any length of time, but never uncovering the eggs. Towards the end of the 33–5 days' incubation the pen rarely leaves the nest at all.

The chicks all hatch on the same day, which may be any time from August to November, once more depending on location. The colder the temperature, the stronger the chicks, which accounts for the parents' instinctive anxiety when the weather turns warm during the breeding season. A good fertilisation rate is 84·4 per cent. The pen never leaves when the hatching starts, she turns the eggs with her bill, and the male is exceptionally aggressive. The chicks are very weak at first—the first-born may try to climb up to the edge of the nest, but they fall back and the pen helps them to their feet with her bill and neck. Should some eggs be infertile she will abandon the nest, taking the chicks with her. They can only walk very clumsily and fall over after three or four steps, but after the second day they go on the water with their mother and there they are more sure of themselves, spending most of the time swimming, and eating everything within reach.

The Coscoroba chicks have a much stronger marking on their down than the other swan chicks and in this respect they resemble the whistling ducks. Their down is greyish-white with a bold, blackish patch on the forehead, divided by a black line with a white crescent under their brown-grey eyes. The thin, grey line starting from the nape broadens as it reaches the back and runs down to the rump; a dark band along the wings is connected to this darker down on the back and there is another band across the sides above the thighs. The bill is grey, tipped and edged with pink, and the legs and feet are pale-pink tinged with grey. On average the Coscoroba has a larger brood than the other swans and this may account for the parents not carrying the chicks on their backs.

They are both very attentive, and care for and instruct their young, brooding them on land, and, for the first days, keeping them near the nest. By 70 days the cygnets are one-third the size of their parents and by 250 days they reach the adult size.

The parents and mature swans have a prolonged moulting period from November to April. At the end of this time the cygnets are able to fly north with their parents. As they lose their down their dark markings change to a strong, brownish-grey and even after they have obtained their first plumage they still retain some grey patches on the wings until the second year. In immatures the irises of both sexes are light brown, the bill is reddish-grey, with the borders, the lower mandible and the nail a fleshy-white. Their legs and feet are a pinkish, flesh colour.

By virtue of its broad, strong bill the Coscoroba is mostly a dabbler and eats the leaves and stems of submerged and floating aquatic plants. The young chicks graze on the marginal vegetation of the coastal districts while their parents keep them near to the land, but as soon as they are allowed free access to the water they eat the same food as their parents. The Coscoroba feeds while wading in shallow water and prefers the coast which provides different forms of vegetable matter, aquatic insects, fish spawn and sometimes small crustaceans. They also eat a substantial amount of seeds and fruits, but they never up-end to stretch for the roots and tubers deeper in the water. Although they come ashore they confine their grazing to the coastal margins and rarely graze in open grassland.

During the winter the swans that have bred in the colder regions are migratory and leave their breeding grounds to travel hundreds of miles to the warmer northern districts of tropical South America, rarely venturing further north than 25°. As there has been no ringing

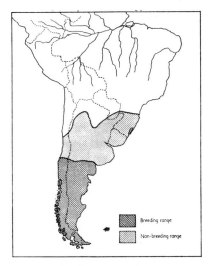

Habitat of the Coscoroba Swan

or population counts of the Coscoroba there is no record of its actual movements, and it is even more hard to determine the extent of its movements by its inconsistency in favouring unexpected localities and ignoring the well known waterfowl habitats. Coscorobas are not as abundant as the Black-necked Swans, and although they are widely distributed they are less easy to find because they do not flock together as much as their more gregarious neighbour but keep in family parties. It is estimated they have a population of some tens of thousands.

There is no record of the swan's longevity in the wild but its life expectancy in captivity is 7·3 years although it has been known to live for 20 years. It has the same predators as the Black-necked Swan and also falls to the hunter's gun, but because its meat is not appreciated, it is not greatly sought after and its numbers have not diminished greatly during the last twelve or so years. Being a dabbler it suffers from cattle trampling over and destroying the vegetation of the marshy areas it frequents—unfortunately for the wildfowl few marsh areas in South America are fenced.

There are no reports of the Coscoroba having died from lead-poisoning. It is unique among swans in having had a tumour of the liver—in spite of their long life-span swans do not suffer from tumours as a rule, although they are usually found in other, older animals. In common with the Bewick's Swan, the Coscoroba has been found to suffer from *Stappyloccosis*, the bacteria which gains access to the body through cracked or calloused feet. Infestations of *Cyathostomia bronchialis*, one of the gape-worms, has been recorded in the Coscoroba, and another disease to which it has been subject is endocarditis (valvular disease of the heart). So far it is the only swan that has not been found to suffer from feather lice, although it may do so. In common with the Black-necked Swan, the Coscoroba has never been known to cross with any other species of bird: it mates for life in the same manner as others of its species.

Although it is believed to have been a native of South America since the Pleistocene period, the Coscoroba was not scientifically described until 1782. The Indian tribes which hunted both the Black-necked Swan and the Coscoroba classed it as a goose, and to many of the natives it is still thought of as such. In Argentina it is called 'Glauso Blanco' (White Goose); in Chile it is known by the name of 'Cisne Blanco' (White Swan) or 'Coscoroba'; and in Patagonia they refer to it as 'Caporova' because of its call, or as 'Cisne da Patagonia'.

In 1870 the London Zoo became the first place in Europe to receive the Coscoroba. As with the later attempts at breeding, although the pair nested they did not hatch their eggs. The earliest breeding success in Europe took place at Woburn Abbey around 1910—the female hatched several chicks but was very restless and lost all but one. This particular cygnet became very tame and attached itself to the Duchess of Bedford, accepting food from her hand and causing much amusement by its quaint antics and by the way it followed the duchess around. From these poor results it is apparent how difficult the Coscoroba is to breed in captivity. A pair at Slimbridge have reared a cygnet, but although they have attempted to breed twice a year, having a second clutch after a month to six weeks, there has been no further success in hatching. Philadelphia Zoo has been slightly more successful. A pair of Coscorobas received there in 1948 successfully hatched two chicks in July 1950.

Although breeding is not often achieved, the Coscoroba thrives well in the temperate zones of Europe and North America, but it is rather susceptible to contagious diseases. Once a chick is successfully hatched it grows without difficulty, thriving on the usual diet for young swans, such as duckweed and egg yolk in the first days, followed by bread and milk, boiled rice and grain. Cygnets reared in the Zoological Gardens in Buenos Aires were strengthened by a daily three or four drops of cod-liver oil.

CHAPTER ELEVEN

Swans and Man

Before civilisation there was a natural balance between swans and man. Natives hunted them for food, for their feathers, and used their bones for making tools, beads and pipes; but, with the vast areas of wetland at their disposal, swans thrived. As man discovered new continents swans entered the commercial field, and the arrows of the natives were replaced by guns, or by trapping. Moulting birds were driven in their flightless state, together with their young, into corrals, such as the Heligoland trap which was set up by a trapper named Götke, a century ago.

As far back as the thirteenth century a great deal of profit was made out of swans for the table. They were fattened by placing large numbers in pens, as it was found they fed better in flocks. Poorer gamesters only had small pens made of hurdles, with a small pond or pit dug in the centre. Those gamesters in the habit of selling 'table-birds' went in for something more elaborate, and their artificial pits of water within grassed enclosures were called swan-houses or swan-pits.

St Helen's Hospital, Norwich, formerly possessed the largest swan-pit in England. It was constructed in the sixteenth century in a meadow behind the hospital. Today a swan-pit constructed in 1793 is still there, and up to the 1880s it was occupied by about eighty cygnets. After that period swan-keeping gradually died out and the hospital was the last place in England to keep swans for food. In Europe swans were marketed in quantity until after World War II, but with the coming

of the war, grain became short in England and it was then that the
hospital discontinued keeping swans.

Well grown cygnets were preferred for the table. The hospital sent
them out plucked, trussed and ready for the oven with the following
printed instructions:

> Take three pounds of beef, beat fine in a mortar,
> Put into the swan—that is, when you've caught her.
> Some pepper, salt, mace, some nutmeg, an onion
> Will heighten the flavour in Gourmand's opinion.
> Then tie it up tight with a small piece of tape,
> That the gravy and other things may not escape.
> A meal paste (rather stiff) should be laid on the breast,
> And some whited brown paper should cover the rest.
> Fifteen minutes at least ere the swan you take down,
> Pull the paste off the bird, that the breast may get brown.
> To a gravy of beef (good and strong) I opine
> You'll be right if you add half a pint of port wine:
> Pour this through the swan—yes, quite through the belly,
> Then serve the whole up with some hot currant jelly.
> NB The swan must not be skinned.

When dressed, the swan has the appearance of a dark-coloured
goose, but it does not taste as good, for although being plumply
fleshed and carving well, the meat is leathery and rather oily.

The only places where swans are still served are at the annual 'Feast
of Cygnets' at the halls of the Dyers and Vintners. At Vintners' Hall in
the City of London a cygnet is borne into the hall on a vast silver dish,
preceded by a heraldic banner, and to the sound of trumpets. The
Dyers' traditional ceremony opens with a singer singing a song entitled 'The Swan', while a procession enters the room.

Besides being hunted for material reasons, sportsmen found swans'
great white bodies a challenge both in the Old and New Worlds, with
the result that the Whooper Swan has left its former breeding grounds
in Greenland, the Orkneys, and part of Finland; and the Whistling
Swans no longer frequent the Perry River in Arctic Canada. This ruth-
less hunting nearly exterminated them in some coastal waters but
during this century they have come under protection in most countries
of the world.

After being placed under protection in some parts of Sweden as far back as 1910, the Euroasian swans were granted full protection by both the Swedish and Danish governments. In England all three species are protected under the Protection of Birds Act, 1954: anyone found guilty of killing a Whooper or Bewick's Swan is liable to a fine of £25, and there is a fine of £5 for killing a Mute Swan. Tame swans come under the Protection of Animals Act, 1911, and anyone stealing a domestic or tame swan is guilty of theft. Killing, maiming, or wounding a domestic swan is an offence under the Malicious Damage Act, 1861. Farmers are permitted to kill a Mute Swan if they have sufficient grounds to prove it is damaging their property, and Mute Swans' eggs may be sold for the purpose of breeding.

The Black Swan is protected in Australia, and the Black-necked Swan has some measure of protection in South America. It is illegal to kill either species of the North American swans under the Migratory Bird Treaty Act of 1918, which was signed between Great Britain and the United States of America for the protection of the migratory birds moving between Canada and the United States. Unfortunately some hunters still ignore this Act.

Now that the hunting and exploitation of swans is virtually a thing of the past they are being subjected to other forms of extermination. Wetlands, the areas of marsh and shallow water favoured by swans, are particularly vulnerable to the rapid destruction and pollution occasioned by technological advances. Also they are one of the most unstable of ecological types, and if they are left to their own resources, rapidly evolve to dry scrublands. In England half the nation's marshlands have been progressively drained by the growth of human populations and the spread of industry. The destruction of much of the Black Swan's habitat by development in Australia, and the industrialisation around the South American swans' marshlands in the area of Buenos Aires, have already been discussed. In North America the problems of conserving waterfowl are different from those in Europe. The prairie and pothole regions within the provinces of Alberta, Saskatchewan and Manitoba in Canada, and the states of North and South Dakota, and Minnesota in the United States, are the breeding regions for ducks and the non-breeding range of the Whistling Swan. The Canadian provinces contain rich agricultural land and extensive areas of wheat, the rainfall is low, and there are fluctuations of wet and dry conditions which sometimes lead to severe droughts when many potholes dry up. These potholes make ideal nesting habitat when they are filled, and in the United States' north central states, water has been put back into them. The federal refuges have been developed from Canada to the Gulf Coast, consisting of artificial ponds with hundreds of acres of wildlife food plants planted in them. During the severe drought of 1960, conservationists, aware of the waterfowls' danger, made sure they were preserved. North America also had another problem regarding the preservation of waterfowl. After World War I the improvement of roads, the influx of the motor-car, and the increase in trade hunters, reduced many species of waterfowl, including the Trumpeter and Whistling Swans, to danger point. By 1934 it was estimated that only 10 per cent of the waterfowl population had survived as compared with the number in 1900.

Swans now also risk pollution by crude oil, oily wastes and oil products. The oil boom of the Arctic Slopes of Alaska, although near the ecological limit of swan habitat, is a breeding area for the Whistling Swan. The Prudhoe Bay–Valdez pipeline route was approved by the Secretary of the Interior early in 1972 but was opposed by environmentalists which delayed it being passed through Congress until November 1973, when it was finally signed into law. Its opponents are allowed 60 days in which to challenge it in the courts, but it is doubtful whether they will be able to muster sufficient arguments in so short a time. The necessary permits for building the 789 miles long pipeline from the North Slope oil fields to Valdez will no doubt be issued by the end of 1973. The danger to wildlife from this pipeline will not be so much from the oil development itself as from the development of the now virgin wilderness for servicing the installations which could affect much of the Arctic coast in future years. Some swan nesting areas must needs be affected in this event, but many it is hoped will remain untouched. The breeding grounds of the Whooper and Bewick's Swans in Arctic Siberia are indirectly threatened by Soviet plans to water the central deserts by reversing the flow of the great rivers Yenesey and Ob.

Encroachment on habitat, and pollution by oil are not the only dangers to rivers and coastal waters; they are affected by sewage, industrial effluents, detergents, fertilisers and pesticides. Some 200,000 birds were killed by pollution around the British coast in 1970. Avian populations have taught man a great deal about environmental pollution; it is doubtful whether DDT and its relatives would yet have been restricted in Britain were it not for the evidence against them accumulated by the deaths of wild birds. DDT is passed from one continent to another in dust and rain and it has been found harmful to waterfowl by rendering their eggs so thin-shelled and subject to hairline cracks that the mother bird cracks or breaks them during incubation.

The dangerous practice of pumping untreated sewage and industrial waste directly into rivers, lakes, and the sea, has resulted in even the major rivers in western Europe, including Britain, becoming open sewers. Some of Europe's main rivers drain into the Mediterranean and the Baltic seas, and unless these rivers are kept clean the seas could become dangerously polluted. In Russia, industrial effluent from the town of Irkutsk is pouring into Lake Baikal, the largest and deepest expanse of fresh water in the world. In America, Lake Erie's 10,000 square miles of water is clogged with sediment of between 30 and 125ft. It will take many years to 'purify' it. The lake is bounded by Ontario, Canada, on the north, and four states belonging to the United States of America on the south, which presents international and inter-state complications. The United States government has taken action against the most flagrant polluters, but the lake's shores are covered with massive industrial and residential development, and it is crossed by many shipping lines. In these greatly populated areas sewage effluents, if left untreated, de-oxygenate rivers and lakes. The nitrates in fertilisers in agricultural areas percolate from the fields via rivers, and enter lakes where they stimulate the toxic algae to such vigorous growth that all other life in the lake is killed. Australia has scattered poisonous insecticides and weedicides over its land, and the toxic effluxes her rivers pour into the sea have begun to affect wildlife as far away as Antarctica; fortunately the Australians are now actively engaged in research and anti-pollution measures.

Pesticides have affected Whooper Swans in the British Isles—some 30–40 swans found dead in Scotland had traces of mercury in their stomachs, no doubt ingested with the wheat upon which they had been grazing. Other Whooper Swans have been found dead in Scotland and they were suspected of having been poisoned by pesticides. Benzine hexachloride and dieldrin have been discovered in Mute Swan cygnets and also in Mute Swan's eggs.

Lead-poisoning has already been described at some length among the Trumpeter and Whistling Swans of North America. Soft iron for shot has been developed by one American manufacturer and used experimentally in a wildlife management area. This seems to have promise within a normal shooting range but it has not yet been proved whether the iron shot erodes the choke of the shotgun, in which case it would open the pattern of the shot string and decrease the killing range, thus defeating its purpose by crippling, instead of making clean kills, such as have been made with lead. Lead-poisoning accounted for the loss of several thousand Canada geese on Maryland's eastern shore last winter. The Whistling Swan's restricted feeding areas may have accounted for them not suffering likewise: the nature of the bottom of these areas is favourable to the swans, there is an availability of natural gravel, and the softness of the bottom facilitates the speed of the shot so that it buries itself deeper than on hard beds. Other metallic poisonings have been reported in Europe—copper sulphate was found in the gizzards of two Mute Swans in Switzerland, and in England fragments of brass were found in two Mute Swans.

Fortunately the protection of wildfowl is becoming an international concern, largely due to the pioneering spirit of a number of nations. Britain has played a leading role in furthering the idea of international responsibility for the conservation of wildfowl, thanks to the efforts and enthusiasm of Peter Scott, the founder and director of the Wildfowl Trust. The International Wildfowl Research Bureau was founded in 1954, and it has been housed and serviced as an independent organisation by the Wildfowl Trust at Slimbridge since 1969. Dr Geoffrey Matthews is the Director of the IWRB. The bureau has no political affiliation and any country with wildlife and wetlands is welcome to have official representation. Some countries in Asia and Africa have correspondents appointed by the bureau to maintain the essential liaison. Such countries as the United States of America, Australia, New Zealand, and Canada have their own conservation and research programmes.

The IWRB has been concerned from the start with the project known as MAR, which is an international effort directed at the conservation of wetlands; it is so named because the word for 'marsh begins with these three letters in many languages. An authoritative document was prepared listing more than 200 wetlands of international importance in Europe and North Africa, and it provided invaluable support for efforts aimed at averting many drainage and reclamation schemes. MAR now covers Asiatic waters and also those of equatorial Africa. The bureau has created a wetland convention by which governments are encouraged to make a public statement that they recognise certain wetlands in their countries to be of international importance, and to pledge themselves to conserve them to the best of their ability.

International meetings of the IWRB have taken place all over Europe, and in February 1971, the International Conference on the Conservation of Wetlands and Waterfowl was held at Ramsar, Iran, on the southern coast of the Caspian Sea. This was a historic occasion with some seventy delegates from twenty-three countries in Europe, Asia and Africa attending, and also eight international organisations. The conference opened with a personal message from HIH the Shahanshah Aryamehr, read by his brother HIH Prince Abdorreza. This ended with the statement that Iran would be prepared to place one of its wetland ecosystems of special global significance in joint trust with a suitable international agency. Iran was the first nation to undertake to forego part of her sovereignty for the benefit of the international community, and it is hoped it will lead to other countries doing likewise.

The following countries were represented at the conference:

Belgium	Iran	Sweden
Denmark	Ireland	Switzerland
Finland	Jordan	Turkey
France	Netherlands	Union of Soviet
Federal Republic	Pakistan	Socialist Republics
of Germany	South Africa	United Kingdom
India	Spain	

The governments of Bulgaria, Hungary, Rumania, Greece and Italy sent observers.

During the conference the main areas in danger of disturbing the habitat of waterfowl by development and pollution were considered, and recommendations were made to the countries concerned to delay further development until the ecological situation had been studied. The areas in question were all relevant to swan habitats. Plans for the reclaiming of the Wadden Sea was the chief concern; fortunately these plans now no longer appear to be operative. Other areas were the Thjorsarver area in central Iceland which the Icelandic government proposed to flood for hydroelectric purposes; North Bull Island, Ireland, the only wetland of international significance within a capital city in Europe; lakes in Afghanistan; and the Medway Estuary in Kent, England, which was being considered as a site for a marine industrial development area. Besides being populated by flocks of Mute Swans this area is the alternative wintering ground for the Brent goose when it is displaced from Foulness, the proposed site for the new London airport.

It was also recommended that strict supervision and further research should be made of oil pollution, and that the use of persistent pesticides such as chlorinated hydrocarbons, should be banned or severely restricted; also that governments and all departments and institutions concerned with natural resources should assist in wetland research.

Finally the conference recommended that the wetlands in all parts of the world should be brought within the scope of UNESCO's new programme on 'Man and the Biosphere' (MAB), which involves worldwide research into, and advice upon, the best way to conserve and utilise the major habitats.

It may appear inconsistent that the Wildfowlers' Association of Great Britain and Ireland, known as WAGBI, should be represented on the council of the International Wildfowl Research Bureau, but they, in common with such bodies as the Wildfowl Trust, the Royal Society for the Protection of Birds, and the International Council for Bird Preservation, have interest in the welfare of wildfowl and their conservation. Some wildfowlers are naturalists, and although their chief aim is to harvest the proceeds of the conservationist's care, without the WAGBI it is doubtful whether any vital interest would have been created in wildfowl. The Wildfowl Trust, with the help of WAGBI, has studied the food preferences of individual species of waterfowl, and carried out a full survey of wildfowl and their habitat in Great Britain.

At Sevenoaks, Kent, the WAGBI has the most concentrated nesting area in Kent. Besides rearing 1,393 young ducks at their Wildfowl

Trust Experimental Reserve, Mute Swans have been attracted there and have averaged over 500 in the years 1966–9. Whooper Swans also come to rest on its waters—73 were seen in 1962–3, and also 7 Bewick's Swans.

Besides Abbotsbury, already mentioned as a sanctuary for Mute Swans in England, there are other wildfowl refuges in the British Isles where the Northern Swans of Eurasia are to be found. Whoopers migrate to Lindisfarne National Nature Reserve, Northumberland; the Statutory Sanctuary at Hamilton Low Parks in Lanark, Scotland; and the Achray Forest Reserve in the Trossachs, Perthshire. Bewick's Swans are to be found on the Ouse Washes; much of these wetlands are in Cambridgeshire and belong to the County Naturalists' Trust and the Royal Society for the Protection of Birds. In Norfolk, the Welney Marshes constitute 600 acres belonging to the Wildfowl Trust; Bewick's winter here and at a local nature reserve at Breydon Water, Norfolk. Many Bewick's fly to 'Swan Lake' at the Wildfowl Trust, Slimbridge during late October and early November.

Ireland stands at the end of two main wildfowl flyways: one from Greenland and Iceland, and the other from the north-west European mainland. Unfortunately the country is on the brink of massive destruction of wetland habitat by drainage and pollution. There has, however, been a great awakening of interest in wetland conservation, which in January 1969 culminated in the Irish Wildfowl Committee of the Republic merging with the Irish Society for the Protection of Birds and the Irish Ornithological Club, to form the Irish Wildbird Conservancy. With everyone co-operating, it is now thought that the disastrous situation of the wildfowl in Ireland can be saved. Many important reserves have been established, including Wexford North Slob, Tern Island, Lower Lough Erne, and Lough Neagh. At Strangford Lough efforts are being made to control the spartina grass which is choking the *Zostera*; and at North Bull Island, Dublin, a tidal wetland inside the city, the corporation propose to reclaim the channel between the island and the mainland at Clontarf. At Lough Cara, County Mayo, the Mute and Whooper Swans are thought to be on the increase.

There is an increasing interest in conservation in Europe. Scandinavia has widespread regulations for the protection of wildlife. In her report at the 1971 conference, Sweden listed twenty protected areas. Denmark has saved wetlands from destruction—the island of Saltholm lying between Denmark and Sweden is a bird sanctuary where Mute Swans nest. Holland has an enlightened outlook on conservation; all the displaced swans and geese from Germany moved there and the number of reserves is increasing steadily as part of a 10-year programme. About 3,000 Bewick's Swans, the largest number anywhere in north-west Europe, winter there. Germany is suffering from tourism besides industrial development—the habitat of the Whooper and Bewick's Swans at Assler Sand on the lower Elbe, and inland waters in Lower Saxony and the north Rhine are threatened in this way, although some of them are protected areas. A reserve, Sreberna-See, in Bulgaria, is a nesting ground for Mute Swans, and Bulgaria has declared both Mute and Whooper Swans protected.

The Soviet authorities tackle their conservation problems in a vigorous and relatively enlightened manner. Their wetland is also diminishing and leading to a decrease in wildfowl, but in the western Siberia–Baltic–North Sea population they have slightly increased. This is the only wintering area in Europe where an adequate chain of reserves has been established. In the tundra, reserves extending for 175,000 acres supply habitat for all the main moulting and wintering concentrations of waterfowl. They are under national control and every endeavour is made to keep them quiet and retain their natural conditions. All swans, eiders and Brent geese are protected, and since 1970 a complete prohibition of spring shooting has been introduced.

Iran has many wetlands of international importance. Fourteen at least have been granted legal protection, including three swan habitats: the Bay of Gorgan and the Miankaleh Peninsula; the marshes of Pahlavi Mordab in the regions of Siamkesheem and Selke where 50,000 to 80,000 wildfowl feed each winter; and Lake Rezaiyeh and its islands.

Australia's management of the country's fauna is a matter for the individual states and the only co-ordinating body for the protection of waterfowl is the Australian Waterfowl Committee which is composed of a research worker from each state and from the Commonwealth. The most urgent needs of habitat retention and restoration, and the importance of maintaining the flow of inland streams, have been recognised and acted upon. In Victoria steps are being taken to create reserves and sanctuaries throughout the state. New Zealand takes a keen interest in protecting and controlling the Black Swan population on Lake Ellesmere.

There is a high degree of international co-operation between the United States of America, Canada and Mexico: a treaty was signed between the United States and Mexico in 1937 which brought the most southerly of wildfowl winter quarters under jurisdiction. By the example of the Whistling Swans in the Klamath Basin, North America has discovered that it is more advantageous to provide extensive refuge areas for swans than to spend large sums of money on deterrents. By 1963 the United States had established 220 wildfowl refuges covering just over 2 million acres of wetland, and in addition 66,000 acres of potholes had been acquired. Canada has also contributed to the North American network of refuges with a remarkable conservation project —founded by duck shooters in 1937 under the name of 'Ducks Unlimited'—which was probably the greatest private enterprise for wildfowl conservation ever undertaken. Wildfowl breeding grounds were restored, 800 dams were built, and over 750 new lakes and swamps were formed. In 1962 Reifel Island generously leased to the British Columbia Waterfowl Society 40 acres of foreshoreland for thirty years at $1 per annum, and in 1963 the Provincial Government of British Columbia agreed to allow the society 700 acres of marshes as a provincial waterfowl refuge, to the advantage of the Trumpeter and Whistling Swans who inhabit these sanctuaries.

The Red Rock Lakes Migratory Refuge in south-west Montana, acquired by the United States government in 1935, is now administered by the Bureau of Sport, Fisheries and Wildlife, principally for the perpetuation of the Trumpeter Swan. Yellowstone Park, where the swan also breeds, is the United States' first and largest park; its wildlife was protected under the Lacey Act, 1894, but unfortunately subsequent legislation was too late to prevent the extermination of the Trumpeter Swan over most of the United States' breeding range. The Migratory Bird Treaty Act of 1918 placed a closed season on both species of swans and saved the few Trumpeters still existing in the park.

Conservation in South America is more backward than in the rest of the world—some laws do exist but are so ineffectively enforced as to make them almost meaningless. The National Institute of Agricultural

Technology has done some good work and several ornithologists have contributed to the general knowledge of waterfowl habits and distribution, but apparently there is no government-sponsored research. Argentina has made some effective efforts at conservation: conferences have been held there in 1965, 1966 and 1968, and there was a joint one with Mexico and Brazil in 1967. The White Lake National Park in the province of Neuquen has a large reserve for waterfowl and a biological station was set up in 1963 to study the arid zone and also birds and their environment.

Japan has taken the Whooper Swans to her heart, and calls them the 'Angels of Winter'. The swans' pure white, elegant forms, appear on the northern Japanese skyline from September when they migrate southwards from Siberia. Swan settlements in Japan are to be found at Lake Furen in Hokkaido, Ominato Bay in Aomori, and Lake Hyo in Niigata on the Japan Sea coast. Kominato Bay in Aomori is one of the swans' midwinter resorts, and some hundreds of them swim here against a background of snowy hills; they have been protected as messengers of the Raiden Shrine and the bay is now a natural monument.

In Niigata Prefecture in north-eastern Japan, an obscure lake, named 'Hyoko', in the town of Suibara, has become a centre of attention since hundreds of swans have made their winter home there. A farmer named Juzaburo Yoshikawa discovered Whooper Swans alighting timidly on the lake in January 1950, and by February their number had increased to forty-six. Yoshikawa fell in love with them and succeeded in persuading the mayor and the local huntsmen to reserve the lake as a sanctuary for swans, where hunting would be prohibited.

When the swans reappeared the following year Yoshikawa redoubled his efforts to protect them and pleaded with all his neighbours to co-operate. He even tried to control the dogs and traffic near the lake in order not to frighten them. By 1952, no matter how severe the weather, he was feeding the swans morning and evening, and even kept a vigil over them at night. As a result of his efforts the town allocated money to him to purchase food for the swans, and hired a watchman to protect them. Money was also granted to Yoshikawa for expenses incurred in his 'swan hospital'. On the lake, resting-places were constructed, and the water was kept from freezing.

In 1954 the swans of Lake Hyoko were proclaimed natural monuments, and that same year the wild birds started eating out of Yoshikawa's hand. They knew his voice and would come only to his call. His sweater-clad figure, complete with hunting cap and rubber boots, became a familiar sight at the lake's edge with all the swans around him. But in 1959, after insisting on going out one very cold day to feed his cherished birds, Yoshikawa died. His work is now being carried on by his son, Shigeo, who shares his father's love for swans. Greater plans were made in Suibara to protect the birds, and by 1970 there were over 1,000 swans on the lake, by this time known as 'Swan Lake'.

Japan is certainly becoming 'swan conscious'. Swans on Lake Hyoko are now being studied, and a register of each bird is kept with a photograph to distinguish it by its bill and the colour of its feathers. In this way an endeavour is made year by year to know the sex and age of each swan, and how many times it returns to the lake. In Nemuro, in east Hokkaido, swans have a special clinic which can accommodate six ailing swans in a heated room. Children are taught to know and respect the beautiful winter guests. At Akatsuka High School in Niigata a statue of a swan the pupils cared for has been erected in the school grounds, and in another school the children have a stuffed specimen to study. All the efforts of the Japanese to protect their yearly visitors will be achieved if they teach their children to love and respect them. Success is already apparent—the Forestry Agency recorded approximately 12,000 swans in the northern districts of Japan during the winter of 1970. Most of these are Whoopers, but Eastern Bewick's have increased in numbers during the last fifteen years.

Man does not always take kindly to swans, as has been observed in the chapters on individual species. Complaints have been made of their interference with crops of spring grass. In Scotland, where large flocks of Whooper Swans gather in Aberdeenshire, farmers complain that they graze on their arable land during the spring, and on the young wheat in winter. In Iceland, also, some farmers are disturbed by the swans eating their summer grass to the detriment of sheep, but these are only isolated cases. Fishermen resent swans on trout rivers and on their coasts, but both in Europe and North America swans have been vindicated of serious nuisance. Their feeding habits are useful for

Food: A *eel grass* (Zostera marina); B *common sedge* (Carex); C *amphibious bistort* (Polygonum amphibian); D *bur-reed* (Sparganium erectum); E *Canadian pondweed* (Elodia *canadensis*); F *reedmace* (Typha latifolia)

saving rivers from an over-abundance of water weeds and their droppings enrich the plant life where it is less plentiful.

Even after existing with our technological civilisation for well over half a century, swans still fall foul of overhead cables and cause power failures. They hit pylons, and in bad weather fly into trees and kill themselves. Dead swans found on railways are more likely to have flown into the wires complementary to the trains, than to have been hit by the trains. A death of a motor-cyclist has been recorded after being in collision with a swan, but these birds cannot be rated as a great hazard to motorists; occasionally a stray swan may land on a wet road in mistake for water and be hit by a car, for they become stupefied by the noise and speed of motorways. The serious accident in North America when Whistling Swans collided with an aircraft has led to research into the swans' migratory movements, which should avert further disasters. Although fishermen complain swans interfere with their fishing, the birds suffer many hardships from fish-hooks and blows from oars. Wastage such as glass and plastic bags are thrown into the water and become entwined in the weeds consumed by swans, causing them much suffering and ultimately death. Vandals take a perverse pleasure in persecuting these beautiful creatures, attacking them and disrupting their nests and eggs.

Weighing the pros and cons of 'man versus swans', what undoubtedly emerges is that man has contributed more to the suffering and mortality of these retiring, magical birds than they have inflicted upon man. Even though hunting them is virtually a thing of the past, they suffer greatly from man's encroachment upon their habitat, and from his technological expansion. Swans are essentially wild birds. Some species such as the Mute, the Black Swan, the Trumpeter, and the Black-necked Swan, thrive and breed in captivity, but in common with the three most Northern Swans and the Coscoroba, they are happiest in their own environment. Their only hope of survival is to protect their breeding grounds from exploitation and preserve their waters against all the poisons man has for so long introduced into them.

Because they provide such attractive ornaments for lakes and large ponds man has attempted to keep and rear them in captivity and has had success with all species. Although they can exist on fairly small ponds, such large birds are more fitted to grace large expanses of water that have a plentiful supply of aquatic food, a good amount of permanent grit and lime, the latter in the form of oyster or egg shells, and a surround of grassland for grazing. Considering their strong, territorial instincts it is advisable to isolate breeding pairs.

Swans' diets can be augmented with grain, such as wheat, barley or maize; green food in the form of lettuce, watercress and cabbage; and brown bread. A suitable water-space must be provided where they can swim freely, for without swimming facilities they develop trouble in their limbs which leads to arthritis and cripples them beyond recovery.

All swans are hardy and can sustain severe cold as long as they have open water. In severe weather their diet needs to be supplemented with extra grain and bread. Stagnant water is not beneficial as it can infest the birds with parasitical diseases. Given the correct environment they will reward their provider by destroying weeds and keeping the waters clear. They will come to a familiar whistle, in some cases feed from their owner's hand, and they certainly enjoy being spoken to, the tamer species making friends with and taking part in their owner's outdoor interests.

Additional food is required before and during the swan's moulting period, and should a female be encouraged to breed, she will benefit from poultry-breeder pellets and extra green vegetables. Nesting sites can be provided by growing plenty of reeds and long grass among secluded and protected locations and placing nesting boxes in them. Nesting boxes are made open at the front and underneath so that the eggs can rest on the earth. Their average size is 3 by 1·5ft (91·4 by 45·7cm). Nesting swans can be fierce so it is advisable to avoid confrontations at this time; in emergency an attacking swan can be fended off by the human being standing with arms flung right out, occasionally flailing them up and down in a swan's familiar aggressive action.

The parents are the best providers and protectors for their young, but the chicks' food can be supplemented by chick-starter crumbs, and later, growers' pellets. Swan chicks appreciate a large amount of duckweed (*Lemna*).

A sick bird, or a bird that has to be transported from one place to another can be captured most easily on land. It has to be prevented from being able to take-off or reach water, and once cornered it should be held by the neck, and the wings prevented from flapping by securing them with a long muslin bandage, or failing this, two nylon stockings tied together. After this the swan will offer little resistance but hang its head down limply and emit a few protesting snorts. It can then be placed in a sack with its head protruding. Two British bird hospitals where swans have been successfully treated are Mrs Brenda Marsault's Hospital for Wild Birds at Redgate, Salterton Road, Exmouth, Devon (Exmouth 3073), and The Raystede Animal Centre of Miss Raymond Hawkins, Ringmer, Sussex (Halland 252).

When a swan has spent a number of days in a pen the soiled feathers will lose their waterproofing. If it is allowed on water for any length of time in this condition, it could drown, or die of a seizure or cold. Before releasing a penned swan it should be thoroughly cleaned and only allowed on water for short periods. At any sign of distress it should be taken out and dried.

Education and television have played their part in gaining the public's sympathy for wildlife, and it is evident that man appreciates the aesthetic beauty of such graceful, elegant waterfowl as swans from the vast number of people who are attracted to their sanctuaries and to the great gatherings of swans in North America. It is not enough to admire them: children must be taught at an early age to understand and appreciate nature and be conscious of their responsibility to wildlife in order to ensure that conservation is continued by future generations.

CHAPTER TWELVE

Myths and Inspiration

———◆———

Art of the Stone Age has revealed that man of the Upper Palaeolithic culture was aesthetically attracted by the magical and spectacular beauty of the swan. Rock-carvings of swans by the Cro-Magnon people of the Aurignacian culture have been found at Lake Onego in northern Russia; and paintings 13–17ft long depicting bulls, and galloping ponies together with swans and birds of prey enrich the walls of caves in Spain, France and Italy. All these were created about 18,000 BC, and when this culture ended, the Magdalenian art developed, which is renowned for very fine workings on bone and antlers such as is seen on a swan engraving in Gourdan, northern Spain; and at Teyjat, where an antler was found upon which three swans were beautifully etched. In later paintings in Andulasia, southern Spain, lines of swans with other birds were depicted on rocks.

The belief that swans had a connection with death and represented the external soul was derived from the Stone Age. The Tungus shamans and certain groups of Yakuts in Russia have the swan as their totem: effigies of swans are erected on poles around their coffins, and they never eat its flesh. In many countries it is considered unlucky to kill swans because they embody human souls. Many of the Siberian tribesfolk believe that if a man kills a swan he will die, and that it is dangerous even to point at one. The Buriats of Siberia consider it a dreadful sin to kill a swan, and to handle a feather is also thought to be sinful. They look upon the eagle as their paternal forebear and the swan as the mother of their race. When the swans arrive in spring they drink to them and the women pray to the first one they see. Legend has it a swan brought fire and burnt the tent of a man who robbed its nest.

The swan-maiden myth may have arisen out of the bird-beliefs of the Siberian people. The Buriats alone enact a ritual associated with this myth, and the standard swan-maiden legend is given as the reason for their ceremonies. One day three swans arrived at a lake, they left their feather garments on the bank and went for a swim. A hunter took one of the feather cloaks and when its owner emerged from the water as a beautiful maiden, he married her. After many years he allowed her to try on her swan-garment and she flew out of the tent's smokehole crying: 'Every spring when the swans fly north, and every autumn when they return south, you must honour me with your ceremonies.'

The swan-maiden legend is characterised by the metamorphosis from swan to human form of a beautiful half-mortal, half-supernatural maiden. The maiden must be in possession of her feather robe, wings, crown, chain or ring, before she can assume her swan form. This motif is found throughout Europe and Asia; in Slavic, Icelandic, Finnish, Celtic and Teutonic legends, and in the mythology of Persia, India, Japan, Australia, Polynesia, Melanesia, Indonesia, and in East and West Africa and Madagascar; the Zulus also possess such legends.

Reference to the smokehole in the tent is found again in the Irish legend of Étain and Midir, who, in the shape of swans, flew out of the smokehole of the castle where Étain and her mortal husband, King Eochaid, had lived. Midir, who bore her away, had come to claim her as his wife and as the queen of the fairy mound of Bri Leith, where he reigned as king. In another Irish legend the Quins' chieftain found a strange woman in a cave and she agreed to marry him providing no O'Brien should enter the castle; eventually this happened and she sprang with her child through a window into the lake.

Swans are still birds of mystery and magic in Ireland, and also to a lesser extent, in Scotland. A seventeenth-century poet styled Ireland as 'The Swan abounding Land'. It was tabu to kill a swan there, and in the Hebrides it was considered wrong to kill or hurt one. In some districts of both countries it was believed that anyone who killed a swan would die within a year or that someone else in the parish would die. In County Mayo the souls of virgins were thought to dwell in swans at death, and girls are described metaphorically as swans both in Irish and Greek literature.

Swans figure in a group of Irish tales known as 'The Three Sorrows of Story-telling'. In one of the tales the 'Children of Tuirenn', Brian and his two brothers, were told by the sons of Canute that in recompense for killing their brother, Cian, they must find three apples from the Garden of Hesperides in the Eastern World. Many dangers assailed them, but Brian, having a magic wand, eventually escaped with his brothers by turning them, and himself, into swans.

Another of the tales, 'The Fate of the Children of Lir' is also related to the swan-maiden theme. King Lir's second wife, Dorfe, jealous of his daughter, Fionnuala, and her two brothers, turned them into swans and condemned them to swim on the sea between Ireland and Scotland for nine hundred years, 'until the bells of heaven recalled their spirits from the world'. The three swans sang sweet fairy music which cast a spell on all who heard them, and the birds flocked to listen. When the swans reached the fury of the Waters of Moyle, Fionnuala gathered her two brothers under her breast and wings to shelter them. 'The bells of heaven' eventually reached them in the form of a Christian monk, Saint Caemhoc, who looked after them and linked them together with silver chains. When the Children of Lir were restored to human shape they were so old and decrepit that Saint Caemhoc just managed to baptise them before they died.

Thomas Moore, the Irish poet of 1779–1852, was inspired to write a poem, entitled 'The Song of Fionnuala', about this legend:

> Silent, oh Moyle, be the roar of thy water,
> Break not, ye breezes, your chain of repose;
> While, murmuring mournfully, Lir's lonely daughter
> Tells to the night star her tale of woes.
>
> When shall the swan, her death-note singing
> Sleep, with wings in darkness furl'd?
> When will Heaven, its sweet bell ringing,
> Call my spirit from this stormy world?

Another legend on this swan-maiden theme tells of Angus (Oengus), the son of Dagda, dreaming of a beautiful girl visiting him and of him so desiring her that he fell desperately ill. The dream-maiden was Caer, who lived in a fairy mound with her father, Ethal, and when the men of Dagda discovered this, they threatened to behead Ethal, if he would not divulge where to find his daughter. Ethal told them that next Samain, which was the beginning of the Celtic New Year, Caer would be at Lough Bel Dragon in the form of a bird, with 150 swans wearing silver chains and coronets of gold. When Angus saw the swans he called to Caer and she came to him. He embraced her and they fell asleep together in the form of swans. When they awoke, after circling the lake three times, they flew away.

The swan-maiden theme has been immortalised in the ballet, *Swan Lake* (Le Lac des Cygnes), which originated from a book written by V. P. Begitchev and Geltser. The music was by Tchaikovsky, and the ballet was first produced in Moscow in 1877. One of the famous ballerinas who has taken the dual parts of Odette, the swan-maiden, and Odile, the daughter of the Black Swan—Odette's scheming counterpart—was Pavlova, who developed a great affection for swans after visiting Abbotsbury to study their movements for her most famous dance 'The Dying Swan'. Afterwards she kept a pair of Mute Swans in a small lake in her Hampstead garden.

In this ballet we have Odile, dressed in black: for in the days before the discovery of Australia, mythical black swans were looked upon as symbols of evil. This was not so among the Aborigines of Australia—to them the Black Swan was the bird of the Great One, Byamee, and was called Byahmul. In the legend of Wurrunnah, white swans make their appearance in Australian folklore. It seems inconceivable that the Aborigines should have imagined the symbol of white swans, and it must have been after the coming of the white man that this tale was created. Wurrunnah was a magician, and in order to divert the attention of a neighbouring tribe of women while his men raided their camp, he turned his two brothers into white swans. After his plot succeeded, Wurrunnah forgot about his brothers and they were attacked by eagles who wounded them and ripped off their feathers, with the exception of their pinions. The swans were saved from death by a flock of crows, which noticing their plight pulled the feathers out of their own breasts, and let them fall on the naked swans. Legend has it that that is why the Australian swans are black with white wingtips, and their beaks are stained crimson with the blood from their wounds.

Legend also accounts for the Mute Swan drooping its head mournfully into the water. They are said to have adopted this attitude since Cygnus, the son of Poseidon, mourned his close friend, Phaeton, who was hurled into the River Eridanus after riding his father's sun-chariot wildly over the sky and incurring the anger of Zeus, who snatched a thunderbolt and hurled it at the chariot. Cygnus dived into the river so many times to gather Phaeton's charred remains that when he pined away in grief, the gods had pity on him and allowed him to haunt the river in the shape of a swan. The constellation of stars named Cygnus the Swan was named after him when later he was transformed into a star. Another Cygnus, son of the Ligurian king, Stenelus, was also transformed into a swan. The Mute Swan was once given the name *Stenelides olor*—the Swan of the Son of Stenelus—and in America it was used in various forms in the ornithological check-list.

Another Greek legend tells of the transmigration of souls entering bodies of their choice. Er, a brave warrior of Pamphylia, who was thought to have died in battle and was placed on the funeral pyre to be burned, visited the World of Shades during his twelve days of unconsciousness and watched the wandering souls of the dead enter new bodies. Orpheus chose the body of a swan, and a swan chose the body of a man. The swan is linked with the funeral pyre in Greece because the essential symbols of the mystic journey to the other world are the harp and the swan. The painting of 'Orpheus' by G. Savery, in the National Gallery, has swans in the central position symbolising the mystical connection with Orpheus in 'The Dream of Er'.

In common with many of the Greek gods, the birth of Cu Chulainn, the greatest figure in Irish heroic literature, had connection with birds, and the myth that they are linked with chains indicates affinity with swan legends. Before his birth, Cu Chulainn's mother, Dechtire, in company with her attendant maidens, in the form of a flock of birds, destroyed all that grew on the plain at Emain Macha. King Conchobar of Ulster pursued the birds with a hunting party in nine chariots, but the birds flew away in nine groups, each pair linked with golden chains.

After three years Dechtire and her maidens again met King Concho-bar—in the house of Dagda, the magician. The women joined the king's hunting party, but when they were all asleep Dechtire gave birth to Cu Chulainn, whose father was said to be Prince Lug, chief of Tuatha De Dannan, the fairy stronghold.

Cu Chulainn performed great feats at an early age, and at seven, after killing three men, he brought down first eight, and then sixteen, swans, with single stones from his sling. In triumph he returned home with the heads of the three dead men on his chariot and the live swans tethered around it.

The story of 'The Sick-Bed of Cu Chulainn' has affinity with the swan legends. The men of Ulster were gathered for the New Year feast when they saw a flock of beautiful birds hovering over the lake. Cu Chulainn used his spear like a boomerang and slew the birds. He gave a bird to every woman there except his wife, Ethne—to appease her he promised he would catch the two loveliest birds for her the next time they flew over the lake. When two birds appeared, linked with chains of red gold, they sang so sweetly that everyone fell asleep except Cu Chulainn and Ethne. In spite of Ethne warning her husband that the birds had a special power he tried to catch them, but after three attempts, although his spear went through the wing of one of them, they both flew away. His wife's warning proved correct, for afterwards Cu Chulainn fell into a deep sleep and had a vision which made him ill for a year.

Swan designs are found on an eighth-century slab at Inishkeel, Ireland, and also variations of the bird sun-worship symbols. Other such symbols are found in France and Germany and throughout Eurasia. Swans, and other anserine birds, occur frequently in Bronze and Iron Age art; they are often incorporated with twin-headed horses and sun symbols, which points to swan-beliefs occurring in the cults of metal-using, horse-riding and sun-worshipping peoples. Golden chains and coronets, so often mentioned in Irish legends, may indicate that they came before the Iron Age for by that time the gold in Ireland was exhausted.

Iron in swan myths and legends is an element that opposes these supernatural creatures, and to ward them off, the hero in legends of the Iron Age always wore iron shoes. The Tuatha De Dannan people of the fairy strongholds of Ireland were associated with geese and swans; they were great magicians and craftsmen but were conquered by the Sons of Miled, who, according to Macalisher, an Irish historian, were Iron Age Celtic invaders. If this is correct the fairies' hatred of iron is explained, and the swan's supernatural nature must have been connected with the preceding Bronze Age.

There are many legends relating to iron. The Buriats believe one-legged dwarfs, dressed in skins and living in caves, possess mineral and metal treasures. Smiths were people apart in the Middle Ages; they were generally nomadic, sometimes speaking a different language from the people they served, and certain tribes of Arabs would not intermarry with them.

Wayland Smith was the centre of a swan-maiden myth in England before the Danish Invasion (1016). He was a famous wonder-working smith, the son of a sailor and a mermaid, and king of the elves. Although King Nithnar had ill-treated Wayland, his daughter fell in love with the smith, and in Northumbria, on the Franks Casket, carved from walrus ivory, Egil, Wayland's brother, is depicted catching birds to make wings for his brother so that he could fly away with his sweetheart. In Leeds Parish Church Wayland Smith is carved on a cross, clad in a feather garment, and holding the swan-maiden aloft.

Another legend discrediting iron is that of Wastin of Wastinog, in Wales, who watched groups of women in an oatfield for three moonlit nights; eventually he followed them and they took refuge in a pool. He persuaded one of them to marry him, but she warned him that if ever he hit her with a bridle she would leave him. One day he unintentionally hit her with the iron of his bridle and she flew to the lake with her children and they all plunged in. Wastin was only able to save one child. This legend has many counterparts both in Ireland, Finland, Lapland and Scandinavia.

In Scandinavia the swan was associated with Freyr, the Norse god of sunshine, rain and fruitfulness, and with the white cumulus clouds that formed his chariot. Swans are also linked with the Valkyries, the women warriors who rode to battle over sea and through the air, to choose the slain to bring to Valhalla—the hall where Odin, the great Norse god received the warriors who had died. The Norse Fates, Urda, Verdandi and Skuld, are also associated with swans, in so far as their duty was to water the sacred ash, Yggdrasil, one root of which stretched to the sky and had the sacred 'Spring of Urd' beneath it, where swam the two swans from which all swans were supposed to have originated.

Finnish mythology captured the imagination of Sibelius, and the epic of Kalevala exercised a great fascination for him. He wrote the four legends of Kalevala for orchestra. The first of the legends was 'The Swan of Tuonela'. In this work Sibelius proved his genius by capturing the icy intensity of Tuonela, the land of death, through which runs a river of black waters dividing Tuonela from the land of the living. The Swan of Tuonela floated on these waters, unperturbed, majestic and forever singing. Lemminkainen, a typical hero of Nordic mythology, being both tough and fearless, sought to marry Aino, the Maid of the North. Aino's mother was an ugly old hag, and she agreed to Lemminkainen marrying her daughter provided he shot the sacred Swan of Tuonela, using one arrow only.

Lemminkainen found the swan and was about to draw his bow when a blind shepherd whom he had previously scorned hurled a water-snake at him. He was bitten by the snake and fell into the River of Death which carried him to Tuonela, where he was cut into pieces and tossed back into the water.

The second legend, 'Lemminkainen in Tuonela', was written by Sibelius in the same manner as the first, illustrating the story closely and not leaving the listener to supply his own fantasy. In this legend, Lemminkainen's mother commissioned Ilmarin, the great smith, to make a rake for her measuring 500 fathoms, and then she used it to drag the river for pieces of her son's body. She found them all and brought him back to life by singing magic songs. Restored to health, Lemminkainen still wanted to kill the swan, but his mother pleaded with him and he returned home.

India has many legends connected with swans. Brahma was called One Goose or Swan, and swans towed his chariot which was swifter than thought. Buddha also is linked in legend with a swan. As a young man Buddha found a swan shot with an arrow. When the huntsman came to claim it Buddha refused to part with it, explaining that life belongs to him who saves it. He succoured the swan and the bird helped him in his search for a way of life; in one of his findings of his 'four noble truths' he included abstinence from taking both human and animal life.

A very ancient variation of the swan-maiden legend comes from India. Urvasi, a heavenly woman, deserted her husband when he broke a tabu. When he found her she was with nymphs in the form of swans, swimming on a lake. Although the nymphs all assumed human forms again, Urvasi refused to return to her husband.

About the time of Buddha, the Scythians, who lived north-east of the Black Sea, practiced Shamanism and designed animals in felt, wood and leather. They placed horses, saddlery, and harnesses of leather and felt, together with fine fabrics, in the tombs of their dead kinsmen. Their animal art was highly decorative, what would be described these days as 'psychedelic'. Swans, elaborately designed in felt, have been found decorating a carriage in a Pazyryk barrow, dating around 400 BC. These barrows were placed over the log-lined tombs and were almost immediately robbed. When they became filled with water, the water froze, resulting in the contents of the tombs being preserved as in a deep freeze.

The Greeks came into power during 400 BC. It is thought the swan-song theme, so widespread in Greek literature, originated from the north. The Mute Swan, although wild in Greece, was very rare, and because of this and its great beauty, the ancient Greeks looked upon it as a sacred bird. They believed it to be an omen of fair weather and a lucky bird for mariners. Their belief that it sang before it died has appealed to many poets. Shakespeare refers to it in Othello (V, ii):

> I will play the swan,
> And die in music.

Byron also alludes to the swan singing before death:

> Place me on Sunium's marbled steep
> Where nothing save waves and I
> May hear our mutual murmurs sweep;
> There, swan-like, let me sing and die.

The first mention of the swan in Greek legends is in connection with Leda who was married to Tyndareus, King of Sparta. On the same night as Leda had lain with her husband, she was visited by Zeus, the King of Air and Earth, in the guise of a swan. As a result of her double conception, Leda bore two pairs of twins, each pair enclosed in an egg. The offspring Polydeuces and Helen were said to be the children of Zeus, and Clytemnestia and Castor, the mortal children of Tyndareus. In classical art Leda and the Swan are identified with the Heavenly Twins. Yeats wrote a beautiful poem entitled 'Leda and the Swan':

> A sudden blow, the great wings beating still
> Above the staggering girl, her thighs caressed
> By the dark webs, her nape caught in his bill,
> He holds her helpless, breast upon his breast.

'Leda and the Swan' was the most popular legend with artists. Michelangelo painted a famous picture depicting Zeus, in the form of a swan, wooing Leda; the painting is now in the National Gallery, London. Other paintings on the same subject are by Il Sodoma (1477–1549), an artist of the High Renaissance; Francois Boucher (1703–70), president of the Academy of Paris; and Paul Cezanne (1839–1906). Sidney Nolan, the Australian artist, exhibited a large group of paintings in London during 1960; 'Leda and the Swan' was the central motif. A marble statue of the same theme by Vincenzo Dante (1530–76) is to be seen in the Victoria and Albert Museum, London.

Apollo was the son of Zeus by Leto, who found shelter in the island of Ortygia when she was about to give birth to the sun god and his twin sister Artemis (Diana). Swans circled the island seven times at their birth, and Zeus showered gifts upon them, among which were two chariots drawn by swans. Apollo's chariot has been depicted on works of art. Horses and lions were said to draw him by day, but it was the swans which hauled his bark over the waters by night. On his way to Delphi in his swan-chariot, Apollo stayed for a year in the swans' country on the edge of the ocean where the happy and contented Hyperborean people lived. They made Apollo their god and from then on he always visited them in his chariot at fixed times.

According to a very old Greek legend Apollo's soul passed into a swan, and this may explain the Worshipful Company of Musicians having a swan on its arms as an allusion to Apollo, the god of music.

Aphrodite (Venus), the goddess of love, came to Greece in a chariot drawn by swans. The white swan took the place of the goose in Greek symbolism, and the swan is sacred to Venus as being the image of a naked woman of chaste nudity and immaculate whiteness. It also had erotic symbolism, its long phallic neck symbolising the generative power of the male, and its silky, white, rounded body, symbolising the female. 'The Birth of Venus', by Reubens, has swans and cherubs forming an arc above the central figure of Venus.

In South America an Indian legend involving the Black-necked Swan and the Coscoroba Swan is associated with the sun, and with the soft white body of the swan which cradles the Sunchild. Both the Black-necked Swan and the Coscoroba appear in a sacred light by defending the Indians against the fierce Araucanian tribe. Ollal, Child of the Sun, tried, without success, to reform the Araucanians, and promised he would return later as a holy child. Before he was reborn, his mother was killed by a giant, who, having heard her unborn baby would kill him, cut the child from her womb before eating her. A rat rescued the baby while the giant was feasting, and nursed it until it grew into a young boy. Then he asked four large animals to bear the child to safety. A skunk betrayed three of the animals—an ostrich, a flamingo, and a puma—and for his treachery he has stunk ever since. The fourth animal was the Black-necked Swan. She placed the child on her back and with an escort of Coscoroba Swans swam across the lake and flew to Patagonia. For their chivalry the Coscoroba were rewarded by being given black tips to their wings and pink bills and legs. Since that time the Black-necked Swan has been unique among the South American birds by carrying her young on her back.

As centuries passed, the mysticism and reverence the Greeks held for the swan flowed into the rest of Europe in the shape of the Swan Knight. The Legend of the 'Seven Children changed into Swans' was similar to 'The Fate of the Children of Lir' and was introduced as the origin of the Swan Knight. The children's mother was said to be a nymph and they were born with golden chains around their necks. When the king, their widowed father, went on a campaign, their grandmother tried to get rid of them and took their chains away. The children changed into swans—except the daughter, who went in search of her father and told him of her brothers' fate. As soon as the king persuaded his mother to confess her guilt his sons were restored to their human forms, except for one whose chain the grandmother had used to mend a cup. The Swan Knight would not leave his swan-brother when he went on a journey and they sailed away together. At this stage the legend is connected with the Swan Knight sailing to Nimwegan and rescuing Beatrice of Bouillon.

Wagner was inspired to write two operas on the Swan Knight theme. The first was *Parsifal*, influenced by Wolfram Van Eschenbach's great poem. In this, Parsifal, against his mother's wishes, goes in search of King Arthur's Court. The opera opens with the mystical beauty, solemnity, and holiness of the Grail. The Grail's lord is in anguish for having been seduced, and consequently losing the lance he was to use to fight Klingsor, the wicked magician, who was threatening the Grail. As he prays for help he hears a voice which tells him: 'Made wise through pity, the Blameless Fool—wait for him, my chosen one.' The silence which follows is broken by cries of 'Woe', and a wounded wild swan flies across the lake to fall lifeless to the ground with an arrow in its breast. Parsifal is then dragged on to the stage and admits he killed the Swan. He is told he has committed murder, for in the Grail, man and animal live in peace and trust. As Parsifal sees the king born away, and the swan also taken reverently away on a bier of fresh branches, he experiences his first pang of pity; but Parsifal, 'the Blameless Fool' has a long way to go before he recovers the Grail's hallowed lance.

The German epic of Lohengrin, which dates back from 1260, was adapted by Wagner to suit his own purpose. It was his first real success and led to the young Ludwig II of Bavaria befriending him and providing him with enough money and patronage to enable him to expand as an artist.

Ludwig lived in Hohenschwangan, the capital of the swan country in the Bavarian Alps. Swans were everywhere, and Ludwig had his tapestries decorated with them, together with the legends of the Grail and the story of Lohengrin. He spent much time sketching swans and had a swan for his personal seal.

There are a great many variations of the swan-maiden theme linked with the Swan Knight. One such story appears in Grimm's Fairy Tales. Hans Andersen wrote an elaborate version in his tale 'Eleven

Wild Swans'. In it eleven young princes are turned into swans by day by their wicked grandmother, and their sister Elisa is sent to live in a labourer's cottage. When Elisa has grown into a beautiful girl she finds her brothers one night on their yearly visit to their father's country. The handsome princes turn into swans at daybreak and decide to take Elisa back with them to their sanctuary across the sea. They convey her in a net gripped by their bills, and the youngest swan flies above her to protect her from the elements.

On arrival at the sanctuary the swans leave Elisa to rest in a cave. Morgana, a fairy, comes to her in a dream and tells her she must weave eleven shirts with long sleeves from flax made from stinging-nettles outside the cave, and when finished she must throw the shirts over her brothers to release them from the spell. There was one stipulation— Elisa was not allowed to speak until the shirts were finished, or her brothers would die.

While Elisa is busy weaving, the king of the country, out hunting, finds her and falls in love with her. In spite of her silent protestations he takes her to his palace and surrounds her with every luxury; but she is not happy until the flax and shirts are restored to her.

Elisa soon returns the king's love and marries him, but every night when he is asleep, she steals from the bedroom and spins her shirts. While gathering nettles from the churchyard one night, she is alarmed to see witches digging up graves and eating the contents. The archbishop sees her there, and, to turn the king against her, tells him she is a witch. Later, the king sees her in the witches' company and sadly decides the people must judge whether she, too, is a witch.

Everyone clamours for Elisa to be burnt as a witch; she is thrust into a dungeon where she continues shirt-making. Her youngest brother finds her; he and his brothers go by night to the king to plead for her freedom, but unfortunately the king does not wake up until morning, and only sees eleven swans encircling the palace.

On the way to the stake Elisa tries to finish the eleventh shirt; the crowd, rushing to attack her, are frightened away by the great swans flapping their wings around her. As the executioner seizes Elisa to throw her on the pyre, she flings the shirts over the swans' heads and they turn into princes; but sadly, the youngest prince retains one swan's wing, because his sister had not time to sew the last sleeve.

Free to speak at last, Elisa declares her innocence, but she is so exhausted that she dies. While the princes are telling the king how hard Elisa worked to release them, a perfume, as strong as a million roses, pervades the air, and the pyre of faggots changes into a beautiful red rose-bush, topped with a white flower, shining like a star. The king takes the white rose and lays it on Elisa's breast and she awakes, filled with peace and happiness.

This story inspired Arthur Gaskin to paint a picture entitled 'The Wild Swans'; and symbols are to be found in Denmark of swans with crowns on their heads in recognition of the legend.

Pythagoras, the Greek philosopher (582 BC), originated the belief that all good poets passed into swans at their death. Virgil was known as the 'Mantuan Swan' and Homer the 'Swan of Meander'. Anna Seward, the poetess, was alluded to as 'The Swan of Lichfield', and Henry Vaughan, the Silurist poet, was called 'The Swan of Usk'. Our greatest poet of all time, William Shakespeare, was given the title 'The Swan of Avon' by Ben Jonson. When Shakespeare died, Ben Jonson wrote 'To the memory of My Beloved, The Author, Mr William Shakespeare':

> Sweet Swan of Avon! what a sight it were
> To see thee in our waters yet appear
> And make those flights upon the banks of Thames,
> That so did take Eliza and our James.

What greater honour could the swan have than to be compared with the most versatile weaver of mystic and magical tales the world has ever known?

Appendix

COMPARATIVE MEASUREMENTS

The Mute Swan
(Cygnus olor)

	SIZE OF MALE (AVERAGE)		SIZE OF FEMALE	
Wing:	608·4mm	(23·9in)	566·8mm	(22·3in)
Leg:	112·8mm	(4·4in)	104·8mm	(4·1in)
Bill:	80·2mm	(3·2in)	76·3mm	(3·0in)
Tail:	195mm	(7·7in)		
Weight:	12·2kg	(26·84lb)	8·9kg	(19·58lb)
Length:	1·41m	(55·2in)		

The Trumpeter Swan
(Cygnus cygnus buccinator)

	SIZE OF MALE (AVERAGE)		SIZE OF FEMALE	
Wing:	618·6mm	(24·3in)	594mm	(23·4in)
Leg:	122·9mm	(4·8in)	121·7mm	(4·79in)
Bill:	112·5mm	(4·4in)	107mm	(4·2in)
Tail:	232·5mm	(9·1in)	232·5mm	(9·1in)
Weight:	11·9kg	(26·2lb)	9·4kg	(20·7lb)
Length:	1·56m	(61·4in)	1·5m	(59·1in)

The Whooper Swan
(Cygnus cygnus cygnus)

	SIZE OF MALE (AVERAGE)		SIZE OF FEMALE	
Wing:	615·6mm	(24·2in)	597·2mm	(23·5in)
Leg:	124·1mm	(4·9in)	116mm	(4·6in)
Bill:	109mm	(4·3in)	103·6mm	(4·1in)
Tail:	180mm	(7·1in)	167·5mm	(6·6in)
Weight:	10·8kg	(23·76lb)	8·1kg	(17·82lb)
Length:	1·52m	(59·8in)		

The Whistling Swan

(*Cygnus columbianus columbianus: Olor columbianus*)

	SIZE OF MALE (AVERAGE)		SIZE OF FEMALE	
Wing:	538mm	(21·2in)	531·6mm	(20·9in)
Leg:	111·9mm	(4·4in)	107·2mm	(4·2in)
Bill:	102·6mm	(4·1in)	99·9mm	(3·9in)
Tail:	170·8mm	(6·7in)	165·3mm	(6·5in)
Weight:	7·1kg	(15·6lb)	6·2kg	(13·64lb)
Length:				

The Bewick's Swan

(*Cygnus columbianus bewickii*)

	SIZE OF MALE (AVERAGE)		SIZE OF FEMALE	
Wing:	531mm	(20·9in)	510mm	(20·1in)
Leg:	106mm	(4·2in)	102mm	(4in)
Bill:	94·7mm	(3·7in)	90·9mm	(3·6in)
Tail:	165mm	(6·5in)		
Head:	163mm	(6·4in)	157mm	(6·2in)
Weight:	6·4kg	(14·08lb)	5·7kg	(12·54lb)
Length:	1·27m	(50in)	Slightly smaller	

The Black Swan

(*Cygnus atratus*)

	SIZE OF MALE (AVERAGE)		SIZE OF FEMALE	
Wing:	489mm	(19·2in)	461mm	(18·1in)
Leg:	97mm	(3·8in)	95mm	(3·7in)
Bill:	69mm	(2·7in)	63mm	(2·5in)
Tail:	138mm	(5·4in)	123mm	(4·8in)
Neck:	782mm	(30·8in)	675mm	(26·6in)
Weight:	6kg	(13·2lb)	5kg	(11lb)
Length:	1·29m	(50·8in)	1·16m	(45·72in)

The Black-necked Swan

(*Cygnus melanocoryphus*)

	SIZE OF MALE (AVERAGE)		SIZE OF FEMALE	
Wing:	443mm	(17·4in)	408mm	(16·1in)
Leg:	87mm	(3·4in)	79mm	(3·11in)
Bill:	80mm	(3·15in)	72mm	(2·8in)
Tail:	172mm	(6·8in)	163mm	(6·4in)
Weight:	5·4kg	(11·9lb)	4kg	(8·8lb)
Length:	1·25m	(49·2in)		

The Coscoroba Swan

(*Coscoroba coscoroba*)

	SIZE OF MALE (AVERAGE)		SIZE OF FEMALE	
Wing:	465mm	(18·3in)	444mm	(17·7in)

Appendix: Comparative Measurements

Leg:	93mm	(3·66in)	92·9mm	(3·66in)
Bill:	68mm	(2·7in)	64·4mm	(2·5in)
Tail:	155mm	(6·1in)		
Weight:	4·6kg	(10·12lb)	3·8kg	(8·36lb)
Length:	1·15m	(45·3in)		

Bibliography

ARMSTRONG, E. A. *The Folklore of British Birds*. London: Collins, 1958

ATKINSON-WILLIS, G. L. 'The Mid-Winter Distribution of Wildfowl in Europe, Northern Africa and South-West Asia', *Wildfowl*, 20. 1969

BANKO, W. E. *The Trumpeter Swan*. Washington: US Fish & Wildlife Service, 1960

Birds of Isla Grande. Washington: Smithsonian Institution, 1970

BRAITHWAITE, L. W. *The Black Swan*. Australian Natural History, 1970

BRYANT, SIR ARTHUR. 'The Age of Chivalry', Chap 5, Vol 2, *Story of England*. London: Collins, 1940

Brewer's Dictionary of Phase and Fable. London: Cassell, 10th ed, 1967

CARP, E. *Ramsar Proceedings*. Slimbridge: International Wildfowl Research Bureau, 1972

CLAIR, C. *Unnatural History*. New York: Abelard Schuman, 1967

CLARK, SIR KENNETH et al. *Sydney Nolan*. London: Thames & Hudson, 1961

CORTISSOZ, ROYAL. *Decorations of Francis Boucher*. New York: Wm Bradford, 1944

CROSS and GLOVER. *Ancient Irish Tales*. London: Harrap, 1935

CURRY-LINDAHL, K., HANSTROM, B. and JOHNELS, A. G. 'Acta Vertebratica', *Studies of the Mute Swan in Sweden*, II, 2, 1963

DACIUK, J. 'The Fauna of the White Lake National Park', *Annals of the National Parks of Argentina*, II, 2 (1968), 225–304

DAVIDSON, G. *Stories of the Ballets*. London: Laurie, 4th imp, 1952

DELACOUR, J. *The Waterfowl of the World*, Vol I. London: Country Life, 1954

——. *The Waterfowl of the World*, Vol IV. London: Country Life, 1964

DUNBAR, C. O. *Historical Geology*. New York: J. Wiley, 2nd ed, 1960

ELTRINGHAM, S. K. 'The British Population of the Mute Swan, 1961', *Bird Study*, 10 (1963), 10–28

FESTETICS, A. and LEISLER B. 'Ecology of the Danube with Special Reference to Waterfowl in Lower Austria, *Wildfowl*, 21 (1972), 42–60

FISHER, J. *The Shell Bird Book*. London: Ebury Press and Michael Joseph, 1966
—— and PETERSON, R. *The World of Birds*. London: Macdonald, 1964
FRITH, H. J. *Waterfowl in Australia*. Sydney: Angus & Robertson, 1967
FROHAWK, F. W. *British Birds*. London: Ward Lock, 1951
GODAY, J. C. 'Evaluation of the Natural Resources of Argentina', *Fauna Silvestre*, I, Chap VIII (1963), 299
GUILER, E. R. 'Breeding of the Black Swan in Tasmania', *Emu*, 70 (1966), 3–8
Harmsworth's Universal Encyclopedia. London: Amalgamated Press, 1920–3
HARRISON, J. G. *A Wealth of Wildfowl*. London: André Deutsch, 1967
—— and OGILVIE, M. A. *Immigrant Mute Swans in S.E. England 1967*, Wildfowl Trust Annual Report, 18 (1967), 85–7
HILPRECHT, A. *Hoskerschwan, Singschwan, Zwergschwan*. Wittenberg: Neue Brehn-Bircherei, rev ed, 1971
HULL, A. V. *Trumpeter Swans, Their Management and Preservation*. United States Biological Survey, Montana, 1939
Ingersoll's Birds in Legend, Fable and Folklore. London: Longmans, 1923
'Japan's "Angels of Winter" ', Japan, 2 (magazine), 1971
JEWSON, C. B. *The Great Hospital, Norwich 1249–1949*. Norwich: The Great Hospital, 1949
JOHNSGARD, P. A. *Comparative Behaviour of the Anatidae and Its Evolutionary Implications*. Annual Report Wildfowl Trust, 1960
——. *Handbook of Waterfowl Behaviour*. London: Constable, 1965
JOHNSON, A. and HAFNER, H. 'Winter Wildfowl Counts In South-West Europe and Western Turkey, *Wildfowl*, 21. 1970
JOHNSON, A. W. *The Birds of Chile and Adjacent Regions*, Vol 1. Buenos Aires: Platt Establecimientos Graficos, 1965
KIKKAWA, J. and YAMASHINA, Y. 'Breeding of Black Swans in Japan', *Emu*, 66 (1967), 377–81
KING, J. G. 'The Swans and Geese of Alaska's Arctic Slope', *Wildfowl*, 21. 1970
KORTRIGHT, F. H. *Ducks, Geese and Swans of North America*. Washington: American Wildlife Institute, 1943
LACK, D. *Ecological Adaptions for Breeding in Birds*. London: Methuen, 1968
——. 'The Proportion of Yolk in Eggs of Waterfowl', *Wildfowl*, 19 (1968), 67–9
LAYTON, G. *Sibelius*. London: Dent, 1965
LEACH, B. A. 'A Slimbridge in British Columbia', *Wildfowl*, 21. 1970
LINDUSKA, E. J. (ed). *Waterfowl Tomorrow*. Washington: Bureau of Sport, Fisheries and Wildlife, 1964
LONDON NATURAL HISTORY SOCIETY. *Birds of the London Area*. London: Hart-Davis, 1964
LOWERY, G. H. *Louisiana Birds*. Louisiana: State University Press, 2nd ed, 1960
MACAN, T. T. *Freshwater Ecology*. London: Longmans Green, 1963
MACSWINEY, MARQUIS. *Six Came Flying*. London: Michael Joseph, 1971

MARSHALL, A. J. *Biology and Comparative Physiology of Birds*. New York and London: Academic Press, 1960

Marvels and Mysteries of the Animal World, Chap 11, London: Reader's Digest (1964), 22-4

MATTHIESSEN, P. *Wildlife in America*. New York: Viking, 1959

MIERS, K. H. and WILLIAMS, M. 'Nesting of the Black Swan at Lake Ellesmere, New Zealand', *Wildfowl*, 20. 1969

MINTON, C. D. T. 'Mute Swan Flocks', *Wildfowl*, 22 (1971), 71-88

——. 'Pairing and Breeding of the Mute Swan', *Wildfowl*, 19. 1968

MONCRIEFF, A. R. H. *Classic Myths and Legends*. London: Gresham, 1912

MOORE, THOMAS. *Irish Melodies*. Dublin: Gill & Macmillan, 1963

MUNRO, I. S. and MUNRO, K. M. *Index to Reproductions to European Paintings*. New York: H. W.Wilson, 1956

NAVAKE, E. 'The Waterfowl of Mongolia', *Wildfowl*, 21 (1970), 61-8

NEWMAN, E. *Wagner Nights*. London: Putnam, 1949

OGILVIE, M. A. *Population Changes and Mortality of the Mute Swan in Britain*. Wildfowl Trust Annual Report, 18, 1967

Pears Cyclopaedia. London: Pelham Books, 1966

PERRIN, C. M. and REYNOLDS, C. M. *A Preliminary Study of the Mortality of the Mute Swan* Cygnus Olor. Wildfowl Trust Annual Report 18, 1967

PETERSON, R. T. *The Birds*. New York: Time-Life International, 1968

POULSON, H. *Dansk Orn For Trids* (concerning Mute, Whooper and Black Swans), 47 (1948), 173-202

——. *Dansk Orn For Trids* (contributions to the ecology of swans), 800B (1948), 173-202

RADFORD, E. and M.A. *Encyclopaedia of Superstitions*. London: Hutchinson, 1969

RIVIERE, G. *Cézanne le Peintre Solitaire*. Paris: Librarie Fleury, 1933

ROBINSON, H. S. and WILSON, K. *Encyclopaedia of Myths and Legends of All Nations*. London: Edmund Ward, 1967

ROSSI JOSE, A. H. 'Contributions to the Study of the Biology of the *Coscoroba coscoroba*', *Physis*, 21 (magazine) (1960), 69

SALOMONSEN, F. 'The Moult Migration', *Wildfowl*, 19 (1968), 5-24

SALZMAN, L. F. *Edward I*. London: Constable, 1968

SCOTT, D. 'Bewick's Swans in the Netherlands', *Wildfowl*, 21 (1970), 152-3

——. 'Wild Swans at Slimbridge, 1968-69', *Wildfowl*, 20 (1969), 157-60

SCOTT, P. *The Wild Swans at Slimbridge*. Wildfowl Trust, Slimbridge, 1970

—— and THE WILDFOWL TRUST. *The Swans*. London: Michael Joseph, 1972

SEDGWICK, L. M., WHITTAKER, P. and HANSON, J. *The New Wildfowler in the 1970s*. London: Jenkins, 1970

SELOUSE, E. *Evolution of Habit in Birds*. London: Constable, 1933

Shell Country Book. London: Dent, 1966

SIMPSON, G. S. *An Introduction to Biology*. London: Routledge & Kegan Paul, 1970

SLADEN, W. J. L. *Studies of the Whistling Swan 1967-68.* Trans-North American Wildlife Conference, 34, 42–50. Washington: Wildlife Management Institute

——, GUNN, W. W. H. and COCHRAN, W.W. *Studies of the Migration of the Whistling Swan, 1969.* Proceedings of the World Conference on Bird Hazards to Aircraft, Canada, Sept 1969

SOPER, T. *The Bird Table Book.* Newton Abbot: David & Charles, 1966

Standard Dictionary of Folklore, Vol 2. New York: Funk & Wagnall, 1950

STEWART, R. E. and MANNING, J. H. 'Whistling Swans in Chesapeake Bay', *The Auk,* 2, 75. November 1958

THOMSON, S. *Motif-Index of Folk-Literature,* Vol 6. Copenhagen: Rosenkilde & Bagger, 1955-8

TICEHURST, N. F. *The Mute Swan in England.* London: Cleaver Hume, 1957

——. 'The Mute Swan in Kent', *Archaeologia Cantania,* XLVII (1935), 55–70

TOTTENHAM, K. *Bird Doctor.* London: Nelson, 1961

TREFETHEN, J. B. *34th North American Wildlife and Natural Resources Conference.* Washington: Wildlife Management Institute, 1969

WAGNER, SIR A. *Archaeologia Relating to Antiquity,* XCVII (1959), 127-38

WELLER, M. W. 'Comments on Waterfowl Habitat and Management in Argentina', *Wildfowl,* 20 (1969), 126–31

——. 'Notes on Some Marsh Birds of Cape San Antonio, Argentina', *Ibis.* (1967), 109

WETMAN, J. *Ducks, Geese and Swans.* London: Museum Press, 1968

WETMORE, A. 'Observations of Birds of Argentina, Paraguay, Uruguay and Chile', Bull 133, 1–448 (1926), United States Museum

——. 'Observations on the Genera of Swans', Washington Academy of Science, 411 (1951), 338-40

WINCHESTER, A. M. and LOVELL, H. B. *Zoology.* New York and London: Van Nostrand, 2nd ed, 1970

WITHERBY, H. F., REV JOURDAN, TICEHURST, N. F. and TUCKER, B. W. *The Handbook of British Birds.* London: Atherley, 1940

Acknowledgements

I am grateful to the following people and organisations who have given me patient and persevering help throughout my work on this book: Jean Bowden; the British Museum (Natural History Department); the British Trust for Ornithology; the Deputy Librarian, Australia House, London; the Icelandic Embassy, London, and the Natural History Museum, Iceland; Japan Information Centre, London; the National Reference Library of Science and Invention (Bayswater Division); Naturhistoriska Riksmuseet, Stockholm; the Office of Ornithology, Facultad de Ciencias Naturales Y Museo, Argentina; the Reference and Public Libraries, Bexleyheath, Kent; the Royal Society for the Protection of Birds; Professor William J. L. Sladen, John Hopkins University, Baltimore; F. John Turk, the Royal Swan Keeper; the Universitetes Zoologiske Museum, Copenhagen; the Wildlife Management Institute, Washington DC, and particularly Mr J. B. Trefethen; the Wildfowl Trust, Slimbridge, Gloucester; the Wildlife Research Division, Commonwealth Scientific and Industrial Research Organisation, Canberra City, Australia; the Worshipful Company of Dyers; the Worshipful Company of Vintners; and the Zoological Society of London. I must also thank my husband who has accompanied me on my hunt for swans from south-west England to southern Sweden with enthusiasm and practical help.

Index

Abbotsbury, 65, 194
Anatidae, 9, 16, 23
Andersen, Hans, 66, 214
Anseres (sub-order), 28
Anseriformes, 10, 15
Anserinae, 10, 11, 18
Anserini, 9
Aphrodite, 213
Apollo, 212
Archaeopterex, 27–8
Archosauria, 27
Aurignacian culture, 203

Bewick's, 9, 31, 36, 38, 39, 131–45, 188, 189, 194, 195, 217
Bill, 11, 44, 63, 72, 74, 76, 78, 95, 110, 131, 146–7, 165
Black-necked Swan, 9, 10, 22, 165–75, 188, 200, 213, 218
Black Swan, 9, 10, 21, 22, 32, 35, 44–6, 146–64, 188, 196, 200, 206, 218
Brahma, 210
Breeding, 20–2, 48–57, 81–5, 98–100, 114–15, 133–6, 149–56, 169–70, 179–81
Bronze Age, 36, 209
Buddha, 210–11
Buriats, 209
Byron, 211

Captivity, 94, 109, 129, 141, 163–4, 169, 175, 183, 184–5, 200–2
Census, 60–1
Chicks, 22, 54–6, 85–6, 100, 115, 136, 155–6, 170, 182

225